FALLEN ANGEL

William Fotheringham writes for the *Guardian* and *Observer* on cycling and rugby. A former racing cyclist and launch editor of *procycling* and *Cycle Sport* magazines, he has reported on nineteen Tours de France as well as Six Nations rugby and the Olympic Games. He lives in Herefordshire with his wife and two children.

Also by William Fotheringham

Put Me Back on My Bike: In Search of Tom Simpson

Roule Britannia: A History of Britons in the Tour de France

WILLIAM FOTHERINGHAM

FALLEN ANGEL
THE PASSION OF
FAUSTO COPPI

YELLOW JERSEY PRESS
LONDON

Published by Yellow Jersey Press 2010

4 6 8 10 9 7 5

Copyright © William Fotheringham, 2009

William Fotheringham has asserted his right under the Copyright, Designs
and Patents Act 1988 to be identified as the author of this work

First published in Great Britain in 2009 by
Yellow Jersey Press
Random House, 20 Vauxhall Bridge Road,
London SW1V 2SA

www.randomhouse.co.uk

Addresses for companies within The Random House Group Limited can be found at:
www.randomhouse.co.uk/offices.htm

The Random House Group Limited Reg. No. 954009

A CIP catalogue record for this book
is available from the British Library

ISBN 9780224074506

The Random House Group Limited supports The Forest Stewardship Council®
(FSC®), the leading international forest-certification organisation. Our books
carrying the FSC label are printed on FSC®-certified paper. FSC is the only
forest-certification scheme supported by the leading environmental organisations,
including Greenpeace. Our paper procurement policy can be found at
www.randomhouse.co.uk/environment

Printed and bound in Great Britain by
CPI Group (UK) Ltd, Croydon, CR0 4YY

To Caroline, who took me to Italy

CONTENTS

ILLUSTRATIONS

A NOTE ON CURRENCIES

I have used both Italian lire and French francs throughout as appropriate.

It should be noted that, pre-war, the Italian lire was worth roughly 100 to the pound sterling, and roughly 20 to the dollar.

After the Allied invasion, the initial exchange rate was set at approximately 500 to the pound, or 120 to the US dollar; this rate was reset at 625 lire to the dollar in 1949.

The French franc was revalued in January 1960; in Coppi's era the currency is what was known as the 'old franc'. In 1949, when Coppi won the Tour de France for the first time, the exhange rate was roughly 1000 to the pound sterling (350 to the US dollar); by the end of the 1950s, it had declined to approximately 1400 to the pound (roughly 500 to the dollar).

CHAPTER 1

THE LETTER AND THE PHOTOGRAPH

At a quarter past four on 25 May 1949, Aunt Albina sits down next to her radio and begins to write on a single sheet of squared paper. Soon the afternoon's coverage of the Giro d'Italia will begin, and the announcer, Mario Ferretti, will tell her how Faustino and Serse have fared on the road to Salerno in Italy's national tour. This is the time of day the Coppi family shares with its two boys; in another house in the little village of Castellania, their mother, Albina's sister Angiolina, is also sitting, waiting for Ferretti to pick up his microphone. Just outside, in the little field they call Campo del Mù, Albina's husband Giuseppe is cutting the hay; for the three weeks of the race, each day's work is planned so that he will be within reach of the house now, ready to run to the radio.

How to tell Faustino and Serse what they all feel? The boys are always on their minds. What could be more natural? The Coppi brothers have won such fame, Faustino with his Giro d'Italia wins and his Italian national titles, Serse with his unstinting work in support. Each time they come back from their great races – as far away as Naples or Rome, sometimes even France or Switzerland – they bring back fine things: Angiolina's fridge, her radio. The family have such good clothes now and want for nothing; no one in the village has seen anything like Faustino's new Fiat. But it is not so long ago that the brothers were at Albina's school, inseparable even then. Faustino had always been mad about that bike of his;

one day, she had had to mark him 'absent' in the register when he went out cycling and forgot to come back. How she had told him off.

Giuseppe is certain Faustino will win on the climbs; Albina can say that in her letter. She must tell them of the prayers the family say each day for their boys' safe return, the tears she and Angiolina shed each time Faustino wins, and she can remind them to wear their medallions with the image of the Pilgrim Madonna. She must be sure to have Angiolina sign the letter, and Giuseppe, so that the boys know they are all thinking of them. Above all, she must make a point of including Serse, so often in his elder brother's shadow, but so loyal, and as lively still as when Faustino first brought him to school.

Aunt Albina writes with a script so close and neat it might have come off a printing press. A lady of precise mind, she times and dates the letter. Many years later, it will be passed on to Faustino's daughter Marina. Sixty years on, the letter seems surprisingly formal. Perhaps it is because Albina is the village teacher and thus elected to write on the family's behalf. She sends the 'most fervent' prayers of this 'church family' – Albina and Angiolina's uncle is a priest. The Immaculate Madonna will bless them, will give Faustino the strength to be victorious, to pull on the pink jersey awarded to the race leader.

'Obviously we discuss what is going on,' she continues. 'Your uncle talks about you with a fervour and affection that you cannot imagine. On the days you finished first I cried, and I'm still crying for joy. Well done, Faustino, well done, and go on. You will be carried along the way you have chosen by your intelligence, your good sense and your experience.'

To Serse, she writes: 'With your good character, your willpower, your strength, you will be the finest and greatest help to your big brother. You will give him encouragement even if you go through difficult times.' She sends hugs and kisses, 'with the greatest affection, your most affectionate uncle and aunt Giuseppe and Albina'. There is a scribble from Angiolina on the bottom of the letter: 'love from Mamma, hope all goes well'. Uncle Giuseppe's signature is heavier, thicker.

Aunt Albina's close, regular handwriting evokes a lost world, a pastoral idyll of summer haymaking. The women sit in the parlour, listening for news, waiting for the return of the men who have left the land to seek their fortunes. Whether they quite understand the intricacies of the faraway world of bike racing is unlikely. That does not matter. Faustino and Serse may be a long way from home, but they will understand their import-ance to their family, feel the simple power of their relatives' love, know the depth of their Catholic faith.

*   *   *

The photograph, on the other hand, is more troubling. Four years later, Fausto Coppi stands on the podium of the world road race championship in Lugano. He has just pulled on the winner's rainbow-striped jersey. As he waves the victor's bouquet, his face comes as close to a smile as he ever manages to muster. The lower lip curves; the upper remains straight; only the creases in his cheeks show that this is a moment of pure joy. He has just clinched the only major title that has so far eluded him. There can now be no debate: he is the greatest cyclist ever. His title, *campionissimo* – champion of champions – is not mere hyperbole.

By 30 August 1953 Coppi had twice achieved the 'double' everyone thought was impossible: victories in the Tour de France and Giro d'Italia in the same year. At the World's that day he dominated the race in the style that was to become his hallmark: he waited for the moment until he felt the opposi-tion tiring, then dramatically raised the pace until no one could stay with him. The final fifty miles were a triumphant, if painful, procession in front of the hundreds of thousands of fans who had flocked over the Italian border.

Coppi's rainbow jersey doesn't quite fit over the deep blue tunic of the Italian team, stained with sweat after 165 miles in the sweltering heat on the hilly circuit above the lake. Alongside the cyclist are the usual dignitaries in suits and ties, the mayor of Lugano, the cycling federation president; behind are onlookers craning their necks.

At the shoulders of the men in suits, however, stands a woman. A woman with immaculately coiffed dark hair swept back from her forehead, eyebrows tightly plucked into two perfect lines, dazzling teeth, a chunky gold bracelet on her right wrist, a distinguished black dress and a jawline that hints at the unstoppable force of a battleship's prow.

It was the presence of the woman, Giulia Locatelli, which made a routine podium photograph into one of the most reproduced images in Italian sport. To this day, no one quite knows how Coppi's mistress cajoled, argued, pushed her way into forbidden territory to pass him the flowers in an almost peremptory gesture captured by the television cameras. She was alongside her lover in his moment of triumph, to share the acclaim of the hundreds of thousands of Italian fans, to be pictured alongside him in the next morning's newspapers. It was the moment their love affair became public, because she had decided that it should be so. For an Italian, the image has the same power as the moment in the Profumo scandal in Britain in the early sixties when Mandy Rice-Davies answered: 'He would say that, wouldn't he?'

The affair had been going on for some months. It had been rumoured in the closed world of cycling that the biggest name in the sport had a dark-haired mistress. All was not well, it was said, with his marriage of nearly eight years, in spite of Coppi's love for his daughter Marina. Cycling champions often strayed as they flitted from race to race, and in most cases what happened on the road remained hidden. They were good husbands at home so people turned a blind eye. But Giulia's determined move put the affair in the public gaze. In 1950s Italy adultery was still illegal. This was an act of colossal daring, many would say sheer folly.

When Coppi left his wife Bruna for Giulia soon afterwards, such an act of open immorality could not be allowed to go unchecked. The Pope publicly expressed his displeasure and became involved in fruitless moves to restore the marriage. The police dragged Giulia and Fausto from their beds in an attempt to prove their illicit liaison. The woman, the guilty party in the eyes of the law, was briefly thrown into prison. The adultery trial was brief but vicious, the bitter little details of marital breakdown mulled over in public. The children were called as witnesses. The sentences were suspended, but the case remains a landmark nonetheless: a major public figure and his mistress prosecuted for adultery just as Italy was turning into a secular society, developing into a modern European state.

The Lugano world championship marked a turning point for Coppi in another sense. It was one of the last major races he won. He was nearly thirty-four: his glittering career was all but over, his decline inexorable in spite of his best efforts, the more marked because no matter how poorly he performed he could never be anonymous. When he struggled, it was noticed. Inevitably, the scarlet woman was blamed for his decline; even for his premature, controversial death. Within cycling, she would never be forgiven, not on moral grounds, but for emasculating the champion of champions.

Coppi is Italian sport's immortal hero. '*Coppi viva, Coppi il mito*' – Coppi lives on, Coppi the myth – say the placards at the great races, the Giro, the Tour de France, and they are right. He remains a mythical figure nearly fifty years after his death. Walk into the reception at *La Gazzetta dello Sport*, the paper that embodies the spirit of Italian sport, and there in front of you is a life-size black and white picture of a man on a bike: Coppi. Not a Ferrari, not a footballer, but the cyclist. In the Giro each year, the highest mountain is given the title *Cima Coppi*, the Coppi summit. No French or Spanish champion is remembered this way in their home Tours. And who can count the number of Italian cycling clubs called Gruppo Sportivo Coppi?

Every era is marked by the emergence of a possible 'new Coppi' amid much speculation. On the fortieth anniversary of his death, a video of his life sold 60,000 copies in a few days. Half a billion lire was spent on an elaborate memorial in Turin. And it was Coppi who was voted the most popular Italian sportsman of the twentieth century, ahead of the great skier Alberto Tomba and the motor racing legend Enzo Ferrari. Not a footballer within a mile of him.

Coppi has moved way beyond his sport. He is now immortalised in opera, film, television docudrama, experimental works by classical composers, sculpture, painting, ceramics and T-shirts as well as in print. Memorials to his name stand on high Alpine passes and obscure climbs in distant parts of Italy. The writer Bruno Raschi called the obsession with *il campionissimo* 'inexplicable . . . an irrational over-reaction to his memory and to his earthly image. No athlete is wept over in this way. No other has brought forth so many memories or has had a destiny of this kind. And no one has decided that it should be so.'

No one decided that Coppi should be wept over, in the same way that no one quite knows why the obsession with Coppi has endured. The answer lies in the gulf between the letter and the photograph, between the world of Aunt Albina and the image snatched at the world championship in Lugano. In the four years and four months between the two, her

Faustino, the boy from the tiny hamlet of Castellania, had become Fausto, the greatest cyclist in the world, a figure who dominated his sport. The photograph subverted and transformed the image of Italy's greatest sports star of the post-war years. It marks the moment when the idol was shown to have feet of clay, when the simple country boy of the letter suddenly became a far more complex and controversial figure. Coppi's mythical status, the tears that are still shed, stem from one essential question: how did the Faustino of the letter become the Fausto of the photograph?

CHAPTER 2

TO RACE A BIKE, YOU NEED TO BE A POOR MAN

Castellania is almost the end of the road. Only a few hamlets and farms lie beyond the village, where the foothills of the Apennines rise up, wave after wave, steep green valleys, wooded hilltops, pocket-handkerchief vineyards, lonely towers. Like the other villages in this part of north-west Italy, Castellania is not thriving. Not all the houses are lived in and there are few signs of active agriculture, although the Catholic organisation Opus Dei is investing in the village in a move which may well revitalise it. The population has declined as the small farms no longer support more than one or two people. At one time there were ten families called Coppi in the village; today there are only four. The population is now well below fifty, where once it was three hundred, and those who are left are ageing: only three children have been born here in the last twenty years. The school closed in the 1960s. The hills feel empty, silent but for birdsong.

Armando Baselica is warming himself in the April sun, sitting in an old chair repaired with planks. Behind him, a maize field slopes away and the mountains rise up, their summits still flecked with snow. If there were anything of note happening in Castellania he would have a grandstand view, but the village is sleeping. At eighty-four, Baselica, wizened and bullet-headed, has earned the right to a little rest. He is the last man here whose life ran parallel with that of the village's only famous son. He was born in 1922, went to the village school with Faustino Coppi in the late 1920s during the rise of fascism, left his studies to work in the fields, quit the hilltop to fight in Mussolini's war, returned a changed man. Had cycling not intervened, had he not been successful, Coppi might well have ended his life like this old man: sitting in peace in the spring sun watching a very small world go gently by.

Coppi and Baselica were part of the last generation who can bear witness to a lifestyle that has now all but disappeared from Italy. The world of subsistence farming by small peasant communities had changed little in its essence since medieval times, but it is now largely a memory, and even those who can recall it are dying out. This is the life from which Coppi escaped, as did so many, because the road out of the village was the only one offering any relief from hard labour and little reward. Baselica can describe life here in a single word: 'miseria'. Poverty.

The hills are attractively rounded and green as they rise from the plain. The vineyards stand in neat rows. The maize fields swish gently in the spring breeze. But the fields were not easily worked when the work was done by hand, ploughing with oxen, swinging the double-pronged spade known as the zappa to break the clods for planting. The fields are clay and turn to mud when the autumn rains come. 'It takes the thighs of a horse to lift your feet out of the mud,' said the journalist Gianni Brera.

Up here, 1,000 feet above sea level, a living had to be scratched from the land, supplemented by selling wood, maize, and the relatively poor wine from the local grapes. The peasants kept chickens, rabbits, a pig or two – vital as the source of hams and salami that would last a year – and perhaps a cow. Once a week, they made bread in a wood-burning oven, bread that, says Baselica, improved over the eight days it was kept. The houses contained only the essentials: one book, perhaps, passed down from brother to sister, might have to last ten years.

Isolation and the shared need for survival meant the people in the village were closely knit, 'like a big family', as Baselica puts it: tasks such as harvesting maize were shared cooperatively; the maize would be ground with a handmill to make the flour for *polenta*, the staple form of carbohydrate. *Miseria*, Baselica may call it, but it was not unremittingly grim. The day dedicated to the village's patron saint, San Biagio, was celebrated with two days of dancing and eating: 'rice, meat, chickens, *agnolotti* on the second day'.

In part of *Love and War in the Apennines*, a classic tale of life as an escaped prisoner of war in Italy between 1943 and 1944, Eric Newby documented daily life in a peasant household further south along the mountain range from Castellania. By the midday meal Newby and his fellow workers on the farm are already sleeping over their food through physical exhaustion. 'I had always thought of Italian *contadini* as a race of people who sat basking in the sun before the doors of their houses while the seed which they had inserted in the earth in the course of a couple of mornings' work burgeoned without their having to do anything but watch this process take place. I now knew differently. These people were fighting to survive in an inhospitable terrain from which the larger part of the inhabitants had either emigrated to the cities or to the United States or South America.'

*   *   *

Casa Coppi, Fausto's home until he left to seek his fortune on two wheels, is one of the biggest of the twenty-five or so houses in the village, a three-storey yellow building on the south side of the cluster of dwellings and barns. It follows what is clearly a typical local pattern: a long, thin house, alongside a two-storey open-fronted barn used to store hay, maize and piles of stakes for growing tomatoes. The house has barely changed since Coppi's time: the cyclist's mother Angiolina lived here until her death in 1962, after which it was shut up until it was turned into a museum in 2000.

Today, the contents are a curious mix of traditional peasant fittings and slightly incongruous, highly polished furniture from the 1940s and 1950s, presumably bought as Fausto's winnings accumulated. The large kitchen on the ground floor still has its sloping stone sink, but alongside is a new-looking wood-burning cooking range. Sadly, there is no sign of the fridge, which was Coppi's first gift to his mother. She never knew exactly what it was for and kept her underwear in it, he said, while at other times she used it to store kindling for the fire. He would never have the heart to tell her its real purpose.

The sitting room has the single-channel television Coppi bought for the family – the first in the village – but retains the myriad hooks in the ceiling for hanging hams, grapes and salami. Upstairs, both Fausto's and Serse's bedrooms contain 'preti' – priests – the sledge-like contraptions containing an earthenware pot, used for heating the beds with coals from the stove, which were the cause of many a house fire. The cot Coppi slept in as a child, with its uncomfortable looking metal frame, still stands in his parents' room, a cord still attached to one side so it can be rocked from the bed.

The Coppi family were small peasant farmers like the rest of the population, but they were slightly better off than many of their neighbours: a four-ox family where the norm was two, farming some thirteen hectares, some of it rented, but still well above the average for a holding in rural Italy. It was not enough to feed everyone, however, and Fausto's father, Domenico, had no choice but to hire his services out to other local farmers. Thin-faced, moustached, Domenico was a good-looking man, reputed to have had an eye for a pretty face.

According to one biographer, Jean-Paul Ollivier, Domenico's marriage to Angiolina Boveri, the niece of the local priest, was a shotgun affair. Their elder daughter Maria was born three months after the wedding.

Angelo-Fausto was their second son, their fourth child after their daughters Maria and Dina and their eldest son Livio. He was born on the ground floor of the house at 5 p.m. on 15 September 1919 while Domenico was working in the fields. It was his father who wanted to christen him Fausto, the family name; his mother felt he should be named Angelo after his grandfather and he was always referred to in official documents by both names. From his father, he would inherit a long, thin neck and almost Slavic cheekbones; from his mother a prominent Roman nose in the middle of a roundish face. He soon acquired the nickname Faustino, the diminutive due partly to his slender physique but also to distinguish him from his uncle of the same name.

The Coppis had lived in these parts since the seventeenth century, and were more than mere labourers, although Faustino's family were not the best educated or the most ambitious of the clan. While Domenico worked the land, his brother Giuseppe Luigi was the mayor, his sister-in-law Albina the schoolteacher. The other brother, Giuseppe Fausto, had left to make his fortune as a sea captain, and appears to have ended up as the honorary head of the family. Initially Domenico and Angiolina lived in the house behind Casa Coppi, a smaller building which has recently been turned into the Grande Airone restaurant. Gradually they took over the larger property in front across the courtyard, and eventually its ten rooms were the home of an extended family of eleven people including various aunts, Fausto and, briefly, his wife Bruna.

Later, much was made of the fact that Fausto Coppi was transformed from a physically unprepossessing youth into the greatest athlete of his generation. Writers speculated over the reasons for his scrawny physique. There was a theory that Faustino and his younger brother Serse, born in 1923, were both slightly stunted because their father's genes had been affected by the strong liquor given to him when he was a soldier in the First World War before they were conceived. Another popular myth was that Coppi suffered more broken bones than the average cyclist because his frame was weakened by a vitamin deficiency similar to rickets. Small and skinny he may have been, but he was clearly strong, although Livio must have been exaggerating when he recalled 'he could carry 100 kilos on his shoulders when he was eleven'.

Faustino was not a brawny boy, but this was nothing exceptional. A photograph from the early 1930s shows Livio, Dina and Faustino with the outsized eyes and stick legs of undernourished children, looking old beyond their years in their heavy outdoor boots and oversize, handed-down shorts. All the local children were like that: as Baselica recalls, the youngsters in the single class of pupils from Castellania and three or four surrounding villages were 'like organ pipes: thin and small, thin and medium sized, thin and tall, thin and bald, thin and hairy. All thin.'

Faustino and Serse were already close in spite of the four-year difference between them, a relationship that lasted until the younger brother's premature death in 1951. Faustino had begun Serse's schooling for him by refusing to go to class unless his little sibling went as well. Despite their closeness, they were 'like night and day', Baselica recalls. Fausto was well behaved at home, 'Serse was never still', less obedient, merrier.

Fausto worked hard at school, where their attendance would depend in part on whether they were needed in the fields; when they were there they were taught about Romulus and Remus, the River Po, Mont Blanc and the difference between animal and mineral by Faustino's lively, tough little aunt, Albina. She maintained discipline with the help of a collection of sticks kept behind her desk: thin, thick, supple, knotty, 'the right one for each infraction'. Put your hands out, she would order. But I'm your nephew, Serse, Faustino or their cousin Piero would reply. Put your hands out, you big ugly boy, she would repeat. At catechism in the church, an uncle Coppi presided with the help of a collection of sticks to match their aunt's at school. Not surprisingly with the church connection on Angiolina's side of the family, the Coppis were 'gente di chiesa', religious people: missing a service meant trouble, recalls Piero.

When not at school or working alongside their parents on the farm, the boys played a version of hopscotch, and sometimes stole fruit, which wasn't mere mischief: they were always hungry. They played soccer with a ball made of rags until it split, or until one of the boys went to tell the owner of the field that they were ruining his grass; out would come the peasant brandishing a stick, and they would run away laughing fit to burst. Serse tended to be the prankster among the children; Fausto was as serious a child as he would be as an adult.

Coppi's first bike was a reject, picked up from a corner where it had been abandoned because it was virtually unusable. He had no money, so he restored it to working order as best he could. He remembered a frame with the chrome cracking off it, so big that he had trouble getting his leg over the crossbar. On 17 October 1927, Albina wrote the letter A, for absent, against the boy's name in the school register. The eight-year-old Faustino had gone out on his bike that day and played truant, so she made him write out one hundred times: 'I must go to school and not ride my bicycle.' On their clunky old machines, the boys played at bike racing, running time trials where the lack of a stopwatch did not matter: one of them would count the seconds out loud. One such bike racing game was the Giro d'Italia.

That reflected the fact that in the time before the rise of football, cycling was Italy's most popular sport. Although cycle ownership was lower than in France or Britain, the bike was the main means of transport for most of the population. Since its foundation in 1909, the Giro had drawn the country together, bringing its glamour and festival atmosphere to the most far-flung areas. As well as the great one-day Classics such as Milan–San Remo and the Giro di Lombardia, monuments of the sport even today, a host of regional one-day races such as the Giro del Veneto, Tre Valli Varesine, Milan–Turin and the Giro del Piemonte drew massive crowds. The *tifosi* thronged to watch the stars at exhibition events on short circuits and banked velodromes, and the start contracts for the cyclists were correspondingly fat.

The first great national rivalry of Italian cycling, between the *campionissimi* – champions of champions – Alfredo Binda and Learco Guerra, had caught the popular imagination. Internationally, Italy could boast the first world road champion in Binda (1927) and a brace of Tour de France wins for Ottavio Bottecchia in 1924 and 1925. Together with Tuscany to the south and Lombardy to the east, the Piedmont of Coppi's childhood was a hotbed of the sport, producing champions such as Gerbi, Brunero and Costante Girardengo, whose home was in Novi Ligure, on the plain below Castellania. As well as the *campioni* and *campionissimi*, the men who made the serious money, there were decent pickings to be had for the *gregari*, the lesser lights who helped the great men in the big races and made up the numbers in the exhibition races.

When a journalist went to Castellania with Coppi in the 1940s, the cyclist said simply: 'Do you understand now why I became a cyclist? What could I do other than go off on my bike?' The parallels between subsistence farming and the life of a professional cyclist are surprisingly close: both entail hours of repetitive physical labour in the open air, in all weathers, with no certainty that all the effort will have its due reward. For all the drama of the breakaway or the sprint, the podium girls and the chance of prize money, there was a distinctly unglamorous side to cycling in those days: saddle boils from the poor roads, sickness from an uncertain diet, the bizarre remedies peddled by team helpers. The professional cyclist had to accept adversity – punctures, crashes, stronger rivals, capricious team managers, poor wages – with the stoicism with which a peasant views the weather.

Cycling was physically demanding, but it was better than the unremitting drudgery of working the land. As the Irish farmer turned racer Sean Kelly said two generations later, at least when you were on your bike you got paid more for being out in the rain all day. That was ever the case for professional cyclists who were not *campionissimi* or even *campioni*. Coppi's contemporary Alfredo Martini explained: 'When I left to go training early in the morning, the peasants were already in the fields; my father, my brother, bent over the spades thinking only of work and fatigue. I would ride two hundred kilometres in training and when I came back in the evening, tired but happy from the long trip, I would see the same people still thinking only of the same tiring and repetitive work.'

'Cycle racing opened the doors to a world forbidden to mere mortals,' writes the historian Daniele Marchesini. As well as the financial rewards and the chance to eat foodstuffs never seen on peasant farmers' tables, cycle racing offered the chance to travel, a glamorous business at a time when the nearest market town was a major excursion for many. Martini told of the pride he felt on returning home with the labels of the best hotels in Paris and Brussels stuck on his suitcase. 'Cycling meant leaving the status of peasant behind and travelling the world, getting to know other people, other languages, meeting famous people and – not the last thing on our minds – earning more than normal.'

*   *   *

At twelve, Coppi was out of school and working alongside his father on the farm; a year later, however, in 1932, he moved away from home to work at a butcher's shop, Ettore's, in Novi Ligure, twenty kilometres away on the plain. Such a move was common among the children of peasants: the land could only support the parents. The seagoing uncle Fausto, *il comandante*, was the man who found him the job. Coppi recalled the day he left: a cool spring morning, walking alongside his father who was on his way to the fields, pushing his bike, this one lent to him by his brother Livio, 'an enormous heavy machine with regal handlebars and tyres like lifebelts', carrying his lunch in a checked handkerchief. Domenico said goodbye to his son at the foot of the first hill.

Coppi did not stay long at Ettore's. He moved to another butcher's shop, run by Domenico Merlano at Via Paolo 17 – a single room opening onto the street under a stone lintel in the Roman style, with vast hams and salamis swinging from the door frames and two colossal pigs' heads hanging from the wall.

Initially, Faustino stayed the entire week in Novi, but soon he grew homesick and asked his boss to allow him to sleep in Castellania and ride daily to and from his work. And here, it seems, the bike suddenly gained in importance, with a round trip of forty kilometres each day to build his young muscles and the long climb back up to the village from the *pianura* to develop the heart and lungs that would power him in the future. Angiolina would wake him at six, but Coppi liked to stay in bed as late as he could in the mornings. 'To avoid the clips round the ear that would be waiting for me, there was only one solution: make up on the road the time I had wasted in bed. And so I ended up sprinting the twenty kilometres to the butcher's. No one ever timed me, but none of the cyclists I met along the way could hold onto me.'

The downhill run to Novi would turn into a time trial, with a slap from his boss if he failed to make the cut. He would 'go lorry hunting', looking for a vehicle that was moving slowly enough for him to tuck into the slipstream. Sometimes he met local amateurs, and the story goes that, in the style of the best film scripts, one morning he met a string of them, apologised for not riding with them because he was late for work and whizzed away on his heavy bike, to their utter consternation.

Cash, meanwhile, remained scarce. The Castellania priest would walk with Faustino to catch the bus at a stop outside the village to save half a lira. So it must have been a huge gamble when one day, probably in 1933 when he was thirteen or fourteen, Faustino and Livio took their savings out of the bank in order to buy new bikes. The bank accounts had been opened for the brothers by an uncle, Cico, with ten lire apiece; *il comandante* Giuseppe Fausto, the sea captain, had gradually filled them up so they had 400 lire each. Livio bought a Maino, Faustino a Girardengo, and they rode them together, always over the climb at Carezzano, unsurfaced like most of the roads, up to one in six at its steepest. Here they would meet local amateurs and professionals; Faustino could leave them all behind. Among his victims was a cyclist named 'Piass', who had raced the Giro, and who refused to speak to the youngster after being left behind.

However, the butcher was less than entirely happy with the scruffy boy who turned up each morning on his bike: Faustino took far too long to do his rounds of the neighbouring villages. Unknown to Merlano, every time he rode out into the countryside he chose a route that took in a village called Gavi, an extra ten or fifteen kilometres, including a long climb. To avoid Merlano's clips round the ear, he had no choice but to ride the circuit faster and faster. When the butcher did find out, he had trouble believing quite how quickly his delivery boy could ride his bike.

CHAPTER 3

THE BLIND MAN AND THE BUTCHER'S BOY

The Museo dei Campionissimi in Novi Ligure is a large, yellow building just outside the town centre, surrounded by cycling sculptures – a final sprint, a cyclist on a mountain – while inside is a celebration of the town's two cycling greats: paintings, photographs, cuttings from magazines, cartoons, all devoted to Coppi and his predecessor Costante Girardengo, nine times Italian champion and six times winner of the Milan–San Remo Classic after the First World War. Here, cycling roots still run deep. Leave the station and the first thing you see is a statue of Coppi in a small park with tired-looking goldfish in a pool. Coppi spent much of his life in Novi, and his daughter Marina still lives in the town.

Visit Novi and you can understand why Coppi became a cyclist: the town lived and breathed the sport. This was a centre of the Italian cycle industry, home of the Santamaria and Fiorelli manufacturers; when Coppi came to work here, Girardengo was the town's most famous inhabitant. Here, in the early 1930s, the *campionissimo* and the men who raced with him and lived off him were hard to avoid. The baker opposite Merlano's boasted that he had delivered his brioche to the champion. Gira' also bought meat from Merlano: on one occasion, Coppi had to take him some salami but the great man showed little interest in the bony youth on the butcher's bike.

Domenico Merlano had a number of regular clients who

would sit in the shop and put the world to rights over slices of sausage and a glass or two of wine. One of these regulars, a recently blind man named Biagio Cavanna, spent more time there than the others as he came to terms with his disability. With his Ray-Bans and his stick, Cavanna was a distinctive figure in the little town: thickset, heavy jowled, and now weighing 120 kilos due to the loss of physical activity with the onset of blindness. His bad temper was well known. The blind man had worked as a masseur and team manager; he had a dogmatic way about him as they discussed the merits of this cyclist and that footballer.

There are at least four versions of and several different dates for the first meeting between Cavanna and Faustino Coppi; it is variously said to have been through the butcher or through various cyclists trained by Cavanna who met Coppi on the road and reported back to their master. The masseur and the youth met some time between the end of 1937 and the summer of 1938 and that is all that matters. It was a key moment in Coppi's story, probably the single most important event.

Cavanna was Fausto's cycling father and the most import-ant influence on his cycling career. Cavanna drove the budding champion forwards in his formative years and was behind him in his greatest ones, providing far more than massages. He taught him how to train, how to ride his bike, how to behave as a professional sportsman should. Eventually, he provided him with team-mates, sympathy and magic mixtures to make him go faster.

Before his blindness struck, Biagio Cavanna had noticed Fausto Coppi as a fifteen-year-old working in Merlano's shop, a 'reed-thin lad with joints of meat on his handlebars'. The man who made the champion would never know what his protégé looked like at his peak, would never see the colour of the yellow, pink and rainbow-striped jerseys he won.

He would only know Coppi's voice, and his body: the tone of each muscle, the temperature and texture of his skin. The sound of the young cyclist's voice was still in the ears of the old man twenty-two years later after Coppi's death. 'A bit timid and awkward, the voice of a young boy from the country.'

Cavanna had started out as a cycle racer of some talent, then turned boxer, where he had a reputation as a clever fighter who could not take punches and was willing to play dead to escape a nasty bout. After his sporting career was over, he had settled for a backroom role. He had looked after Girardengo and had been the confidant of the legendary Learco Guerra, the 'human locomotive', world road champion and winner of the Giro d'Italia with ten stages along the way. He had travelled Europe to the indoor cycling tracks of Belgium and Germany and had followed the Giro and Tour de France. This was exotic enough, but there was talk of murkier links. Cavanna had been a close friend of a legendary bandit, Sante Pollastro, who had gone on a Bonnie and Clyde style spree of robbery and killing across Lombardy. There was a story that he and Pollastro communicated by whistles; on one occasion, it was said, Pollastro had whistled while Cavanna was at a Six-Day race in Paris and he had upped and left the track centre. It may or may not have been true but it reflected Cavanna's larger than life aura.

It was some time in 1936 when Cavanna first began wearing the sunglasses which would be his trademark. His blindness had been a gradual process over three years, the sight going first in the right eye, then in the left. The precise reason was never clear, but the gossips, inevitably, said it might be syphilis. Cavanna himself claimed it was as a result of getting hot smuts from a steam engine in his eyes when he was on a trip to Brussels. Perhaps understandably for a man who had been deprived of sight, Cavanna liked to be in control of the world around him and the people in it. His wife would read him the papers. He controlled the family's cash by touch. Through his work he came to manage entire careers and dictate the pace of men's lives.

Traditionally, Cavanna is described as a *soigneur* – French cycling jargon for a team helper, who gives massages, providing race food and lends a sympathetic ear as he rubs his charges' legs. The term is no longer officially used, because since the dawn of cycle racing, the *soigneur* has also been the provider of secret remedies that range from old wives' tales about training and diet to the latest wonder drugs. But the blind man was more than a leg rubber and witchdoctor.

One old cyclist of the era, Alfredo Martini, calls him *un maestro*, which variously translates as a teacher, a master, an expert in his field. He was talent scout, tactician, trainer, team manager. Behind his back Cavanna was called '*l'umon*' – dialect for *l'omone*, big man. He had been christened Giuseppe, but this was long forgotten. He was always Biagio, Biasu in the local dialect, Signor Biagio to his pupils. There were other nicknames: the Miracle Maker, the Muscle Wizard. He was an intimidating figure to his protégés, by and large ill-educated young labourers and peasants, who had never been far from their home villages. As one of them said: 'I wasn't afraid of God or Fausto [Coppi], but I was scared of Cavanna.'

Post-war, he ran a legendary cycling 'college' at 4 Via Castello, where the courtyard is still recognisable from old photographs, although the frescoes have long since faded and fallen. To the left through the arch was the kitchen, in which *il maestro* would hold court. The yard, however, was the hub, with its workbench and tools, dismantled bikes, empty petrol cans, sheets, and jerseys and shorts hanging on the washing lines. The dining table would be placed outside the kitchen window, or under the arch when it rained in winter; wheels were hung on hooks on the walls. Rooms were rented above the arch where the riders slept, and there were other rooms about the town, where the riders 'camped out like gypsies'. Cavanna would never use a massage table; the riders lay on the bed in the room and he went to work. There was a small toilet in one corner of the yard, a thirty-foot-deep well in the opposite one, with a winch formed from a tree trunk for bringing up the water.

*   *   *

To this day, blind masseurs carry particular status within cycling. As recently as the 1990s, the ONCE professional squad set great store by one Angel Rubio, but sixty years ago, among sportsmen who lacked education and experience of the wider world, a *soigneur*'s market value was based only partly on what he actually knew. Just as important was the mystique these figures carried with them, which added a whole psychological side to their treatment and their remedies. Given the intensity of superstitious belief in rural Europe at the time, they had a ready market. Whatever the degree of his expertise, Cavanna inspired both fear and faith among those he treated.

Cavanna's blindness added to the aura created by his connections and his personality. All those treated by him would maintain that his massages were better than others', because he had *il tatto*, the healing touch, in both hands. The *soigneur* was happy to build on the mystique by claiming he had supernatural qualities: 'My hands can see better than any human eye and my ears can hear sounds inaudible to the normal person. My hands and my ears never lie.'

Asked further about the blind man's sense of touch, Alfredo Martini simply grabbed the scruff of my neck. 'There were points in the physique which let him understand if you were strong, if you were weak,' he said, and this was one of them. 'A thin neck is worth nothing', the blind man would say.

Cavanna also claimed that he could assess the strength of a rider's heart by taking his pulse, then he would move up the arm to check the musculature, to see if the cyclist was willing to do hard physical work. When he got to the neck, the muscles there would tell him if the rider had tried hard in training and could sustain the workload. The muscles of the lower back and buttocks would show the cyclist's strength and ability to change pace – the 'cartridge belt', Cavanna called it.

His charges also remember the things he said, in the didactic, semi-mystical phrases typical of such eminences grises. One motto was '*niente fumo, niente donne, niente vino*': no smoking, no women, no wine. Another was 'Enjoyment of any kind is a cyclist's worst enemy.' On sexual activity he subscribed to the view of some modern day team managers, that it is not the act but the hunt that is harmful to the athlete, hence the maxim 'Don't fool about with girls, they'll leave you in bits. It's better to go to a brothel.' Most important of all was the call for absolute obedience: 'If you want to be a cyclist, don't ever ask questions. Do what I say and remember that others have done the same before you.'

Cavanna 'could go inside the mind of the athlete, indicate to each guy how to prepare,' Martini told me. There was a practical side to his work. He taught his pupils skills such as how to remove gravel from their tyres with the palm of the hand, and invented a primitive kind of tyre saver that skimmed flints off the tyres before they could be driven through the cover, a vital aid on the unmade roads of the time. As well as training, the pupils were taught 'behaviour with women, with journalists, at table, how to look after the bike'. He had made Girardengo shift baskets of gravel in a riverbed over one winter in order to strengthen his back. He had an obsession with position on the bike and with training in different, usually difficult conditions. His method of assessing whether a cyclist was ready to turn professional was simple. There were two sweet factories nearby; one in Novi, the other in a village called Serravalle, seven kilometres away, and if a rider could travel from one to the other in seven minutes, averaging 60kph over the distance, he was good enough.

*   *   *

Faustino Coppi may have been whizzing ever faster around the Piedmont hills on his butcher's bike, but as a racing cyclist he was the rawest of recruits. He had begun racing unofficial local events for Spinetta Marengo, the club nearest to Castellania. A photograph of this time shows him on a machine that clearly does not fit, with balloon tyres and floppy brake cables. Coppi's shorts are baggy around his stick-thin legs but his hair already has the neat side parting that would be his trademark. His uncle remembered one event in particular, in 1936, held at a nearby hamlet, Buffalora, to celebrate the return of troops from one of Mussolini's African wars. The sixteen-year-old Coppi rode up to the startline from Novi Ligure, won on his own by five minutes and took home fifty lire and a salami. Other records show him riding an event on 1 July 1937, over a course that started and finished in Buffalora, in which he punctured and failed to finish.

Cavanna initially had his doubts about Coppi but it was nothing to do with his cycling ability. One of his criteria for accepting 'students' was that they should be neither well off nor well educated. In his view, only the poverty-stricken had the hunger to make a champion. He liked carters, masons, builders, peasants. He hesitated to take Coppi because he had a job and might be soft, but he changed his mind when he heard that Coppi had worked in the fields at Castellania. Coppi, on the other hand, knew all about Cavanna when the blind man came into the butcher's shop and asked to meet *il Faustino*.

By the late 1940s the diminutive would be gone and Fausto Coppi would be legendary for his perfect pedalling style on the bike and his sartorial elegance off it. A 1938 description by fellow cyclist Luigi Malabrocca underlines the Cinderella-like transformation effected with the support of the blind man. In those days, he said, Coppi was 'in a right state, only fit for the dustbin. Shoulders hunched as if he was choking, sickly, pallid, twisted to one side, nervous, with feverish eyes, the eyes of a man possessed, and up front a big pointed nose. A shabby jersey and flapping breeches, fixed to his gaiters with clothes pegs. A military haversack around his neck and an old gate of a bike.'

According to Cavanna's later accounts, Faustino pedalled with his head in the clouds and his toes pointing at the ground. In spite of the balloon tyres on his heavy bike, he punctured time after time, and Cavanna realised it was because he was not looking where he was going. That habit had to be brow-beaten out of him. It took time, and so did persuading him to give up the wine he had always drunk, as peasants always did. Instead, he was put on a diet of minestrone made with greens, which he disliked. Faustino was made to sleep as if he was on his bike, lying on his right side with his knee brought up to his body.

Cavanna's school had yet to grow to the scale it reached when Coppi's career, and the blind man's reputation, were collectively at their zenith, but at the time he had three *allievi*, pupils. Coppi was put to train with the best, Borlando. It was not an easy life. 'The principle was: ride your bike. On your bike every day. Even rest days,' recalled Michele Gismondi, who went through the 'nursery' when Coppi was in his prime. Gismondi would have preferred any other life, 'alive or dead', it was so hard.

First thing in the morning, Cavanna would bang on the bedroom door with his stick, thwacking the planks as if he wanted to break it down. Some former pupils have it as early as 4 a.m., others 7 a.m.; presumably it depended on the time of year. Cavanna's contacts in Novi would have let him know if any of his charges had been seen in a bar, or in female company. They would receive their instructions – 'andate di qui, di là, di sù, di giù', here, there, up, down, as one protégé told me, quoting Figaro – and they would be waved off as if it were a race. All Cavanna lacked was a finish flag, said another. Each training circuit had its set time which the riders had to better. One typical circuit was 190 kilometres, westwards over the Apennines to the Mediterranean and back again, partly on unmade roads, to be done in six hours, the riders propelled by bottles of water, caffeine and the stimulant simpamine, a mild form of amphetamine that students took to get them through their exams. 'It won't make you campioni, but it will help you concentrate,' their master would say.

'When we came back Cavanna would come to us. He would be waiting with his hands to feel whether we had sweated, whether we were thin, whether we were dry, in form, or still had work to do,' said Riccardo Filippi, whom Cavanna guided to a world amateur championship. If the blind man's hands felt that a cyclist's neck was dry, he would be sent out to sweat some more. One protégé recalls that they would sometimes get round him by wetting their collars with water.

Cavanna was paid in kind – a basket of fruit, a chicken, a demi-john of wine or a big bottle of oil – and he would take a cut when he placed cyclists with professional teams. His allievi would put their prize money into a common pot to pay for their rent. As aspirants to the senior categories – they would make the transition via the intermediate category of independent – theirs was a primitive, relentless life: riding to races with their kit on carriers on the front wheel, sleeping in schools on overnight trips further away. But it was better than labouring, and it was not without its lighter moments.

On one occasion the *allievi* caught a goose while they were out training and brought it back to the master, who could tell from its terrified protestations that it was not a young bird. He was right: it took three days to cook.

*   *   *

Soon after he began working with Cavanna, Faustino gave up his job at the butcher's and began working part-time on the farm, riding down from his home in Castellania to meet the *maestro* and his fellow pupils for training. At this time, having saved up 300 lire from his earnings to buy his first racing bike, he had to deal with poverty as well as the demands his new master made on him. He would ride home from races in the dark, because he did not have the cash to rent a room for the night. Sometimes he and his family would be unable to find the ten or twenty lire he needed to enter a race. He would leave home with only the start money and a few hard-boiled eggs in his pocket, and most often he would return with his pockets empty.

If the scruffy young amateur lacked style, he did not lack ambition. Coppi took his first win in a race on the official calendar early in 1938 at the age of eighteen at the town of Castelletto d'Orba, racing in the jersey of the Dopolavoro di Tortona (one of the sports clubs set up by the fascist government to improve the moral and physical health of the nation). It earned him an alarm clock with a statue of a hunchback on it, which he gave to his mother. *Il gobbo*, the hunchback, is a symbol of good fortune for Italians, and Aunt Albina said the figure would bring him luck. It did not do so immediately, however, as after that successes were few and far between: he won only one more race that season, and had eight near misses.

In most of his races, Coppi was affected by crashes,

punctures or mechanical problems; this is perhaps because he was still learning to keep his eyes on the road, or because he was unable to afford the best equipment, at a time when the quality of a cyclist's machine mattered far more than it does now. Bikes, and particularly tyres, took far more of a hammering because of the poor-quality roads, and, in the event of a problem, assistance from team vehicles was slow at best, and could not be taken for granted anyway. As a result of the lessons learned during these early setbacks, at his peak Coppi was obsessed with the quality of his kit, and would hire the finest mechanic of the time, Pinella di Grande.

It was not the races but the return trips home that enabled the young man to keep faith. As he rode back towards Novi with the other local boys, trying to save money on train fares and board and lodging, he would notice that towards the end his legs always seemed stronger than those of his companions. Not surprisingly, however, with no return for his money and his effort, he would often wonder if it was worth continuing to compete.

More worryingly, so too did his family, according to Cavanna. 'They didn't have a great belief in cycling, were afraid he was wasting time and only got enthusiastic when he won.' His mother was already worried that cycling was not a proper career and her son would be better off working in the fields or behind the counter of a butcher's shop. One day towards the end of 1938, Coppi came to the blind man 'with the look of a dog that had been beaten' and told him his family wanted him to stop racing and to work. Such is the nature of subsistence agriculture: there is no room for passengers.

At this, Cavanna lost his temper, went to Coppi's parents and offered to pay the boy's keep himself and provide his equipment, as long as he could continue to race. As he pointed out later, it was hardly a risky investment. Coppi's rise was meteoric: less than eighteen months after his first win in an official race, he was being tipped for stardom. The break-through came in 1939, when the nineteen-year-old Coppi moved up from amateur to independent, an intermediate category of riders who were permitted to compete with the professionals. 'He was incredibly thin, long legs, big thighs, no superfluous weight, like a tall wading bird,' says Fiorenzo Magni, who competed with him that year. Another observer noted that he was a 'skinny little thing who looked pretty funny in his kit. His calf muscles didn't promise much, because they were pretty scrawny.' 'More like a thin, starving goat than a cyclist,' said another.

Whatever Fausto's looks, Cavanna believed in him. The blind masseur wrote to Giovanni Rossignoli, the organiser of a race in Pavia: 'Dear Giovanni, I'm sending you two of my colts. One is called Coppi and will take the first prize, the other will do what he can. Watch Coppi: he is like Binda.' In 1939 the nine-teen-year-old won seven races, including the Italian independ-ents' championship at Varzi in early May, in which he opened up a seven-minute lead over the next man. This was heady stuff for a youth with only eighteen months' apprenticeship behind him. Each victory demonstrated the pattern that would be his hallmark in future: not only the ability to race alone at great speed, but also, most importantly, his instinct for choosing the right moment to attack the field. Just as promising, however, were his placings in his first one-day races against profes-sionals: second in the Coppa Bernocchi, third in the Giro del Piemonte and the Tre Valli Varesine.

Well before the end of 1939, two professional teams were vying for Coppi's services. In late May, Cavanna's old squad Maino, now managed by the blind masseur's former charge Girardengo, approached Coppi through his family. An agreement was reached, a contract signed, but Cavanna was outraged and turned up shortly after Girardengo had left Castellania to demand that the family renege on the deal: Cavanna had negotiated a contract for Coppi with Eberardo Pavesi, manager of Gino Bartali's Legnano team. In any case Coppi stayed with Maino the night before the Giro del Piemonte, sleeping on a camp bed pushed in between two of the riders' beds.

The pipe-smoking, garrulous Pavesi was a major figure in Italian cycling, a team manager into his eighties, variously nicknamed 'l'Avocatt', the lawyer, 'il mago', the mage, and 'il Papa', the Pope. His racing career had begun in the pioneering days of the Giro and Tour, just after the turn of the century, and as a manager he had been in charge of such legendary figures as Alfredo Binda, winner of six Giri and the first world professional road title, as well as, ironically enough, Girardengo. As for Bartali, he was the Italian No.1, winner of two Giri d'Italia and the Tour de France in the last three years. Coppi was to wear the olive green of Legnano from the start of 1940, for 700 lire a month, on a deal that provided for him for ten months of the year. The rest of the time he would have to earn a living like anyone else. Cavanna's commission was 1,000 lire and a bike from Legnano.

On the road, the transition from impoverished also-ran to budding champion took less than five weeks. At the Italian national championship for independents on 14 August at Varese, the head of the Italian cycling federation (FCI, the Federazione Ciclistica Italiana) came close to throwing Coppi out of the race, because his jersey was so scruffy it was considered to contravene the rules that contestants had to present themselves in a fit state. Coppi was allowed in, under protest, and duly won. The next day he took the flowers to the church in Castellania. His mother, befitting a careful peasant woman with an eye for appearances, said 'they must be worth at least ten lire; pretend you have bought them'.

Soon there would be no need to pretend: on 17 September, two days after his twentieth birthday, he was paid appearance money for the first time, to start the Circuito di Susa, which he also won. On his first attempt at track racing, he raised eyebrows by finishing third in a pursuit match, on a borrowed bike, to the Italian champion Olimpio Bizzi. In his final race of the season, again on the track, he beat Bizzi by forty metres.

By the end of the 1939 season, the newspapers were tipping Coppi for great things. *Il Lavoro* of Genoa described him as 'a formidable climber in spite of his height and weight'. 'We watched him racing: he has a supple pedalling style, effortless and stylish, he is one of those youths who are born to race a bike,' wrote Guido Giardini in *La Gazzetta dello Sport* on 11 November, noting, as so many other journalists would, that Coppi was 'a man of few words, shy, meek-mannered'. It had, said Giardini, only taken the few minutes in which he matched the best in the Giro del Piemonte 'to make us understand that Coppi had the makings of a champion'.

*   *   *

Gino Bartali and his 'greens' in the Legnano team had been Coppi's heroes in his amateur days. Bartali would spur him onwards and upwards for the rest of his cycling career. Their lives would be entwined for more than twenty years: initially as leader and *gregario* (team worker), then friends and legendary rivals, finally, ephemerally, team manager and team captain. They had raced together on 9 April 1939 in the Giro della Toscana; Coppi broke a wheel after 140 kilometres so there had been no confrontation. They had first come head to head in the Giro del Piemonte on 4 June. The youngster, wearing a bright yellow jersey, made an experimental attack on one of the hills and went into a solo lead, only for his chain to come off. He had to stop, and put it back on the wrong gear; even so he eventually finished third behind Bartali. That evening he went to the Legnano team's hotel with Cavanna to sign his first professional contract for the 1940 season.

Bartali told the journalist Rino Negri that, given everything Cavanna had said about the youngster, it was probably better to have him in his own team than riding against him. After all, Coppi was already being described as 'the most elegant pedaller in Italy' and had ambitions that went beyond merely enabling his team leader to win. At their first team meeting, before the opening one-day Classic of the year, Milan–San Remo, Coppi raised his voice, questioning the older man's choice of tactics. But as that year's Giro d'Italia drew near, there was nothing to suggest that the slim youth from Piemonte might be about to usurp his leader's place. Bartali had won Milan–San Remo and the Giro della Toscana in fine style. Coppi's preparation had been held up by a training accident. He had been well placed, but nothing more, finishing eighth in Milan–San Remo and twelfth in the Giro del Piemonte; his selection for the Giro in his first professional season showed that Pavesi felt he had made rapid progress in spite of his lack of wins.

The three-week Giro hinged on a single split second, during the second stage between Turin and Genoa, when Bartali hit a dog, crashed and dislocated his elbow. He was advised by his doctors to quit the race, as they estimated he would need three weeks off to recover. He refused to go home, although he rapidly lost fifteen minutes after failing to stay with the leaders as a consequence of the injury. Coppi, meanwhile, suffered more than his fair share of problems – two crashes, a broken handlebar – but had ridden consistently enough to lie in second place by the start of stage eleven, from Florence to Modena, where the riders had to cross the Apennines over the Abetone Pass.

It was on the slopes of the Abetone, in snow, cold rain, thunder and lightning, that the pattern for the rest of the race was set. Coppi had been told by Pavesi to ride his own race and escaped alone; Bartali had briefly stopped because he had a mechanical problem, with a crank coming loose. Once Coppi had flown, the older man had no choice but to remain with the other team leaders as they spent their energy chasing his team-mate; if they caught Coppi, it would be his turn to attack.

Bartali later claimed he was at least as strong as Coppi on the day, but what is not in doubt is that this was the moment Coppi emerged from obscurity. Orio Vergani wrote in *Corriere della Sera*: 'He seemed to be whistling as he went . . . on the road lashed by the frozen, cutting rain. People at the road-sides huddled under umbrellas, trying to read the number stamped on his frame, looked for his name in the paper that corresponded to the number . . . Coppi, an unknown . . . Fausto, an even more unknown name . . .' Another commentator recalled spectators yelling 'Isn't that the skinny guy who rides for the green rats?' At the finish, he took over the pink jersey of race leader amid general astonishment.

Coppi was as shocked as anyone else. The only time he had spoken about wearing the pink jersey was as a joke, shared with his room-mate Mario Ricci. Ricci had noticed that his young team-mate only wore black socks and asked him why. Coppi replied that as an independent he could not afford white ones, which got dirty far more quickly and were harder to wash. 'We joked that when he won the pink jersey, he would get white socks to go with it.'

As the Dolomites approached, Coppi grew stronger and Bartali's strength declined. The Legnano leader began to mutter about quitting the race but was told that his public image would be better served by staying where he was and assisting his young, inexperienced team-mate. He and Pavesi also had in mind that a three-week Tour was a test of stamina better suited to the more mature man. Debutants who are given the unaccustomed responsibility of leading a major Tour tend not to be up to the pressure, and, although Bartali was half an hour behind, there was still a strong chance that the youngster would not be able to make it to Milan without falling apart.

Coppi's crisis came on the stage to Pieve di Cadore in the Alps, when he made two elementary errors: firstly, eating too much at once, secondly, stopping for a moment. He had a stomachful of chicken sandwich when a rival, Vicini, attacked at the feeding station. He panicked. 'Trembling, I began to chase him,' he wrote. 'These were terrible moments – the cars in the caravan had created a dreadful traffic jam on the road and got in the way of the chase. And the chicken I had eaten was weighing on my stomach like a brick.' By the next mountain pass, the Col de Mauria, he had caught up with Vicini, but he was already exhausted; as the leaders tackled the climb, he was left behind.

'Overcome with sickness, I had to stop by the ditch, vomiting up all the food that I had tried to get down. One by one, all my fellow competitors overtook me as, bent double with sickness, unaware of what was going on, my eyes swimming, I barely realised that I was losing the pink jersey.' It was Bartali who saved the youth. Their roles had been reversed: it was the man who had begun the race as leader who performed the loyal team-mate's duties that Coppi had been hired to carry out for him. By a lucky coincidence, the older man had been delayed by a series of punctures. 'He stopped next to me . . . put his arm around my shivering shoulders and passed me a bottle of water. As I lay on the grass and tried to recover, Gino Bartali, the great Gino Bartali, gently began to lecture me, to persuade me that I should go on and win.'

The pink jersey was saved, but next day came the toughest mountain stage of the entire race, finishing in the town of Ortisei; only 110 kilometres long, it included three massive climbs, the Falzarego, Pordoi and Sella. With only a rest day and two more days' racing to follow before the finish, this was where the race would be decided. To make sure his riders would have the extra kick they needed, Pavesi set out the night before and drove up both the first two passes. In a café at the top of the Falzarego he provided the café owner with two bottles and told him to fill them with coffee and hand them to the first two riders over the pass. 'How do you know they will be your riders?' asked the proprietor. 'One will be wearing red, white and green [Italian national champion, the jersey worn by Bartali] and the other will be in pink,' answered the manager.

He was correct in his prediction that Coppi and Bartali would ride the stage together, but the precise account of what happened depends on the point of view: *Bartaliano* or *Coppiano*. Bartali made the running early in the stage, with Coppi struggling to follow him. Twice Coppi punctured, with Bartali waiting. On the final climb, however, it was Bartali's turn to have a flat tyre. Coppi attacked at once, only to be told by Pavesi that he must wait: 'Pacts are things that you must respect!' In his autobiography, Bartali was adamant: 'If I'd been from another team he wouldn't have won the Giro. He was not experienced and had his limits on the climbs, he would suddenly have nothing in the tank. When that happened in the Dolomites I was the one who saved him from disaster. I didn't do it for him, but for Legnano who paid my wages.' He added that if he had helped Coppi he had done so unwillingly, 'because he asked for things he shouldn't have'.

One eyewitness, Beppe Pegoletti, writing for *La Nazione*, described how Bartali waited for Coppi, shouting encouragement, pacing him 'with patience, even with love' as the young man struggled to hang on to his wheel. At one point Coppi stopped, and Bartali took a handful of snow and rubbed it on Coppi's forehead, then he dropped it onto the nape of his neck. Towards the end of the stage, on the descent to the finish in the little town of Ortisei, Coppi missed a turning and punctured: it was Bartali who gave him his wheel.

Coppi rode into the vast Arena in Milan two days later, the clear winner of the Giro at his first attempt at the age of twenty. The 27,000-lire first prize was his, including a 10,000-lire *Premio del Duce*. The entire Coppi family had travelled to Milan to welcome him in the great open-air stadium, deliberately built to resemble an ancient Roman amphitheatre, on the edge of the Sempione park. The men of the family – Domenico, Uncle Fausto, Livio, Serse – had listened to the mountain stages around the one radio in the village, which was kept in the schoolroom. They had received occasional postcards from their Faustino, two or three of them with a brief message: 'Don't worry, the *maglia rosa* is on its way.'

Whatever the extent of Bartali's assistance, it was a remarkable achievement in a race of such complexity and distance. Usually, stage races favour the older rider: winning such an event at twenty is truly rare. Suddenly Coppi was thrust into the limelight, as he recognised in his memoirs *Le Drame de Ma Vie*, published in 1950. 'It's a curious thing, becoming a star. In one day, a hundred new friends turn up whom you didn't know the day before; the cinema, press and radio take you over. Your legend is born in such a different form compared to the reality that it astounds you. Another Fausto Coppi came into the world, who bore no resemblance to the Fausto Coppi I felt I had quite a few good reasons to know.'

It was also the first act in what would become Italy's greatest sporting rivalry. Bartali clearly resented playing second fiddle to his young team-mate. 'You can rest but don't have too many illusions: give it a year and I'll put things back how they should be,' he told Coppi. Instead, they had to wait six years for the Giro to be run again.

CHAPTER 4

'A VERY REGRETTABLE PHENOMENON'

Two days after shocking Italy with his Giro d'Italia win, Coppi was called up. The transformation from obscurity to overnight celebrity to infantryman No. 7375 in a couple of weeks must have been bewildering, but this was in keeping with the times. Italy had declared war on France and Britain the previous day, on 10 June 1940. Mussolini was about to perform his 'stab in the back', the attempt to conquer France through the Riviera. Invasions of Greece and North Africa were shortly to follow.

Incongruous as it is to think of sport continuing in a relatively normal way at such a time, the formative years of Coppi's career had coincided with Europe's descent into war. In Italy, the fascist regime had always taken a close interest in cycling. 'A sport of poets', Mussolini called it. Stages of the Giro were run down newly opened autostradas, and ministers put pressure on Gino Bartali to race, and win, the Tour de France, in order to enhance Italy's prestige on the international stage. The coming conflict had had little impact on the sheltered world of two wheels, in Italy at least. In summer 1939, the world track championship had been cancelled after the French, Belgian and Dutch Federations pulled their riders out. In autumn that year, the Giro di Lombardia had gone ahead with only one car in the caravan due to fuel shortages.

But as Coppi was learning the art of cycling with Cavanna in 1938, Italy was coming to terms with Mussolini's anti-semitic laws, which placed Jews on the same footing as in Nazi Germany. The newspapers that described his first victories in the late summer of 1939 had Hitler's invasion of Poland and Britain's entry into the war on their front pages. In May and June 1940, even as Coppi and Bartali scrapped in the Dolomites, Hitler's armies were marching on Paris. Italy had its mind elsewhere in those weeks: when would Mussolini take his country to war?

Italy entered the conflict on 10 June, the day after Coppi had returned to Castellania in triumph and given his young cousin Piero a new bike. *La Gazzetta dello Sport* had summed up his win in martial terms: 'Fausto is the conscript who has broken with tradition and won the Giro on his debut . . . this Giro was won by a little soldier with permission to take his leave.' This was actually more than a standard metaphor for a team worker who had won with the approval of his leader; Coppi's military service had been postponed by a month to enable him to ride that Giro. Soon, however, he was a conscript for real.

Coppi said later that the notion of having to kill another man revolted him, but he did not see action for two and a half years. Initially he was posted to Limone Piemonte, near the Alpine front; when the brief French 'campaign' was over, he was sent to Tortona, just up the road from Novi Ligure. His commanding officers were sympathetic, so his life barely altered, even though he was now in barracks: he kept his bike in a workshop behind the barracks, continued training and racing and went to Cavanna's almost daily for massage. By his own admission, he was not a good soldier: something was always missing when his kit was inspected, and 'four or five times a day', he said, he had trouble with his puttees.

There was another significant change, but it occurred more gradually. In late August 1940, a shy, brown-haired girl named Bruna Ciampolini came to ask the star for his autograph at a race. He promised her a signed postcard, but never delivered;

eventually she wrote to him at Castellania, addressing her post-card simply to *Corridore Ciclista Fausto Coppi*, politely asking if he could provide the card. Bruna was a couple of years younger than Fausto and came from a suburb of Genoa called Sestri Ponente, where her parents had a grocer's shop. For the duration of the war, to avoid the bomber raids that were expected over Genoa, she had been sent to stay with her aunt at Villalvernia, a village between Castellania and Novi.

They were both shy individuals, and the relationship devel-oped slowly. This was a small world, though, and there were connections. Bruna and Coppi would happen to meet as they both rode their bikes down the road between Novi and Tortona; they went to the same bike shop, Rossi's, in Tortona. One of Bruna's friends was related to a team-mate of Coppi's. They were photographed in a courtyard, among apple blossom and budding vines, the kind of image that must have been repro-duced in hundreds of thousands of photograph albums across the world in those years. The young soldier is in his fatigues, leaning casually next to his girl; Bruna wears a striped skirt and plain jumper. By the time he left for the front in March 1943, they were engaged to be married, according to one version because it was the only way they could get permis-sion from her old-fashioned father to go to the cinema together.

Life in Italy remained relatively normal in those early years of conflict. There was limited rationing – and, being Italy, ways were found to get round it – cinemas and theatres continued to open, and the *calcio* (football) champion-ship continued. As in much of Europe, cycle racing never quite came to a complete halt. The Giro d'Italia stopped with the outbreak of war, although in 1942 and 1943 the author-ities arranged for a circuit of eight one-day events that carried the name. Criteriums – circuit races on a short course run for a paying public – continued, but professionals were made to compete for free as their contribution to the war effort.

Following the example set by Nazi Germany, the Italian Federation took upon itself to scrutinise those amateurs who applied for professional licences, to filter out 'undesirable' cyclists.

Nicknamed the 'rocket express' by his fellow conscripts, Coppi was allowed to train three days a week as long as he was back in barracks for curfew, and he was allowed to race, though only to boost the prestige of his regiment rather than to fill his own pocket. Wrapped up as he was in his own sporting world, he cannot have been the only Italian to have felt, as he put it, that the conflict did not really concern him at this time. The war, he said, was 'a very regrettable phenomenon, but one which happily had only a moderate effect on my personal life and my cycling career. I paid a sort of tax, by being in barracks four days a week, and that was all I had to do.'

The rivalry with Bartali became intense, even though the two cyclists were still competing together in the colours of Legnano, and Bartali was nominally his leader. In the autumn following his Giro d'Italia win Coppi was close to matching the older man in the Giro di Lombardia. He escaped from an early break on the climb leading to the chapel at Madonna del Ghisallo, only for his stomach to play up – a recurring weakness – enabling Bartali to overtake him 300 metres from the top. In 1941, however, Coppi scored a string of wins in the other provincial single-day events that are the mainstay of the Italian calendar: Giro dell'Emilia, Giro del Veneto, Tre Valli Varesine, Giro della Provincia di Milano. He was still working with Cavanna, with the blind man on a percentage of his prize money. Within Legnano, he had recruited at least one team-mate, Mario Ricci, to work for him rather than Bartali, who had, he said, begun to try to sabotage him by making him eat more than his fragile stomach could stand before a race.

Most significantly, and most bitterly for Bartali, Coppi opened his 1941 season by winning the Giro della Toscana: this event was in the Italian No.1's backyard, in front of his home crowd. Coppi rode the final forty miles ahead of the field to finish three minutes ahead of Bartali, in spite of heavy, chilly rain that turned the roads on the main climb, the Colle Saltino, into heavy mud and made the gravelly descent highly dangerous. The fourth rider was twenty-four minutes behind. Coppi, already, was showing the ability to judge a solo effort and the smooth pedalling style that would be his hallmark. In victory, he was opening up huge margins, and the implication was that the young upstart, in only his second season as a professional, was about to overtake his master.

During 1941 it became clear that Bartali and his young team-mate were ahead of all the opposition, although *La Gazzetta dello Sport* felt that Coppi was 'the strongest cyclist of the season in Italy'. In 1942 Coppi edged ahead in the stakes by beating Bartali once more, in the national road race championship. He did so after it seemed a puncture had put him totally out of the running, and he recalled Bartali's shock when he finished and found out who had relieved him of the title. 'He went as grey as ash. He shook, as if the news weighed more heavily on his legs than the kilometres he had just ridden. His *soigneurs* hurried to support him.' Bartali, on the other hand, took the first 'Giro di Guerra', the regime-backed circuit of eight events that had replaced the three-week Giro.

In one area, however, Coppi was in a class of his own. His ability to judge his pace translated well to one discipline on the track: pursuiting, in which two riders start on opposite sides of a velodrome and 'pursue' each other over a given distance, in those days 5,000 metres for professionals. Pursuits would draw the paying crowds because the stars of the road racing world – a Giro winner, a Classics specialist – could be hired to ride: the stars were visible for the whole six minutes or so that a pursuit lasted, it was easy to work out who was winning and the confrontation could be hyped up even if the stars were just there for the fee.

In a pursuit, Coppi was so superior to the other riders that he would usually close the half-lap gap on his opponent, ending the race early. Three weeks after winning the Giro he took the Italian national pursuit championship, at an average speed verging on 50kph, precociously fast for a twenty-year-old. His fame spread, within the bounds of a Europe at war; he was invited to race in Berlin, and on the Oerlikon track in Zurich in a contest against the rising Swiss star Ferdi Kübler. These were Coppi's first trips abroad and it showed: en route to Switzerland he was not permitted to change money, on arriving he could not find a taxi, so he had to walk the four miles to the stadium, asking the way as he went. At the stadium, the guard had no idea who he was, did not speak Italian and would not let him in until an angry crowd had gathered insisting this was indeed Fausto Coppi and not an imposter. In front of a home crowd numbering 10,000, Kübler was over-taken after less than four kilometres.

Coppi rode twenty pursuits during 1940, 1941 and 1942; both invitation events and the Italian championships in each year. He remained unbeaten in the discipline, a feat which is rarely remarked upon, mainly because events elsewhere made sport largely irrelevant. The war had yet to reach its crisis in Italy but, elsewhere, France had fallen, Dunkirk had been evacuated and Britain had been defended by 'the Few'. Russia was close to collapse; the Battle of the Atlantic was at its height and Italians were fighting in North Africa. In Italy, however, cycle racing continued up to the moment that the government took the side of the Allies in 1943, and Italy was not unique: occupied France, for example, also had a racing calendar right through the war. Apart from bombing raids, the conflict had not yet been unleashed on Italian soil. The campaigns were all abroad, and although they were not going well it was still possible for life to continue in a relatively normal way.

Coppi's cycling career was gaining momentum within the confines imposed by the war, but it stuttered at the end of 1941, with the first in the sequence of premature deaths that would eventually lead to talk of a 'curse of the Coppis'. As soon as the telegram was handed to him in his barracks, Coppi must have felt something was wrong: his family only communicated deaths and births in this way. His father, Domenico, had died on 29 December, from the after-effects of an accident in which he had been crushed while yoking a pair of oxen. He was not yet fifty. His final act had been to ask that his window be opened, so that he could see the land where he had toiled twelve hours a day for so many years.

'I loved my father, because he more than anyone else had convinced my mother to let me race. For weeks, destroyed by the event, I could do nothing. I was completely lost,' recalled Coppi. 'It took all the authority of my brother Serse and the affectionate remonstrations of my comrades and officers to make me train again.' This was not the first time, or the last, that Coppi would be on the point of giving up cycling when adversity raised its head.

*   *   *

Today the Vigorelli velodrome is a cycle racing track in name only. The imposing art deco towers still flank the ceremonial entrance, not far from the Milan exhibition centre and the San Siro stadium, but it has not hosted a serious competition for over twenty years. The boards on the fearsomely steep bankings are so splintered and cracked that no tyres will roll here again until major restoration has been carried out. Unfortunately, there is no prospect of that happening.

When I visited, it had been turned temporarily into the Fiat snowpark. *Bambini* in bright ski jackets on their Christmas holidays were bouncing at high speed on plastic seats over the moguls of a giant ice rollercoaster. The shrieks of delight and pumping music were a tantalising hint of better days, in spite of the chained-up entrance, the shadowy, deserted tunnels, the dusty ranks of seats. It was hard to envisage what went on in the terraces: 20,000 people moving as one when the sprinters attacked, and the most aggressive fans attempting to force the barriers to get at a rider who had just pulled a dirty move. The great track's decline mirrors the increasing marginalisation of the sport itself.

The future of the Vigorelli has been in jeopardy since the roof collapsed under the weight of a snowfall in winter 1985. But until track cycling faded away and ceased to be a major spectator sport in the 1970s, this was one of Europe's legendary venues, together with the Vélodrome d'Hiver in Paris, the Oerlikon in Zurich and the Sportpaleis in Antwerp. For European followers of sport, not just cycling fans, it had the lustre of Barcelona's Nou Camp or Manchester United's Old Trafford. This was once the fastest track in the world. The high canopies – designed by the German architect Frans Schurmann under commission from Mussolini – provided shelter from the wind, and its maple-wood planking was famously smooth. From the Second World War until the end of the 1960s, the Vigorelli was the chosen venue for record attempts, and it was here that Coppi's career took its second great leap forward with an attack on the world hour record.

The hour is often called cycling's Blue Riband. Its appeal lies in its simplicity: a man, on a bike, looking to go further in sixty minutes than his predecessor. Unlike the myriad complexities of road racing, there are no might-have-beens.

The cyclist is either quick enough, or he isn't. In terms of concentrated effort it is cycling's hardest event: the rider is alone on the track, with nowhere to hide, and there is absolutely no respite.

It had taken Coppi most of 1942 to recover from his father's death, and the idea of entering came to him and Cavanna while he was in the process of winning that year's Italian national pursuit title. They had ample time for reflection; this was a uniquely drawn-out affair. Coppi had crashed heavily while warming up on the Vigorelli between winning the semi-final and contesting the final, where he was up against one Cino Cinelli, who later went on to fame as a handlebar maker. He broke his collarbone, and Cinelli should then, according to the rules, have been awarded the title in a rideover. Cinelli showed sportsmanship that was truly Corinthian; or, more probably, he was aware that he had more to gain from a noble defeat than from a lucky win. He agreed to postpone the final from the end of June to the start of October, although he must have known that he stood no chance of victory.

While Coppi was recovering, he was persuaded to tackle the hour. It has been suggested that it was in part a forlorn attempt to postpone his departure for the war, as more and more troops were sent to prop up the disastrous front in North Africa, but there were other reasons as well. Winning in Italy was all very well, but the war meant there was no chance to compete on the international stage. 'Only a great exploit would allow me to lift myself above the rest, to dominate the ranks of international roadmen,' explained Coppi. A record attempt was all that was possible: this was the only form of competition that was internationally recognised, but which did not require cyclists from more than one nation to be present. The record would be a victory well above the status of anything he could achieve in Italy, and that might just tip the balance with the authorities when it came to sending him to fight. Moreover, the hour was a feat Bartali had never attempted.

The record was held by the Frenchman Maurice Archambaud, with a distance of 45.840 kilometres. Coppi could ride quickly enough in a five-kilometre pursuit: he averaged around 48kph, once as high as 50.3kph, so on paper riding at just over 45kph for sixty minutes was not impossible. Even so, in hindsight, it was a crazy enterprise as Coppi was not yet in his best form, having been two months without cycling after his broken collar-bone. It was the conditions imposed by the war, however, that made the attempt truly bizarre. Petrol rationing meant that it was impossible to carry out motor-paced training, the usual way of gaining the ability to ride at a sustained, set speed necessary for the hour. The Vigorelli itself was being used by the army as a clearing station, so it could not be used for training, and special permission had to be given for it to be opened for the attempt. To practise, Coppi located a straightish, flattish bit of road, the same stretch between Novi and Tortona where he had met Bruna.

When he set off at just after 2 p.m. on 7 November, the crowd was sparse apart from a few workers from the nearby Alfa Romeo factory, but that was hardly surprising. The news from abroad was bad and the war had begun to strike the Italians at home. Almost a quarter of a million Italians were by now in prison camps abroad. The Milanesi had been living under blackout since British Bomber Command had begun raiding on 24 October. The previous evening, Genoa had been devastated. The Vigorelli's roof had already been damaged in bombing raids. Fortunately the day was foggy, reducing the chance of a visit from Bomber Harris's aircraft; the record attempt had been specifically timed for the early afternoon, because the Allies tended to bomb at lunch-time and during factory hours to disrupt production. The post-prandial siesta was usually quieter. Even so, the tunnels under the track's grandstands were kept clear, so they could be used as air-raid shelters if necessary.

Notwithstanding a dose of camphorated oil filched from a military hospital, Coppi was never quite on the pace. He started too fast, by half-distance he was behind Archambaud, and then came the hardest part. The final thirty minutes of an hour record attempt are unforgiving, as the strain of sitting on the bike in a fixed position tells. There are no changes of gradient or wind to give a little relief, no chance to freewheel for the odd corner, as in a road time trial. Coppi clawed back the deficit and then began a painful final third in which he repeatedly gained a tiny advantage but slipped back each time, 'furiously snatching a lead then slowing to regain my breath or my strength', as he put it.

Coppi's ghost-written account of the record is compelling: 'Finally, centimetre by centimetre, I managed to catch up with the demonic clock. I could not see the figures on the black-board. I only knew that I could not fall behind the clock any more, that I had to overtake it, even if it was only by ten metres, in order to win. My chest was like a red hot furnace, my brain knew only the order of the clock: faster, faster, faster!' He was still level with seven minutes to go and the eventual margin registered by the judges was tiny: a mere thirty-one metres better than Archambaud's record.

That final effort left its mark: Coppi never attempted another hour, partly because he feared the suffering involved, partly because he dreaded the stress of the build-up. No chal-lenger came forward to attack his distance, and provoke a response, until he was too old. He may also have been keen to keep the record in the past, because it was not a clear-cut success, in spite of the initial euphoria. The documentation for the record never made it to the UCI (Union Cycliste Internationale, the world governing body for cycling) in Switzerland because of the war, and, after the war was over,

Archambaud protested that the attempt had not been carried out in legal conditions. When the lap splits were published they showed that Coppi covered the laps in such irregular times as to suggest he may have had a case. The record was not validated until February 1947, and then only after Archambaud's times had been re-examined as well: both men's distances were revised downwards, offering plenty of material for conspiracy theorists both French and Italian.

By the end of his career, Coppi had begun to regret his decision not to make a second attempt: given the dominance he would attain in the late 1940s and early 1950s, he would surely have gone further, and the result would have been an undisputed record. Hindsight led him to realise that the 1942 attempt was carried out without sustained, specific preparation, due in part to his injury and also to the war conditions. He had made no concessions to aerodynamics, wearing a jersey with flappy pockets and a crash hat with leather bars. To warm up, he had ridden to the track from Castellania. The clinching factor, however, was that he had ridden without using drugs. There were, he said, 'no chemicals. [In the 1950s], "chemicals" [would] increase performance in an hour record by at least 30 per cent, anyone who says it's not like that doesn't know what it's like riding with amphetamine in them.' The record would stand until the arrival of Jacques Anquetil, in the mid-1950s. He, if anyone, knew how to use 'chemicals'.

*　　*　　*

As with the Giro victory, there was no time to savour the hour. Legnano's promised 25,000-lire bonus would never be spent, or at least not by the man who had earned it. Even as Coppi was suffering on the Vigorelli, the war in North Africa had turned definitively against the Axis, after two and a half years

of advance and retreat along the Mediterranean coast.
Montgomery had broken out at El Alamein three days before,
on 4 November. On 6 November General Alexander had
sent Churchill a message saying that he had captured
20,000 prisoners, 350 tanks, 400 artillery pieces and
1,000 vehicles. As the fighting swept eastwards along the
North African coast in the coming months, Mussolini's generals
prepared to throw their remaining troops into one final effort,
if not to stave off disaster then at least to ensure that defeat
could be depicted as an heroic last stand.

Not only had Coppi lost his father the previous January,
his elder brother Livio was reported missing in western Russia,
surrounded on the banks of the River Don with the
230,000 Italians Mussolini had sent to support Hitler's invasion force. Unlike 75,000 others who perished in the retreat,
including Fausto's former training partner Borlando, Livio at
least returned, given leave to work on the farm because both
Serse and Fausto had also been called up. By happy coincidence, he came back the day after Fausto broke the hour.

A former cyclist, Giovanni Cuniolo, now a car dealer, had
been pulling strings to keep Fausto Coppi out of the war, and
had warned him that if he did not get himself 'into hospital'
he would end up fighting. There were attempts to smuggle
him to Switzerland, and Cavanna had offered to 'make him
ill' to get him relieved of active service, using the combin-
ation of a strange concoction and a Tuscan cigar. He declined
both offers. Coppi was willing to submit to something far
larger than himself. He explained later that he felt if he
evaded service, he would inevitably face public criticism.
'Friends suggested ways out. I was against it. I would damage
my career by going, but I would surely ruin it if I stayed.'
Moreover, Bruna backed his decision, in spite of the dangers
he would run.

The abortive campaign in the French colony of Tunisia was

the last gasp of Mussolini's attempt to recreate the Roman empire in North Africa. Coppi and his unit arrived in March 1943, by which time the Axis troops were clinging on to the Mareth Line, a string of French fortifications at the foot of the peninsula, but they were hopelessly outnumbered and were gradually being pushed into the sea by the Allies. The tone had been set for the 'campaign' when the colonel who sent Coppi and his unit to war accompanied them as far as the railway station, where he told them that duty dictated he himself remain in the barracks.

They 'skimmed the crests of the waves' as they flew from Sicily, a memory which still terrified Coppi years later: it was the first time he had been in an aeroplane. From Biserta, at the head of the peninsula, Coppi sent Bruna a coded telegram: 'Fausto is well, under the palm trees.' A month later, in April, he wrote that he dreamt of meeting her. As for the fighting, he later described an army in which the soldiers had no belief they could win, and in which as many men were falling to illness as to enemy bullets. The news via the radio of massive bombardments at home merely discouraged them further: what would be left if they did ever get home?

In spring 1943, Mussolini told Rommel that Tunisia was 'the fortress of Europe and if it falls the European situation could change for good'. The troops on the ground knew defeat was imminent, however. 'No one believed hostilities would end with victory for us,' wrote Coppi. 'Dysentery, lack of supplies, the bad news that the fascist propaganda couldn't hide all combined to turn us into a defeated army. We retreated night and day across the desert after pulling back from the Mareth Line and were surrounded, out of ammunition, food and courage, when the English captured us.'

The first two weeks of May saw a general collapse among the Axis troops, who retreated to the coast. Coppi was captured at Cape Bon on 13 April, just before the end of the entire

Tunisian campaign. The Italian troops had been cut off from their supply lines for forty-eight hours, with their commander alternately calling on the Madonna and screaming down a dead field telephone, his men firing into the air for something to do. Finally, one of Coppi's comrades tapped him on the elbow and told him to stay still: the English had come. Luckily for him, his general had specified that he would only surrender to the *inglesi*. The French had already acquired a reputation for mistreating their Italian prisoners of war as a crude means of reprisal for the 'stab in the back'. Almost sixty years later, Coppi's former classmate Armando Baselica was still bitter about the way the French had treated him.

In his prisoner-of-war camp at Megez-el-Bab, where about 10,000 prisoners gathered in a valley close to the top of the Tunisian peninsula, Coppi must have felt the same as Baselica did among the French: '[in the camps] you forget about the whole world. I didn't know whether Castellania was still there, whether my girlfriend was alive. You know you are losing the best years of your life.' There were lighter moments: the prisoners found a dog and adopted it as their mascot. Coppi did not smoke, so he was able to swap his cigarette ration for food. He shaved with broken glass; he never quite resolved the dilemma of having only one shirt. If he wore it, it would have to be washed, if it was hung out to dry it might well be stolen. He was spotted occasionally, and his celebrity meant that those who did meet him never forgot. Among them was a British soldier named Len Levesley, a London bike shop mechanic in peacetime, who met Coppi under the strangest of circumstances. An Italian prisoner was called to cut his hair, and the barber proved to be none other than Coppi.

'I should think it took me all of a second to realise who it was. He looked fine, he looked slim, and having been in the desert, he looked tanned. I'd only seen him in magazines, but I knew instantly who he was. So he cut my hair and I tried to have a conversation with him, but he didn't speak English and I didn't speak Italian. We managed one or two words and I got through to him that I did some club racing. I gave him a bar of chocolate that I had with me and he was grateful for that, and that was the end of it.' Later, his cycling club mates would nickname Levesley 'Holy head'.

*   *   *

Coppi eventually found a role as a mechanic, cleaning lorries for the British and ferrying the occasional Red Cross parcel; significantly, he had declared loyalty to the new Italian government after Mussolini's deposition on 8 September 1943, so he was treated as a cooperative prisoner. Equally importantly, early in his captivity he had met another Tortonese, Eteocle Ventura, who put both their names on a select list of just eighteen lorry and motorcycle drivers who would be transferred to Naples, where he landed on 3 February 1945. Once on Italian soil, Coppi was held in a camp in Salerno, just outside Naples, but his fellow countrymen saw to it that the rest of his spell as a prisoner was brief. Initially he worked as batman to a sandy-haired English lieutenant who had no interest in cycling, but who at least let him train. The bush telegraph works fast in Italy, however, and eventually he was directed to the offices of a sports journalist, Gino Palumbo, at a newly created newspaper, *La Voce*. Palumbo later recalled that the guard at the door had no idea who Coppi was, but he recognised him immediately as he stood there nervously in his fatigues, twisting his beret in his hands.

Coppi wanted one thing: a bike. The one he was using in camp was simply too heavy. Palumbo knew that the paper could not provide one – there was no money – so he put an announcement on the front page: 'Who would like to give a bike to Fausto Coppi?' There were just three replies and the one that was taken up was from a carpenter in the nearby village of Somma Vesuviana who brought him an old Legnano. 'I didn't understand at first,' Coppi recalled. 'Then I burst into tears, and he, the carpenter, could only blow his nose when he saw me like that.' Two months later, Coppi would race in Somma as a gesture of thanks.

In early April, he was 'sprung' from the camp in Salerno by two older racers, Romano Pontisso and Pietro Chiappini, and a Roman framebuilder, Edmondo Nulli, who obtained his release documents for him. 'Come on, come to Rome with us,' they told him. Initially, he could not believe it was actually happening. For a fee of 12,000 AMlire, the occupation currency, Nulli became his first post-war sponsor. The backer could hardly have been more appropriate: *nulla* is the Italian word for nothing. Coppi was racing with a big zero on the back of his orange jersey; like his country, he was starting again from scratch.

Initially Coppi's racing was restricted to events in the south of the country, the north being still at war. There were hints of better days to come, however: for a track meeting at the Appio velodrome in Rome, Coppi received 16,000 lire, but in one of his few surviving letters his spidery script betrayed his anxiety: 'I've begun racing again but I can see I am only the shadow of myself and I'm worried I won't be able to become what I used to be. For the moment I'm only interested in one thing: getting home.'

That return took place through a devastated Italy of ruined towns, fresh war graves and broken people. Such trains as ran were intermittent and unreliable, so Coppi rode back to Castellania on his bike, on shell-holed roads lined with minefields. The journey's dangers are summed up by a single episode he told later: at one point he was given a lift on a lorry, laden with returning prisoners and refugees, and was lucky to be sitting on the back, legs dangling above the road.

There was a violent shock, and he was thrown into the road. When he looked up, the lorry had crashed. He grabbed his bike and wheels from the carnage and went on.

His family had had no idea where he was. Initially, he had been reported severely injured in a hospital in Tortona, and later there were rumours that he had been taken as a prisoner to America – one magazine in early 1943 had written that they hoped the Americans would return him as soon as possible. His first stop was Sestri Ponente, the home of Bruna's parents; she was not there, having returned to Villalvernia, where they had first met. He doubled back to find her, together with Serse, who had survived a brief spell fighting for the Repubblica di Salò (Mussolini's puppet state); he had been tried by the partisans but had escaped.

On Coppi's back was a haversack, containing his contract money from Nulli. He did not know it as he pedalled northwards, but it was all the cash he had, although before the war he had saved about 36,000 lire from events such as the hour. 'How many times in Africa did I think of this fabulous sum and the use I would put it to? I wanted to set up home because I had fallen in love. I also wanted to buy a car.' It would be a Fiat, he thought; his old friend Cuniolo would get him a good deal. Unfortunately, the money had been entrusted to his parents, who had converted it to Italian government bonds, which were worthless by the time he rode up the hill to Castellania.

*   *   *

Cycle racing had continued right up to the resignation of Mussolini's government on 25 July 1943, the very day that a young man named Ubaldo Pugnaloni won the national championship; when he finished the race, there were no officials there to present the prizes. Pugnaloni removed the fascist insignia from his jersey the minute he crossed the line; he had to wait fifty years to be given the trophy. That year's Giro di Guerra stopped at its fifth round. The sport resumed after the war in an ad-hoc way, largely under the impetus of Gino Bartali and another influential figure of the time, Adolfo Leoni, a sprinter who would go on to win seventeen stages of the Giro. Between them they mustered as many as they could find of their fellow professionals from before the war; it was this circus that Coppi joined after he was released from detention in Salerno. As the front line moved northwards in 1944 and a form of normality was restored from the south upwards, Bartali, Leoni and company would race with local amateurs on whatever bikes had survived the war.

Tubular tyres were in particularly short supply. For training, riders would use punctured tyres repaired with rags. The prize money was taken out of a hat passed among the spectators, and shared by those present. Leoni converted an old car into a riders' minibus, the *Caroline*, which travelled the newly liberated areas carrying up to ten cyclists, their bikes and their bags. It was, recalls Alfredo Martini, a time of austerity, 'no cars, no enjoyment, just the satisfaction of seeing things reborn. There was a human reaction to the bad times, a desire to rebuild, to go back to being something.' Pugnaloni is less nostalgic: 'it was disgusting. The roads were in pieces, the hotels were all requisitioned by the Allies and water was rationed in some places.'

Much of the racing was on the track, because the roads were rarely fit, and with rampant inflation and a primitive economy often the prizes were in kind. After a race, the winner might be seen riding home through the shell-holes with a gas stove under his arm. Or there were barter deals, such as the one Bartali managed, where Legnano paid him in steel tubing, which he sold on to a plumber in Florence. Riders who were hungry would go for lap prizes such as pigs and bottles of wine, and there were curious awards such as paintings and tortoises.

To compete again, Coppi had to base himself briefly in Rome, where he and Serse stayed in a hotel near Nulli's shop in Via La Spezia, racing in the colours of the Società Sportiva Lazio. 'He had no idea about his future,' recalled Gino Palumbo. 'He thought that the years he had spent in prison had cut short his career. If Serse had not been there, with his optimistic, forward-looking nature, perhaps Fausto's career would have ended that year. But it was Serse who said that their lives had not yet begun and Serse who wanted to race the Giro d'Italia if it had been back on the calendar.'

The need for money and the insecurity of those who had once lost everything would haunt the war generation. Later, they would take on ludicrous schedules of exhibition events purely because they dared not turn down the cash. They had little kit: Serse Coppi raced in the pink jersey his elder brother had won in the 1940 Giro. And, like most of Europe's people, they were hungry.

In early July 1945, Milan, like the rest of Italy, was trying to forget the German occupation, the civil war which had raged for almost two years and the spate of revenge killings which had followed the lynching of Mussolini and his mistress, Clara Petacchi, three months earlier. Any distraction was welcome as Italy attempted to put all this behind it, and bike racing was to be particularly popular. Milan hosted the first official event of the post-war era, the Circuito degli Assi, which drew a crowd estimated at between 50,000 and 100,000.

Coppi returned to the city for the first time since he had broken the hour record, and won, prompting La Gazzetta dello Sport's man on the spot to write of 'his superb pedalling style; the crowds have found their favourite champion again'. Six days later, Italy's northern capital celebrated liberation with a massive street party. There were other criteriums, of which he won several, and there was road racing, including one of the first international victories of the post-war era, just over the Swiss border at Lugano – a place we shall revisit – on 29 September. His then sponsor, Nulli, hailed the win as 'carrying the colours of Italian cycling to TRIUMPH renewing the deeds of the most famous champions and the strongest constructors of the past'. The framebuilder's rhetoric was just a hint of what was to come.

CHAPTER 5

JOUSTING IN THE RUBBLE

Each of Italy's three great cycle races is steeped in its own particular symbolism. The Giro di Lombardia, held in October, is the 'race of the falling leaves', the final major event on the calendar, where retirements are celebrated, farewells said for a few months. The Giro d'Italia is the event that draws the various parts of this surprisingly disparate nation together. Milan–San Remo, on the other hand, is the opening Classic of the year, and sometimes the Italians call it *La Primavera*: spring. It is not merely a matter of the date. The riders' journey is an evocative one: they travel literally from one season to another. Usually Milan and the plain of the River Po are left behind in chilly fog or pale sunshine, with snow on the distant Alps. San Remo, on the Mediterranean Riviera, is decked with palm trees, the sea sparkles as the field snakes along the coast road, and at the finish it's hard to resist pulling on sunglasses and calling for a *gelato*.

The point of transition is the Turchino Pass, the crossing of the Apennines. Today, this is a wide main road, sweeping up a valley in a succession of gentle hairpins to a short tunnel. The summit is only 500 metres above sea level, no major obstacle for a professional cyclist of the twenty-first century. It is nowhere near the scale of the Alps, but in the early years of Milan–San Remo, before the road acquired a proper tarmac surface, it was a climb to be feared, and it was a key strategic point in the race. On 19 March 1946, when the first post-war edition of the Classic went over the pass, the road was still unmade and there were no lights in the tunnel: electricity had yet to be restored after the conflict.

The tunnel itself had only just been reopened, connecting Piedmont to Liguria again. For L'Equipe's writer Pierre Chany, the symbolism was too good to miss. 'The Turchino tunnel is small, only 50 metres long, but on 19 March it took on exceptional proportions in the eyes of the world. It was six years in length.' For Chany, the darkness of the tunnel stood for the darkness that had engulfed Europe between 1939 and 1945. It also represented the suspension of international cycle racing during the war years. Milan–San Remo itself had particular significance: it was the first major international cycle race after the conflict. It was, said an editorial in the organising newspaper La Gazzetta dello Sport, evidence that Italy was coming back to life.

Milan–San Remo had particular significance for Fausto Coppi as well. The early part of the race ran right through his homeland, the Piedmont plains below Castellania, where his friends and family would be watching. That morning, his young cousin Piero and one of his uncles had come down from Castellania with two apples in their pockets to hand up to Faustino, as they still called him: apples from the trees in the village, carefully preserved through the winter. As he sped past, Coppi recognised their call, because no one else called him by his diminutive. He grabbed one apple, but dropped the other.

By the time Coppi reached the roads around Novi, he was already in the lead, to everyone's surprise. The Turchino had yet to be climbed and descended; there were still 200 kilometres to the finish on the Riviera. It was unheard of for a favourite to chance his arm so far from the finish, but Coppi needed to take this race particularly seriously. Much had changed in his life since he had ridden up the hill to Castellania at the end of the long road home from Rome through the shell-holes and minefields: he had a wife and a new home. On 22 November 1945, he and Bruna had married. There was no money to deck the church with flowers, so Bartali, like the good Christian he was, had overlooked their rivalry and rigged a win for Coppi in a criterium so he could take home a bouquet or two. A cook had come in from Novi to help Mamma Angiolina prepare the chickens; she had too much to do simply making the mountains of *agnolotti*. After their wedding, the couple had moved to Sestri Ponente, just outside Genoa, to a little apartment above a stairwell.

Another wedding had taken place three months earlier, on 26 September 1945, in Rimini, on the other side of Italy, again with the disruption of war as a backdrop. An Italian army doctor, Enrico Locatelli, met and fell rapidly in love with a dark-haired Neapolitan girl of spectacular beauty, aged just twenty. Giulia Occhini had been educated in a convent, and had come north to stay with an aunt during the war; she desperately wanted to escape her relation and was engaged to a local boy who worked in a baker's in Ancona. Locatelli was seventeen years older but good-looking, nicknamed '*il bel Valentino*'; 'on the beach, all the girls were fighting over him,' recalled Giulia. Locatelli was not keen to marry, but Giulia was insistent. 'What if we ran away together?' he suggested. Two weeks later – during which time she continued to write loving notes to her previous fiancé – they were married; they eventually settled near Varese, north of Milan.

All over Italy, people were beginning new lives. Coppi had changed employers. When he started that Milan–San Remo, on his jersey was the name Bianchi, the bike manufacturer that would become inextricably linked with the *campionissimo*. At Legnano, Pavesi still doubted whether he had the staying power of Bartali in the long term, and was sticking with the older man, so Coppi had accepted a generous offer – a million lire plus performance bonuses – from the car, motorbike and cycle maker. Bianchi had already approached him before the outbreak of war; they had a distinguished history, and not just in cycling. Tazio Nuvolari and Alberto Ascari, both of whom would become notable Grand Prix drivers, had ridden the company's motorbikes.

The deal included the car he had dreamt of on his way home from the war; more importantly, he took with him the mechanic from Legnano, Pinella di Grande, the man they called *pinza d'oro*, golden pliers. Coppi's relationship with Cavanna, part trainer, part confidant, part masseur, now spanned eight years, and he had long known the importance of having the right man to look after his bikes in the same way that Cavanna looked after his body. Given the state of the roads after the Germans and the Allies had done their worst, it was doubly important now. And with Bianchi, there was the chance of a place in the team for Serse, who had taken out an amateur licence early in the war, then had raced with his elder brother on the post-war circuit. Late in 1945, Fausto engineered a victory for Serse in one of the first road races, Milan–Varzi, and that was enough to persuade Bianchi that he was more than their leader's little brother.

The preparation Fausto had put in under Cavanna's guidance was enough to instil confidence in anyone. A strict diet had got rid of the stomach ulcer that had affected him after he left prison camp. He had also recovered from an attack of malaria that hit him after transfer to a camp in Blida, Algeria, late in 1944. The disease had lingered. His tent-mate of the time later testified that he had still not recovered when he returned to Italy in February 1945, and he had a relapse late that year.

Since the start of 1946, he had ridden 7,000 kilometres in training, sometimes using a fixed wheel to increase his pedalling speed. There had been three weeks of light work before he had begun to lengthen the training rides, eventually getting up to 250 kilometres per outing. Finally, in the two weeks before *La Primavera*, there were the dress rehearsals, in which he would ride alone for 150 kilometres, at a brisk pace but without hurting himself. With those kilometres already in his legs, he would meet Cavanna's amateurs 100 kilometres from home. They were under orders to simulate a race, attacking one by one to make life as hard as possible for him. For the time, this was unprecedentedly systematic, targeted training.

The night before the race, Coppi, Cavanna and the manager of the Bianchi team, Giovanni Tragella, had laid their plans well. They knew that after such a long gap in competition, the serious contenders in the field might well lack confidence, and might be unwilling to chase an early escapee. They also suspected that Bartali was not at his best, due to a dispute over his salary with Legnano. So Coppi was to make an early move, following the track racers who had raced the winter circuit and so had plenty of speed but little stamina; they tended to break away early to pick up intermediate prizes before fading later on.

On the Turchino, the last of the early escapees to remain with Coppi, the Frenchman Lucien Teisseire, dropped his head for a second to change gear. When he lifted his eyes, he had been left behind and Coppi was alone in the lead. His emergence from the tunnel prompted Chany to paint a vignette that perfectly sums up post-war bike racing: clouds of dust that stung the eyes and drifted through clothing like desert sand through canvas; a stream of cars amid the dust; *carabinieri* standing in open-top jeeps frenetically waving batons, green on one side, red on the other. Weaving in and out of the cars like children at a grown-up party were the leather-clad motorcyclists whose goggles made them look like frogs. The organiser, Giuseppe Ambrosini, came by in his car, waving his arms for the road to be cleared; an announcer's dusty, grinning face hung out of the back of the vehicle, yelling the words the crowd had come to the mountain pass to hear: *Arriva Coppi!* The words went down to the valley, bouncing off the rocks, leaving the car far behind. 'Arriva Coppi, Arriva Coppi went the noise.'

Finally Coppi burst into the light, and Chany described the man who would dominate cycling for the next seven years: 'He had slim legs, disproportionately long, a short torso, his head slumped into his shoulders, round eyes and his mouth gulping in air; the parts making a paradoxically harmonious whole. A heron in an Italian jersey, perched on an invisible saddle, with the race scattered behind him. His face, fixed in indifference, betraying boredom rather than effort, more resignation than enthusiasm. He disappeared around a shoulder of the mountain.'

Coppi remained alone in the lead all the way to San Remo, for 147 kilometres of the 290-odd that make up the race. This was the biggest winning margin of his career in a single-day event: a gaping fourteen minutes over the next man, Teisseire. Bartali was twenty-four minutes behind. These were massive time gaps, the more striking because there had been no racing for so long and the performance could not be put in any kind of context. It was a one-off. As publicity for Bianchi, his new boss Aldo Zambrini said, it was worth six months' bike production in the factory. The victory was a colossal state-ment of intent from Coppi himself, setting the tone for the coming years. Here was a man renewed, with huge ambitions. The margin of the win and its crushing style were guaranteed to excite the nation.

As Chany saw it, the cry *Arriva Coppi* would become 'the rallying call and the victory yell for all sporting Italy'. The words were to be the rallying call for a generation of cycling fans, but came to represent much more. The phrase also embodied a new, renascent Italy, in which, briefly, the bicycle and the men who rode it enjoyed huge significance. There was inspiration to be drawn from butchers' boys, masons' sons, farmers' lads earning a living through graft and sweat, but there was more. The Vespa and the Fiat 500 were not yet off the drawing board; Italy was reliant on its bikes. There were three million of them in use, compared to just under 150,000 cars. Post-war, said one writer, the bike was 'sold as a necessity of the first order, on the same level as bread, oil, sugar, coffee, chocolate, petrol, clothes and shoes'.

The vital importance of the bike is shown in the classic film *Ladri di Biciclette* (*Bicycle Thieves*), which depicts an impoverished worker's desperate search after the theft of the bike he so desperately needs to earn his crust. Eventually he resorts to theft as well; he is caught and nearly lynched. It is not merely a fanciful plot: an actual lynching of a bike thief in 1948 near Milan is recorded. The symbolism of a cyclist escaping the pack and riding alone to victory was the perfect metaphor for a country pulling itself up by its bootstraps. An entire country was getting on its collective bike.

*   *   *

A single image encapsulates the post-war Italy through which Coppi rode to victory on that March day. The photograph shows a vast sea of empty tin cans and three women scavenging among them for something to eat. The caption does not say where it was: it could have been anywhere. The Italian economy was devastated, its output a third of what it had been before the war. Wages could not keep pace with inflation that had pushed prices to fifty times the pre-war average, meaning people simply could not afford most goods. Food rationing had pushed consumption back to nineteenth-century levels, the black market was rampant, and food shortages were so acute that in Naples, post-liberation, women and girls would sell themselves for a packet of biscuits. Police would raid restaurants and inspect the diners' plates to see if the proprietor was adding anything beyond the ration. The country's infrastructure was in ruins, with half the country's road network unusable and people living in tents and railway carriages.

Coppi's fellow cyclists had all played their part in the war. Coppi's future *gregario* Ettore Milano, who did not start racing until after the war, was a youthful partisan fighting in the Apennines. He still has the marks to prove it, including shrapnel scars on his fingers and his back, and he managed a cycling career in spite of having one leg shorter than the other after injuring his back. One of Coppi's most faithful team-mates, Sandrino Carrea, spent part of the war in captivity in Buchenwald concentration camp and survived two death marches. Another of that era, Alfredo Martini, used his bike to ferry rucksacks full of Molotov cocktails to the partisans. On the potholed, gravelly roads, that was dicing with death.

Coppi's former team leader, Bartali, never fought, but it later emerged that he had been part of a network based in Pisa, founded by a Jewish accountant, Giorgio Nissim, which assisted refugees. The champion cyclist was one of their 'postmen'; he could get through the checkpoints on the pretext that he was training over the 370-kilometre round trip to Pisa from his home in Florence. Hidden on his bike as he went between the convents used as hiding places were the documents used to make false identity papers. It is estimated that eight hundred lives were saved by the network. More controversially, the third great Italian cyclist of the time, Fiorenzo Magni, was tried after the war on a charge of collaboration, but was cleared.

Two wars had been fought on Italian soil simultaneously between 1943 and 1945. The Allies had made their painfully slow and hotly contested advance northwards through the succession of German defence lines, a highly visible conflict that had seen the levelling of towns such as Cassino and Cisterna in the Anzio landing zone, saturation bombing of the front lines, and the destruction of infrastructure such as railways, bridges and roads as the Germans retreated gradually up the peninsula. The other war was the hidden but dirty civil war, Italian against Italian. Together with German troops, the fascist militia and the thousands of Italians who joined Hitler's SS tried to root out the partisans, many of whom were former socialist opponents of Mussolini's regime. In this conflict there was no distinction drawn between combatants and civilians, with mass executions of villagers who harboured and aided partisans, house burnings and torture as the militia and the Germans hunted down the fighters.

The wave of atrocities scarred the national consciousness well beyond liberation. As the war ended there was a brief month of something approaching anarchy, with summary executions by hastily convened 'people's tribunals', revenge killings and random murders as old scores were settled. There were executions of the wrong people as a result of false denunciations and mistaken identity – Bartali for one would have been shot without the intervention of another cyclist, Primo Volpi. Of the public lynchings, that of Mussolini and Clara Petacchi was merely the most celebrated. The mood of those months is illustrated by one episode from Coppi's native Piedmont, in which a fascist militia commander was paraded through villages in a cage. On many occasions, fascists fearing reprisals committed suicide.

The civil war was the culmination of twenty years of simmering civil conflict that dated back to the murder of Giacomo Matteotti (leader of the United Socialist Party) in 1924 and eventually fizzled out with isolated terrorist acts by the remnants of the blackshirts in the 1950s. The scars ran deep – the questions posed by the civil war were raising hackles as late as the 1990s – but in post-war Italy it was not merely a matter of coming to terms with a conflict which had split families and communities. The nation was awash with arms, poverty widespread, violence commonplace: the result was a crime wave. Politically there was the question of how the entire nation should be governed after the collapse of Mussolini's dictatorship: should the monarchy be restored, should a republic be installed? Italy's very borders were in question: the war had seen the loss of colonies in Africa and raised questions about areas on the margins, such as the Alto Adige and the east around Trieste, where Tito's Yugoslavia was making a strident claim for former Italian territory.

All these factors combined to produce a crisis of identity for a country which was still under Allied occupation and did not have its own currency, instead still using the AMlire issued by the occupation government. Many of the answers came in 1946, starting in June with the referendum for a new constitution, in which women had the right to vote for the first time. The Paris peace conference in July saw Italy take its place among the democracies, with the agreement of war reparations. And the economic leap forward came in October, when the new head of government, Bartali's friend Alcide De Gasperi, launched *la ricostruzione*. This was a massive programme of public borrowing, totalling 231 billion lire, to finance public works and give work to the unemployed. The term would also come to stand for the cultural, moral and social rebuilding of the nation after fascism and civil war.

Amid the rubble and the rebuilding, cycle racing in Italy became both a hint of better times ahead and a symbol of the work that needed to be done. It was also a reminder of the disastrous state of the nation's infrastructure. A picture of Milan–Turin, run on 29 July 1945, speaks volumes: a dirt road, clouds of dust, battered support cars, Coppi and his fellow cyclists using every variant of kit, riding bikes that do not fit. At other times, the cyclists would be in mud that came

JOUSTING IN THE RUBBLE 69

over their tyres. Such roads were called *strada bianca*, and
they played a disproportionate role in every race. Racing on
the roads was barely possible. 'Many of the surfaces had no
asphalt and had been ripped out of the earth, they were like
rivers, with rocks and huge holes,' says one writer of the time.
'It was a massive effort to ride on them.' Well-tarmacked
portions were mentioned in race reports in the same tones
that today we reserve for stretches of cobbles; clearly they
were a rarity.

With Italy's infrastructure in such a state, deciding to restart
the Giro d'Italia was a colossal gamble. But in January 1946,
La Gazzetta dello Sport announced that the Giro would go
ahead early that summer. In February Italian cycling was re-
admitted, 'provisionally', to the international fold; the other
defeated nations such as Germany and Japan had to wait
longer. The prospect of the national Giro and international
recognition rapidly revitalised Italian professional cycling: there
were nine squads with some 110 riders between them and
another 115 unattached riders, and 24 races including the
Giro for professionals alone.

Since its foundation in 1909, the Giro had always been
more than a bike race. That was inevitable for the national
Tour of a country that had been unified for less than half a
century. The race had embodied one message after another:
the unification of the country on its fiftieth anniversary in
1911; inspiration for the impoverished south to follow the
example of the richer north; patriotic rebirth after the First
World War, when the route included the battlefields. So the
1946 race was bound to be more than a mere diversion from
grim reality. It was hardly surprising that *La Gazzetta dello
Sport* baptised the event *Il Giro della Rinascita*, the Giro of
Rebirth.

The race coincided with a turning point in Italian history:
the national referendum over a new system of government,

the first national election for twenty years, took place on 2 June, with massive popular support. On 13 June Italy became a republic. Two days later, the Giro started, 'serving a purpose that is greater than the race itself,' said *La Gazzetta*'s editorial. 'Neapolitans, Torinesi, Lombards and Laziali, Venetians and Emilians, all Italians, all regions with a single society and a single heart, all await the Giro as a mirror in which they can recognise each other and smile.'

'We are bursting with faith,' wrote Bruno Roghi in *La Gazzetta*. 'We have had faith in so many arduous, tremendous things. We believed in the fall of the Gothic Line. We believed in the unification of Italian sport. We believed in the constant improvement of roads and infrastructure. We believed in the work and cooperation of industry. We believed in Italy . . . [we had] faith in the rebirth of Italy, faith that has been transformed into the caravan of seventy [cyclists] as beautiful as a rainbow of hope.' The Giro, he added, would enable the Italian people to 'rediscover themselves thanks to their irrepressible optimism'.

Cultural and sporting landmarks acquired more significance in post-war Italy than ever before. The army was disgraced, politics suspended, the King gone. Sport and culture offered stability, hinted at normality. So *La Gazzetta*'s writers compared the start of their race to Toscanini's first baton stroke at the reopening of Milan's La Scala a month before. The sense of rebirth was not limited to the writers on the recently relaunced *Gazzetta*. The Church – the only national institution that had survived the war – was keen to be involved. Pope Pius XII wrote to the organisers saying that he saw the Giro as an act of 'supreme faith in our country's rebirth, in the spirit of fraternity that unites our people'. He blessed the peloton before the start of the stage from Rome to Perugia. Alcide De Gasperi, newly elected as head of government, watched the race between Bassano del Grappa and Trento on 5 July. The stage was deliberately chosen: Trento was part of the Alto Adige, the German-speaking region in the northern Alps that had reverted to Italy as part of the post-war settlement. The head of state's presence here, watching the event that united the disparate areas of Italy, was a symbolic statement: you are part of our country now.

The riders, too, felt they were involved in something bigger than themselves. 'There was a huge feeling for the *Giro della Rinascita*,' Alfredo Martini told me nearly fifty years later. 'Racing it was a positive, emblematic thing. People understood that Italy had to start from nothing, roll up its sleeves and also think of things that would provide enthusiasm, reignite passion. The Giro offered hope for the future.'

A key part of that future was mobility. The destruction of roads and railways had made it a nightmare merely to travel or carry goods from A to B: getting the cyclists from Milan to Naples and back was an assertion of 'a rapid return to daily normality, or at least the desperate desire to believe that that return had been made,' wrote the historian Daniele Marchesini. 'If the caravan was able to move from north to south it symbolized the fact that the public powers had managed to recreate, in the shortest of time spans, the minimum conditions needed to ensure that the nation could live together in one whole.' In contrast, the first post-war football championship – starting in autumn 1945 – had been divided into north and south divisions because communications were so bad.

The Giro organisers' inspection noted that almost all the bridges on the route were temporary, often shared with railways. In places the riders would have to get off and walk up steps. In Milan, the race had to start several miles from the city's outskirts, due to the abysmal state of the roads. The food available to the riders was a monotonous diet of minestrone and chicken, and that not always good. Prizes offered by local sports clubs along the route included demijohns of wine, furniture, sacks of potatoes, home-made cheeses, tubular tyres, fishing rods, 'sometimes cash' – a reflection of an economy which had been reduced to barter. Pigs and chickens would be awarded as prizes at the stage finishes, then sold immediately by the riders.

The newspapers saw the Giro as offering a first chance to go out and report on the state of the nation, so they sent their best writers, men such Orio Vergani of *Corriere della Sera*, who described the event as 'a sort of unreal joust in the rubble'. Vergani described a race of jarring contrasts: the happiness of the event against the grimmest of backdrops, with constant reminders of conflict and death. He observed that in Ancona, where the Giro started, running water had yet to be restored, and he made a point of visiting the vast swathe of flattened buildings. There was the dust, clouds of it blowing from ruined towns and villages, and 'thousands upon thousands of houses reduced to nothing, good only for bats'. The roads were lined with war cemeteries, each with its sign: English, French, Indian. Ninety-five per cent of the people on the roadsides seemed to be wearing dirty khaki, abandoned military uniforms. Many were bare chested, because shirts were in short supply.

Controversially, the race visited the city of Trieste, claimed by both Italy and Yugoslavia amid bitter post-war reprisals and massacres, and at the time under United Nations control. The secret services were against the stage finish, fearing a violent reaction from the Yugoslav population, who would feel the city's inclusion in Italy's national Tour was an unwelcome statement of Trieste's Italian identity. But they also feared an Italian backlash if the stage were cancelled, and let the organisers go ahead.

Their fears were realised when demonstrators stopped the race at the demarcation line with roadblocks of barbed wire and barrels of tar. Stones were thrown; the security forces accompanying the race responded with rifle shots. The field dived for cover; they recognised the sound. Bartali hid behind a car; Coppi took shelter behind a barrel, and together they led the calls for the stage to be abandoned.

Most of the riders felt it was not worth risking their lives and made for their hotels, but seventeen of the field, mainly from the local Willier-Triestina team, were smuggled through the demonstrators in American military lorries bristling with rifles. They were released eight miles from the finish and raced into the city to a rapturous welcome. The final sprint was rigged, to ensure a victory by the Triestina leader Giordano Cottur. The stage was followed by two days of rioting, fomented by Italian nationalists brandishing a bloodied jersey which had been worn by a rider who had been hit by a stone. Bombs were thrown at the police, buildings connected with Yugoslavia were burnt. The riots left two dead and more than thirty wounded.

As far as the actual racing went, Bartali obtained his revenge on Coppi for his defeat in Milan–San Remo that March. Coppi crashed on stage five to Bologna and broke a rib, but he effectively lost the race on the stage to Naples, nine days in, when he had to stop to adjust a defective brake. Bartali took the opportunity to attack. He was four minutes ahead at the summit of the stage's main climb, the Colle di Macerone, and gained another two minutes on a desperately chasing Coppi over the final 100 kilometres.

The minutes lost in the south proved decisive as the race returned northwards. Although he had been advised by the race doctor to retire, Coppi found his legs in the Dolomites, winning three stages but never gaining enough time to take the race lead. The key battle was on the stage to Bassano del Grappa, the decisive point the Falzarego Pass, high above the ski resort of Cortina d'Ampezzo; here Coppi rammed home the fact that he was the best climber in the race by dislodging Bartali, but the Tuscan saved his lead with the help of another rider from his area, Aldo Bini. Coppi won the next day's stage to Trento, with Bartali two minutes behind, but it was not enough to regain all the time he had lost in the south. In Milan, Bartali won by a mere forty-seven seconds; Coppi's frustrations were summed up when he won the final stage in the Arena, only to be disqualified following confusion over whether he had sprinted on the correct lap: he went for the finish immediately after entering the track, only to find that the rest of the field sprinted a lap later.

There were 30,000 in the Arena, a reflection of the massive crowds that turned out for the entire Giro. The focus for this wave of public support was not hard to find: the rivalry between *il vecchio*, the 'old man', Gino Bartali, and the newcomer, Coppi, who had put himself in the spotlight so spectacularly when racing resumed among the rubble. It was at this race that the rivalry moved to centre stage, where it stayed for eight years, until Bartali quit and Coppi lost his powers. The pair performed in a climate of mutual suspicion and surreptitious alliances which could assume ridiculous proportions. During a stage in Tuscany, the older man spotted Coppi dropping a bottle containing a strange green liquid. At the finish he didn't even wait to get a shower: 'I took the car and retraced my steps. I needed that bottle.' The next day, with the help of a chambermaid – they were staying in his native region, after all – he raided Coppi's room and inspected everything: 'medicine bottles, scent bottles, flasks, test-tubes, even suppositories'. There was nothing suspicious, however, apart from Bartali himself. He got the green liquid from the original bottle analysed, and found it contained a 'common pick-me-up, made in France'. To make sure he wasn't missing out on anything, he ordered a case.

On the critical stage to Bassano del Grappa, Bartali's alliance with his fellow Tuscan Aldo Bini helped him chase down Coppi just at the point when the young upstart was threatening his race lead. Coppi complained publicly, but the day before he had reached an agreement with Bartali to combine forces against the up-and-coming Vito Ortelli. On another Dolomite stage, when Bartali was sick, it was Coppi who got off his bike, poured water over him to clean him up, and offered him encouragement. It was pure theatre, and it was just the beginning. By the end of the 1940s an entire generation of European sports fans would find it impossible to mention one without the other.

CHAPTER 6

THE IMPOSTER

The most eloquent link to Coppi's new life in this new Italy is to be found in the town of Novi Ligure, in a large, elegant house set off a wide avenue of shady trees. Marina Bellocchi née Coppi, born in November 1947, is the image of her father: she has inherited the high forehead, the sweeping hair, the elegant nose and the half-smile in which the upper lip barely moves. But whereas Coppi always appears languid and self-effacing in film footage and television clips, his daughter is lively, laughing, expressive, her appearance belying her sixty years.

Fausto and Bruna moved from Castellania over the Apennines to a flat in the town of Sestri Ponente on the Ligurian coast near Genoa after their marriage at the end of 1945. It was easier to get food near the big city in those times of shortages, and the Mediterranean climate was milder for training than the chillier, foggier winters of Piedmont. A fourth-floor flat in an apartment block with no lift was probably not the first choice for a cycling champion, however. His Bianchi bike (possibly his most valuable possession) was kept in the flat, and when Coppi went out training the *tifosi* would wait outside the building to compete for the honour of carrying his bike up the stairs when he returned, so that his legs would be less tired.

In the mornings before Fausto left to go training, he would have breakfast with his daughter as she prepared to go to infant school. She would have *zuppa al latte*, hot, sugary bread and milk, and Fausto would pretend to steal his daughter's food, much to her consternation. When he laughed, it came out like that of a small boy: eheheheh. On winter mornings, he would stuff a thick layer of newspapers under his woollen jersey to absorb the sweat and keep the wind off his chest: as she was eating he would methodically rip out a triangular space at the top of each sheet to allow him to open the zip at the collar of his jersey.

Marina attended a nursery school between the sea and the Via Aurelia, the coast road where Fausto trained most days; as he passed, he would stop at the huge iron gate and call her over just to say hello. Sometimes, as he went training in the morning, he would carry his daughter to school on the crossbar of his bike, a precarious ride she did not entirely enjoy, although she did not tell him so.

Squashed in the pockets of Marina's heavy coat would be a few of Coppi's favourite cakes, little baskets of flaky pastry called *gubeletti*, made specially for the cyclist by a local baker's called Sidea. Usually they were filled with jam, but the baker's boys took the trouble to fill Coppi's with orange marmalade so that they wouldn't be too sweet for him. His other passion was for small pastry fingers known as *bacicci*, little kisses.

Coppi would ride up to 160 kilometres each day, come home, eat a light lunch, and lie down to rest on the sofa with Marina in his arms. Cavanna would be driven the forty-five miles over from Novi Ligure to give him a massage, and he would go to bed at 9.30 p.m. Already, the Coppis were making plans for the future. He wanted to open a bar or a restaurant after he retired, he said while being interviewed by the journalist Gianni Roghi. Bruna overheard, and said the idea would not suit her; the demands on their time would be too great. 'OK,' said her husband. 'We'll get someone to run the bar and we'll just take Marina out walking around the town.'

*   *   *

Outside his family, to most of those who met him, Coppi appeared distant, ill-at-ease. One former team-mate, Michele Gismondi, told me: 'He always seemed to be fond of us, deep down inside, even if sometimes his mind seemed elsewhere, as if he were thinking of something else.' Jean Bobet concurred: 'Out of his racing kit he looked fine, but the suit never seemed quite to fit him. I had the impression he was not at ease. He was always polite but seemed to be watching everyone else, and looked as if he was watching everyone else watching him.'

Coppi was impossible to pin down. Team-mates and friends find it hard to remember specifically what it was that made his character special. He is not, it should be pointed out, the only cyclist of this kind. Orio Vergani of *Corriere della Sera*, for one, believed that most of the cycling champions of that era were reticent men, never letting too much out in public about the efforts they made, the drugs they took, their childhood, their dreams. They were peasant boys with the peasant's instinct for caution, thrown into a bizarre, dog-eat-dog world where they gambled every day – on their own strength, on the trajectory of a bend, on the line to take in a sprint – and where they were surrounded with people whose aim was to deceive them.

The media found him a mystery, apart from one confidant, *La Gazzetta dello Sport* correspondent Rino Negri. 'Very secretive in what he says and on what he intends to do in a race,' wrote a reporter in 1940. 'Don't try to elicit from him a single word more than he might feel he can say without giving anything away.' 'He was hard to drag out of himself even though he was naturally well-mannered and well brought up,' recalled the historian Indro Montanelli, who felt that this was not something the cyclist actually tried to cultivate, but it had its uses. 'Everyone would look at him and wonder "What is he thinking? Is he on a good day or not? What is he planning to do?" And no one ever knew.' The writer concluded: 'He never had many [words] at his disposal. And he seemed to have great difficulty in getting out the words he did have. Perhaps this was why I never managed to understand if he was happy to be the king of cycling. It seemed he wasn't.'

He was not a chatterer, not a man who opened up easily. 'Often Fausto's silences were long, he seemed a tremendously long way away, closed in his thoughts', said a contemporary, Romeo Venturelli. On the road, travelling between criteriums and track meetings with team-mates, the talk was of practical matters: racing programmes, holidays, the next day's schedule. He was obsessed with the logistics, making sure the scheduling was right, that the train tickets were arranged. He was not a man given to daydreams or reflection, even among friends. Fiorenzo Magni noted, for example, that he did not discuss his experiences in prison camp, other than to mention that it had damaged his career because his digestive system was affected.

Coppi was unwilling to make a spectacle of himself in public. For example, if he gave a gift to a charity, he would be determined that it should remain anonymous. He was a man who never made reckless predictions: he would never say 'Today I'm going to win', merely 'Oggi ci daremo una botta', We'll give them a kick up the backside today. The former soigneur of the Italian national team, Giannetto Cimurri, recalled that the campionissimo had his own way of showing someone when they had been admitted to the select inner circle of people who were to be trusted: Coppi would shake hands with them using his left hand. The rest of the world got the right hand.

Others assert that Coppi had two sides: the public face seen at the races and the quietly humorous man at his home, out hunting with his dogs, relaxing with his brother. 'He was a very timid man thrust into the spotlight,' recalls Nino Defilippis. 'When he went to the cinema, he had to go out while the lights were turned off, because the people wouldn't let him leave once they knew he was there.' Coppi did not like the public eye, although clearly he knew he had to live with the exposure. He told Negri: 'I've always hated shaking hands, especially when I was eating and someone wished me *"buon appetito"* with a vigorous handshake.' Ettore Milano said simply of him: 'We talked, he listened.' And Coppi was aware of his own shyness: 'Popularity always scared me a bit. More than once, until a moment before a party or a ceremony began, I didn't know how to behave and wished I could find a familiar face.'

Coppi was superstitious: his brother Livio recalls him throwing away the jersey he had worn in a race that went badly. On the other hand, he believed that the number 36 was lucky. But in this he was typical of his time and his upbringing. *Christ Stopped at Eboli*, Carlo Levi's account of life among the peasants of the Italian south, in Matera during the 1930s, makes much of their folklore: belief in the powers of witches, wolf-tamers, devils in the form of goats, curses, imps that taunt men in their sleep, love potions. Eric Newby, too, notes the fascination with the occult, and with violent death.

Superstition is a recurring theme in Coppi's life and death, and some of those close to the Coppi clan talk about a curse, or at least an unlucky blight on them. 'A family exterminated by bad luck,' says one former team-mate. Given his background, and the fact that he had been exposed at an early age to life-changing events – sudden success and riches, war, imprisonment, the premature death of his father – public acclaim must have seemed very fragile. If others lived for the moment, Coppi seems to have wondered how long the moment would last.

Coppi wanted people around him, not necessarily to do anything, one suspects, but mainly so that he knew they were there. He made sure he had Serse with him both at school and when racing. He also needed reassurance and support, constantly, from those who were close to him. According to Giannetto Cimurri, this was the most important need he had: 'He needed stimulants but he also needed psychological stimulants, words of encouragement.'

Sporting champions divide into two categories. There are those who have an urge to dominate the opposition in any field from an early age and carry it with them into sport, and those who are more insecure, who discover sporting excellence as an outlet, a means of self-expression, of gaining pleasure from doing something as well as it can be done. 'You become a superstar if, having won, you are never completely satisfied . . .' said Coppi. As his team manager Giovanni Tragella put it, 'He is not a weak man, but sensitive. His mood changes over nothing. Even his confidence in his own strength declines. He prepares every race carefully and if things don't go how he wants, he gets angry and demoralised. Sometimes, he underestimates himself. When he says, "There's nothing to be done", insisting otherwise is like beating your head against a wall. But when he realises that everything is working out, he is unstoppable.'

He was highly observant, with the eye of a peasant farmer buying livestock at an auction: he could spot a rival who had had slightly longer cranks fitted because he felt in form, and he easily read Bartali's attempts to send spies into his orbit. After a crash late in his career, he was visited in his hospital bed by a small boy; Coppi asked him where he lived, was told the name of the village and then went through the place, corner by corner, pothole by pothole, trying to work out where the house was. He was thirsty for information – 'who had done this, what Bobet was up to, who had been chasing behind a break', as one-team mate put it. It would all be filed away for future reference.

Like that other great peasant farmer champion, the Spaniard Miguel Indurain, instances of him getting angry were rare enough to be notable. One *gregario*, Angelo Coletto, saw him lose his temper only twice in the years they spent together: once when the mechanic didn't stick Coletto's tyre on properly and it rolled; another time when Coletto crashed and broke the eggs he was carrying for Coppi. 'If someone yelled something offensive at him, he would not answer, he would look at them as if he were 1,000 kilometres up in the air and they were on the ground, small and useless,' recalled one associate.

There was a simple straightness about him that appealed to the other cyclists: he kept his word, didn't go back on deals, paid up when help was bought or bartered. As a result, he had friends aplenty when it came to calling in favours in races. He had a sense of responsibility – or possibly a fear of being badly thought of, *fare brutta figura* as the Italians put it – that was stronger than his need for money. On more than one occasion he made sure he took reduced fees if a track meeting suffered an unexpectedly small crowd. He won the hearts of the French public by going to watch amateurs race at Paris's Vél d'Hiv, and was capable of gestures such as doling out signed photographs to an entire team of workmen renovating a hotel in which he was staying.

He liked simple pleasures, particularly hunting, which began as a need to get outside in the fresh air, and which he eventually found he loved. 'If I couldn't go hunting I'd be bored to death,' he said. Pictures of him shooting abound: fowling from a small boat in the marshes, proudly displaying the day's catch of pheasants or hares. He also had a passion for hunting partridges; it was his young cousin, Piero Coppi, who would gather them. Before he bought land of his own, he spent hours in the fields around Castellania with his gun and his dogs. Not that he was completely bloodthirsty, as Marina recalls: 'My father was hunting once in Piemonte, hunting boars, which he had never done before, he had his gun at the ready, the boar ran towards him, and he lowered his gun when he saw the beast's eyes. Looking at it, he just wasn't able to kill it.' As a child, he was a dab hand with a catapult; later, Coppi's collection of guns was large and eclectic, mostly donated by wealthy fans; his gundogs were well trained.

When he lived near Genoa, one of his regrets was that he didn't get to the cinema more often. He liked Westerns and was a big fan of Gary Cooper and Ingrid Bergman. Football was also a passion: he said he would rather watch a football match than a bike race. Like many Piedmontese, he fell under the spell of *il Grande Torino,* the ill-fated Turin side that dominated Italian football in the post-war years. He would travel to watch them train; in Genoa he was regularly seen at the Sampdoria ground, and he would take his young family to matches in his spare time. On 14 January 1950, he and Bartali captained teams of cyclists in a game in front of a massive crowd at the Arena in Milan. Coppi's team played a 5-3-2 formation, with Fiorenzo Magni in goal and the *campionissimo* on the right wing, directly opposite Bartali, who was disgusted when his side lost 6–0, with Coppi scoring the final goal.

Coppi had learned to drive while in prison camp, and, like every other professional cyclist before and since, he was fearsome behind a steering wheel. Ubaldo Pugnaloni still gets the shivers thinking about the time they ran over a dog at 200kph on the way to a race. He once commented to Coppi that they were cutting it very fine as they passed other cars a hairsbreadth away; he just laughed. And, like so many professional cyclists, Coppi loved his cars, which were as much a tool of his trade as his bike; if Gino Bartali bought a new one he would go out and buy one bigger. He was particularly fond of his spacious, curvy Lancia Aurelia; having bought one in the Vatican because it was cheaper, he couldn't work out how to turn the heating off so he drove it with the windows down.

Many books on Coppi fail to mention a tragedy involving the cyclist in early May 1947, when Coppi ran down a bookshop owner, Giuseppe Vallino, in the Genoa suburb of Sampierdarena, while returning from the Giro di Romagna. Vallino died in hospital from his injuries, unleashing a series of legal battles that ran on for nearly a year. Due to a lack of evidence, claims for damages from Vallino's widow and his brother were thrown out, as was a requested six-month prison sentence for culpable homicide. Coppi eventually paid the widow 1.65 million lire in compensation. By Italian standards it was relatively uncontroversial, but it was a little foretaste of bigger, nastier legal wrangles to come.

*   *   *

Bruna recalled years later that her happiest memory of their marriage was when Fausto was packing his suitcase to travel to the Giro and little Marina hid in it. This is not a memory of time spent together, but of parting and separation. The marriage was eventually to crumble; Coppi's suitcase, however, is still in existence. It's one of the few relics that the Bianchi bike company has retained of the man who put its name on the map. The wooden sides are covered in canvas in the manufacturer's eggshell blue, edged with leather; the corner plates and locks are in sturdy brass, the cyclist's name on the luggage label.

The suitcase is an apt symbol of Coppi's rapid rise to stardom. It was worked hard in those years immediately after the war. For a cyclist who could switch from road racing in summer to track racing in the winter, there was money to be made all over Europe at indoor venues such as Paris's Vélodrome d'Hiver and Antwerp's Sportpaleis. The velodromes are long gone now. The popularity of track racing as a mass spectator sport depended on the fact that without television fans across Europe seldom if ever saw their heroes in action.

Events such as Milan–San Remo and the Giro d'Italia had saturation coverage on the radio, in the sponsoring newspapers and photoreportage magazines, but prior to television the stars could only be glimpsed at the start or finish of major events, or as they sped past on the road.

On the other hand, at a track meeting at the Vigorelli – rebuilt at speed after being damaged in the war, and reopened on 26 May 1946 – or the Vél d'Hiv, the action was right there in front of the fans. The racing might be largely exhibition stuff, but it was spectacular and fast and, most importantly, the big names were on constant display. The roadmen were the crowd pullers, even though the track boasted showmen of its own: specialists such as the British sprint star Reg Harris and the Italian Antonio Maspes. The record attendance for a meeting with Coppi topping the bill was 20,000, in 1951, and he could earn up to 800,000 old French francs in appearance money.

To give some idea of the travel that was involved in this year-round racing schedule, we can study Coppi's programme for the winter of 1947–8. His daughter was born on 1 November, and *La Gazzetta dello Sport* reports that he raced in Antwerp on 29 November, Brussels the next day, Paris a week later, Ghent the week after that, back to Paris for 19 December, Brussels two days later. After Christmas, it was Paris on 4 January, Ghent on 11 January, Brussels on the 17th, Nice on the 18th, Antwerp on the 24th, Ghent the next day, Brussels on 1 February, and finally Paris on 8 February. Travel in those days was by train, most often overnight.

The format of the race meetings varied. Sometimes there would be an omnium, in which a group of professionals would compete in several events – a points race, an elimination race, an event paced behind small motorbikes, perhaps – for a cumulative prize. The professionals would sometimes be divided into national 'teams', so that the evening's show could be billed

as 'Italy v France' for example: anything to draw the crowds.
All those meetings bar one included a pursuit match against
either another major star of the road, such as the Belgian Rik
Van Steenbergen, or a track specialist such as the Dutchman
Gerrit Schulte. That winter Coppi rode twenty-one pursuits,
and won them all.

The Italian writer Mario Fossati travelled alongside Coppi
over one such winter and described how the *campionissimo*
would get out of the express train in each day's great city with
his bike under his arm. At the station he would find the *soigneur*
who had been appointed to look after him – a young man in a
heavy overcoat in Zurich, a dry-faced senior citizen in a sailing
top in Amsterdam, a guy with teeth like a horse in Antwerp, in
Copenhagen a classy chap in a double-breasted coat who offered
them pastis. There were taxi rides through the brightly lit city;
the dramatic entrance onto the track among the screaming
crowd; the night's victims; the champagne, the flowers; oysters
and steak tartare eaten in late-night restaurants after the evening's
work; the beautiful women lavishing attention on the star.

It was the antithesis of racing on the road with its mud,
dust and potholes, the hours of training in all weathers. At
the end of a road race the cyclist would sometimes be invisible apart from his eyes under a mask of muck, in a state
of near collapse. Here, on the other hand, was access to good
food, glamour, easy money, ready acclaim, popular success.
The star, critically, had to play the part: hair had to be bril-
liantined, sunglasses worn to cover the bags under the eyes,
elegant coats and suits donned for the dramatic entry into
each night's venue before he descended to change in the
bowels of the stadium. It was a world of unimaginable glamour
for the poverty-stricken post-war years, in the Europe of the
Marshall Plan and food queues.

*   *   *

The huge crowds at the velodromes reflected the fact that cycling had rapidly returned to being an international sport in the years after peace was restored. Post-war, the French, Belgian and Italian papers who ran the major races – the Tour of Flanders, Paris–Roubaix, and so on – were quick to combine forces in organising the Challenge Desgrange-Colombo (named after the founders of the Giro and Tour). This new umbrella competition across the major events, national Tours and Classics, drew cyclists out of their national fiefdoms.

The Italians were happy to race abroad, once post-war restrictions were lifted. Coppi had made his first trip to France in mid-September 1946, winning the Grand Prix de la Trocadero, a circuit race held in central Paris, as a prelude to an outstanding victory in the Grand Prix des Nations, a massive 140-kilometre time trial. He was pushed hard early in the three and a half hour race by the Frenchman Emile Idée, but pulled away over the little hills in the Chevreuse Valley, south of Paris, in an effort that left him flat on his back in the centre of the Parc des Princes.

Coppi had picked up more than passable English in prison camp, and clearly had a flair for languages: he ended up fluent in French. He travelled more widely, and enjoyed greater international success, than any of Italy's pre-war champions; he would be joined by Bartali and the country's other post-war great, Fiorenzo Magni, who was the pioneer when it came to racing in Belgium. They were supported wherever they went by the massive diaspora of Italian migrant workers spread across Europe – many of them under a post-war scheme to provide much needed labour. Marina Coppi still has a heavy miner's lantern given to her father by the Italian community in the Belgian mining area of Wallonia: 'They told my father, "When you win, we win because we feel important again." It's a huge responsibility for a sportsman to bear.'

Cycle racing was about to experience its popular zenith.

Now the Tour is the one event in cycling that regularly draws truly huge crowds, but during the 1940s and 1950s vast throngs could be seen at races which now sit on the margins or have long disappeared: the Tour of the West and Bordeaux–Paris in France; the regional *giri* – Lazio, Veneto, Tuscany – in Italy. Thirty thousand might turn up to watch the finish of a Giro di Lombardia; pictures taken at the finish of any race or Tour stage of the time will show crowds twenty deep as far as the eye can see.

At a time of economic austerity, the spectacle of a major bike race could be taken in for free, and it offered a chance to recall the days of plenty. People across Europe needed diversion and they were limited in where they could travel before the car and motorbike became universal. Cycling went to those people. It was a sport in which they could take an active role: the riders liked to have bottles of water handed up, time gaps or the distance to the finish could be yelled out. The more concerned or less scrupulous could reach out a hand on a mountain and give a firm push to a backmarker or a leader as they dropped behind.

As Dino Buzzati wrote: '. . . there they were, the people of all Italy . . . massed along 4,000 kilometres and they weren't what they were the day before. A powerful new feeling possessed them, they were yelling, laughing, the sorrows of life forgotten for a few instants, they were happy without a doubt.' The bike was integral to their lives: they had fled invading armies with suitcases on their handlebars, they had ferried weapons and food to partisans and escaped prisoners; in Rome bike bombs had become a fearsome fact of life as partisans fought occupation. They rode bikes to work and play and they could dream of emulating the champions as they cycled to their factories and fields.

For a brief while, cycling surfed the wave of economic expansion that transformed Europe so rapidly after the war.

For a few years, before the advent of live television coverage, cycling retained the mystique of the heroic days when no one quite knew what had happened out on the road. That in turn freed up the journalists to unleash their imaginations. They hyped up the characters, their nicknames, their clashes of personality, real and imagined.

There was Aldo Ronconi, an Italian who was coached by his brother, a priest who would run after him at stage finishes with his cassock floating in the wind, and who would disguise himself so that he could get round the rule that family members were not allowed in the Tour caravan. There was Pierre Brambilla, who reputedly chopped his bike to pieces after finishing third in the 1947 Tour de France. The Swiss Hugo Koblet – the 'pédaleur de charme' – carried a comb and some eau de cologne so that he could smarten up before crossing the finish line in triumph. A rider such as Luigi Malabrocca became a celebrity merely for finishing last in the Giro; he would devise the most bizarre stratagems to lose time and 'win' his lowly place. The nicknames harked back to the language invented to describe the earliest Tours de France: the elf, the Breton gnome, the menhir, the little goat, glasshead, leather head, the emperor, the ironman, the lion of Flanders, the eagle of Toledo.

In this pan-European soap opera with its cast of larger than life actors, the rivalry between Fausto Coppi and Gino Bartali was the principal subplot. It entailed a constant display of what the Italians term *polemica*, best described as a web of intrigue and dispute. *Polemica* drove and was driven by the sales of the newspapers that sponsored the races. Both men had to perform, on and off their bikes, to keep the headlines running, to keep the crowds interested. It was this rivalry that defined both of their careers.

CHAPTER 7

THE MYSTIC AND THE MECHANIC

'I can't do it alone. I need the help of a madman like you' –
Don Camillo to Peppone

When I first started attending bike races in Italy, in the early
1990s, Gino Bartali was as much a fixture at starts and finishes
as the elderly Campagnolo service cars and the pink *Gazzetta
dello Sport* posters. Bartali was then in his seventies, a gnome-
like figure with deep lines etched into his chestnut-brown
face with its towering broken nose and banana smile. He
would be called onto the podium to mutter a few in-
comprehensible platitudes, but mainly seemed to be hanging
around without a role, in a tacky-looking hat with a sponsor's
name on it. What I did not grasp at the time was that he *was*
the role. His task was to be Gino Bartali, to provide a tangible
connection with the glory days.

As much as anything he had achieved individually, the fans
were celebrating his role in the partnership that defined a
golden age when Italian cyclists seemed to win every major
race. Bartali himself seemed to recognise this, commenting
that he felt that the fans were there for Coppi as much as
for him. It was a generous admission of the fact that for thirty
years he had been fighting an unequal battle. Since Coppi's
death in 1960, fans and press had tended to project the
romantic, mythical qualities of their rivalry onto the younger
man rather than the living great. 'Even the *Bartaliani* became

Coppiani, partly through obligation, partly through conviction, partly through nostalgia,' wrote Bartali's biographer Gianni Brocchi.

Bartali was still dearly loved, if the constant queue of people shaking his hand and asking for his signature on anything that came to hand was any measure. There were estimates in the early 1990s that he was signing 5,000 autographs a day, but his popularity had its price. Bartali had also lost any mystique. He was half divinity, half caricature, like an Indian chief in a Barnum big top. There was something a little pathetic in the sight of him handing out publicity trinkets and posing with models in short skirts. It was hard to connect this doddery old man with the legend who had, it was always said, saved Italy from communist revolution by winning the 1948 Tour de France. All that remained of that Gino was the nose, as long and crooked as in his and Coppi's golden days.

*   *   *

As the focus for an entire generation of sports fans, the Coppi–Bartali rivalry is in the same league as those of their fellow cyclists Anquetil and Poulidor in the 1960s, of Ali and Frasier in the 1970s, Senna and Prost in the 1980s. There were classic elements in the plot: the young upstart Coppi against Bartali, the old champion; Coppi the team worker who rises to take on his own team leader, Bartali. All sports feed off such soap operas, but where cycling is unique is that the great, lasting events in road cycling were founded specifically to provide copy for newspapers, by breeding this kind of intrigue.

The rivalry was, said Orio Vergani, 'a great machine of financial interests'. Both men needed the money the rivalry could bring them – no race was worth organising if they did not participate, so they were paid to start, be it an exhibition event or a regional classic. *La Gazzetta dello Sport* needed the pair to boost its circulation, as did the regional papers that ran their own races. Bianchi and Legnano needed the duo in order to sell bikes. Team-mates of the champions earned far more racing for Coppi or Bartali than they could racing for themselves, even if their devotion meant that they never won a single event.

Coppi and Bartali were friends of a kind, who would work together when they had to – but the pyramid of interests ensured that the rivalry took on a life of its own and created its own momentum, to the extent that the actual sports events themselves could become lost among the miasma of words churned out by the newspapers. Behind the *polemica* – the 'disputes' whipped up by *La Gazzetta dello Sport* et al. – there was real competition, in immense volume. The number of events Coppi and Bartali rode, not to mention the fact that a single race, the Tour or Giro, lasts for over three weeks, meant that the frequency with which they went head to head is astonishing compared to, say, the number of meetings between Foreman and Ali. The rivalry lasted for almost fifteen years, from 1940, when Coppi outshone his team leader at the Giro, until Bartali's retirement at the end of 1954. Even though 1943, 1944 and 1945 were lost to the war, that is still an eternity in sporting terms. Begin with the number of events they rode, add in the pre-race hype, the post-race analysis and the between-race gossip and you can understand the massive, lasting impact on Italian consciousness.

Since Coppi and Bartali, Italian cycling has tended to see itself in terms of such opposing pairs. Most important, and deepest, was the rivalry in the late 1970s and early 1980s between Francesco Moser and Giuseppe Saronni (when I visited Moser seven years after his retirement he was still putting down Saronni), but there were others: Marco Pantani and Claudio Chiappucci, the Irishman Stephen Roche and Roberto Visentini, Gilberto Simoni and Damiano Cunego.

Italy seems made for such rivalries. Argument is a national pastime in a nation whose inhabitants do not understand the notion of sitting on the fence. One of the cornerstones of Italian identity is a phenomenon called *divismo* – opposition between concepts, people, places, sports teams and their stars. You are for one or the other, rarely neutral yet, paradoxically, the urge to argue forms a bond. The most basic oppositions in Italy are between the prosperous north and relatively impoverished south, between neighbouring cities and provinces, and between Milan, the industrial capital, and Rome, the political capital.

There was a proliferation of opposing pairs in the post-war years: in politics the right-wing Christian Democrats and left-wing Socialists; in sport, Juventus and Inter, Varzi and Nuvolari, Maserati and Ferrari; on screen, Sophia Loren and Gina Lollobrigida; on stage, Maria Callas and Renata Tebaldi; on the written page, Giovanni Guareschi's conservative priest Don Camillo and the radical communist mayor Peppone. There was another side to *divismo* in the post-conflict years. Fascism had imposed conformity that went beyond the political, while during the civil war loyalties had been a question of life and death. Arguing the virtues of Lollobrigida over Loren, or Bartali over Coppi, was a harmless outlet for emotion and could be celebrated as part of Italy's return to normality.

After Bartali's win in the 1947 Milan–San Remo, the pair whipped Italy's cycling fans into a state of delirium. As Dino Buzzati wrote: 'The [*tifosi*] have forgotten everything: who they are, the work waiting for them, the illnesses, luxuries, unpaid bills, headaches, love, everything except the fact that Coppi is in the lead and Bartali continues to lose ground.' At that year's Giro two separate police detachments had to be provided, one for Coppi's supporters, one for Bartali's. They were not there to prevent fights, but to stop the two stars being overwhelmed by their respective *tifosi* at the finish. The fans would remain outside the two riders' hotels singing and shouting until the small hours; Pierre Chany writes of being awoken one morning at three o'clock by a scream in the street. Outside the hotel, a *tifoso* was lying unconscious on the pavement, blood streaming from his head. He had climbed up the outside of the building and fallen from the second floor; '*Poverino*,' said his sobbing girlfriend, 'he so wanted to see Fausto as he slept.'

*   *   *

Of the two, it is Coppi who has inspired the artists and writers, who has acquired the lasting legacy, but in the flesh it was Bartali who was the bigger personality, who made the clearest impression on the minds of his contemporaries. To start with, there was one thing everyone knew about him, that truly set him apart: his overt religious belief. Coppi remains diffuse, hard to define: Bartali was and is *il pio Gino*. The most famous image of the man shows him praying at Lourdes during the rest day in a Tour de France, with Fiorenzo Magni alongside him. His eyes are closed in devotion, his arms shine with the cyclist's tan.

When away from home and unable to pray in the private chapel of his house in Ponte a Ema, near Florence, Bartali would often take his squad to Mass before race starts. He dedicated his wins to Ste Thérèse of Lisieux and had her image cut into his handlebars (this was subverted forty years on when the sprinter Mario Cipollini rode with Pamela Anderson's picture on his bike). He raced with half a dozen medallions of Ste Thérèse and the Virgin Mary hanging from his neck and his handlebars. There was a rumour that a little girl in the Tuscan countryside had seen Bartali climbing a mountain with an angel pushing him. On a more earthly note, his closest personal *gregario*, Giovanni Corrieri, said his pious master never swore once in seven years and would get annoyed with riders who relieved themselves during a race on the grounds that it did not look good in front of the public. If this were true, it would make Bartali truly unique among cyclists, who view watering the verges where they race as their God-given right.

For the Catholic Church, Bartali was a gift, with the 'deep and ingenuous faith of a Spanish toreador. He kneels and prays before measuring himself against his bull and kneels and thanks God after getting through the day.' His chastity, self-denial and prayer meant he could be depicted as the perfect Christian athlete. He could produce pithy phrases to link his faith and his sport, worthy of fridge magnets or car stickers today: 'Faith enables me to stand the pain', 'My jersey was often dirty, but my thoughts remained pure'. When he founded his bike company, it was no coincidence that the machines were made by a manufacturer called Santamaria. The bikes, ironically, were of poor quality.

Bartali's sporting longevity, over a career that lasted the best part of twenty years, could be held to represent 'eternal Christian youth', the notion that chastity and piety would lead to eternal life while bringing earthly success. Not surprisingly, given the aura that was created around him, he was treated like an earthly saint: the *tifosi* would strew rose petals in his path and kiss the tarmac where his tyres had been. His stage win at Lourdes in the 1948 Tour was, inevitably, seen as divinely inspired.

Coppi was depicted as an atheist, to his utter disgust: he met Pius XII on at least two occasions, in 1947 and 1949. The first visit was at the instigation of Bartali, and the rumour went that he had not gone willingly. His account of the visit is expansive enough to suggest he was not indifferent: the red-velveted page; the silence of the Vatican's corridors; Pius XII's simple room, full of books and decorated with a large silver cross; the papal blessing traced in front of them with his 'delicate, transparent hands'. Coppi actually had the classic peasant Catholic faith he was brought up with, but, unlike Bartali, he had the countryman's unwillingness to bare his soul. He would mutter dark things about other people who made much of their beliefs in public, referring clearly to Bartali, and add that he was equally devout. It was Coppi who presented all his *gregari* and the team manager, Alfredo Binda, with gold medals depicting the Madonna del Ghisallo – patron saint of cyclists – after his 1949 Tour de France win.

There were, in any case, nuances to Bartali's Catholicism. His faith was overt, but his behaviour was more muscular than Christian once he was on his bike and the competitive instinct took over. His thoughts might have been clean, but he sold many of his races as an amateur. In the Giro in 1947, when a rider called him a 'lying priest', he did not turn the other cheek but delivered a straight left that floored the blasphemer. Several of his contemporaries describe him as tight-fisted, a rider who offered money for assistance in races but never paid or came up with less than he promised. 'Gino never kept the promises he made to his rivals in a race. In certain situations he would ask you for help in return for a favour or something else which never came. Fausto on the other hand didn't say very much but kept his word.' In terms of lifestyle, it was Coppi who lived like a monk, while Bartali smoked and drank with Rabelaisian gusto.

Politically, as well, Bartali's beliefs were much easier to identify than Coppi's, and they sprang from his religion. Bartali's father had been an active socialist – he had asked young Gino to hide his party card when the fascists began rounding up the leftwingers – but *Pio Gino* was a close friend of the Christian Democrat leader Alcide De Gasperi, whom he had met in the Vatican during the war. Inevitably, he was adopted by the Christian Democrats. It was, therefore, hardly surprising that Coppi was approached by the left to endorse Palmiro Togliatti's communists during the 1948 election campaign. Wisely, however, and typically, he turned them down. It was widely held by those close to him that he voted Christian Democrat, but that did not stop the political labels: Bartali was 'De Gasperi in bicicletta', Coppi 'the Togliatti of the road'. There were posters, too: 'Up with Coppi the communist, down with Bartali the Christian Democrat'. As with the pair's religious beliefs, the labels were simplistic.

*　　*　　*

For Coppi at least, Bartali was the person who mattered in every race. He was fixated with the man. One writer recalled sitting in the Bianchi team car behind the pair as they ascended a mountain pass in the Giro, where Coppi was clearly the stronger from the way he was riding. The Bianchi boss Aldo Zambrini was shaking his head: his rider could win, but he didn't dare attack. Then Bartali's chain came off. 'It was only a few seconds, but it was enough. As if liberated from a nightmare that froze his muscles and paralysed his willpower, Fausto did not merely accelerate, he took flight. It was like a bird beating its wings.' Coppi was so mentally fragile that he would complain that Bartali was watching him and only him; the notion would make him want to quit.

Sometimes, the rivalry prompted sheer farce, as in the events of the evening before Milan–San Remo in March 1947. That night, Bianchi were in their usual hotel in the centre of the city, the plushly furnished, marble-embellished Andreola, near the vast Central station. With them were Bartali's Legnano. Coppi was worried about his form, so he instructed his domestiques to nobble his rival. This was not a matter of spiking Bartali's food or letting his tyres down. Instead, Coppi based his plan on the psychology of the individual. It was well known that Bartali liked to stay up late smoking and yarning: Serse Coppi was instructed to get Bartali out on the town and keep him up late. The trek to San Remo would begin early in the morning, and a sleepless night could wreck Bartali's chances. With him Serse took his friend Luigi Casola and Ubaldo Pugnaloni, the uncrowned Italian champion of 1943.

'If Bartali were in this room now, we'd be here [talking] until midnight,' Pugnaloni tells me. 'Coppi had gone to bed early as usual. Serse, Casola and I took Bartali to the cinema, to see *Gilda* with Glenn Ford, we began smoking cigarettes, got back in the middle of the night. Fausto had a good grumble at Serse because they were sharing a room and he didn't come in quietly.' After the film they went to eat, strolled round the station, and 'spun the evening out'. At the back of their minds was one thought: 'losing sleep would cut Bartali off at the knees'.

The plan failed. Coppi's conjunctivitis got the better of him and he abandoned. Pugnaloni had insomnia after smoking too many cigarettes and quit; Casola and Serse Coppi also abandoned. As Pugnaloni told me, 'Bartali put out half the team in an evening, because he was used to staying up late and we weren't.' The winner, inevitably, was the 'old man', amid rumours that Bianchi were getting fed up with paying Coppi his huge salary.

The *polemica* in the 1947 Giro was inevitable. Bartali's win in the Giro della Rinascita had 'burned Coppi up', as one writer put it, because he knew it meant that the older man could claim he would also have won in 1940 if team duty had not meant he had to help Coppi. The Giro di Lombardia in early October 1946 gave Coppi his chance for revenge on Bartali, and he won in straightforward style, or so it seemed, until it was revealed that he had paid the third finisher, a local rider called Michele Motta, 30,000 lire to let him escape from the race-winning break in the final kilometres. The affair dragged on for a while, but did not detract from Coppi's market value or his reputation. 'A win worthy of Binda or Girardengo,' wrote *La Gazzetta dello Sport*.

Bartali had opened the pre-Giro hostilities in 1947, declaring that Coppi would win 'over my dead body'. There were murmurings from Coppi's camp that the Giro route had been designed to favour his rival: why else was there no time trial stage? Early on, Coppi was shaken by the loss of his beloved Serse, who crashed out of the race, but he recovered to use his climbing skill to overwhelm the opposition in the Dolomites. The decisive day was from Pieve di Cadore to Trento over the climbs of the Falzarego and Pordoi. Bartali claimed later that he had trouble with his gears; he also crashed during an epic chase behind Coppi, who won the stage by four minutes and twenty-four seconds and kept the lead to Milan. Bartali did not accept defeat graciously, claiming that his rival had been able to ride in the slipstream of vehicles among the race convoy, and that he himself had been told to let Coppi win, because if Bianchi failed to take the Giro the team would disappear.

Coppi was dominant for the rest of 1947, taking the Italian national championship – decided in a series of one-day races – then adding the world pursuit title and finally the Giro di Lombardia, with Bartali more than five minutes behind. At the end of the season he was elected Italian sportsman of the year. In Milan–San Remo the following spring, Coppi's winning margin was a colossal eleven minutes, but the following months saw *il pio* regain the ascendancy as Coppi's star rapidly waned.

First came the Giro, where Coppi and his Bianchi team pulled out in protest when Fiorenzo Magni received a mere slap on the wrist after his supporters had pushed him up the toughest mountain passes. They had been brought in by the coachload and specially positioned for maximum effect. The Tour de France followed; in the Alps Bartali electrified Italy by turning round a twenty-two-minute deficit to take his second victory in the event, at the age of thirty-three. It was one of the great Tour wins, and had a significance outside the sport, coming as it did the day after an assassination attempt on the communist leader Palmiro Togliatti. The Italian team leader was called that same day by his old acquaintance De Gasperi, who asked 'more as a fan than a president', as Bartali put it, whether he could win the race. While at home the communists set up roadblocks and called for a general strike, and weapons were brought out on to the streets, Bartali won the first Alpine stage and took the Tour. The tension subsided, and, strange as it may seem now, the victory was said to have 'saved Italy.'

That is an exaggeration: while the gravity of the circum-stances cannot be underestimated – the country was just three years out of the war, with plenty of former partisan weapons in circulation – historians feel that Italy would probably have stepped back from revolution even if Bartali had not performed. From Coppi's point of view, it was disastrous: this was Italian sport's first victory at international level, outside the country, since the football World Cup in 1938. It carried colossal pres-tige. Moreover, he had foolishly turned down the invitation to ride himself. And for Bianchi it was a catastrophe: Legnano enjoyed a massive increase in sales, up by about 40,000 bikes a month.

*   *   *

To make the relationship more complex, Coppi and Bartali were the children of different worlds. The age difference between them was a mere five years, but Bartali was rightly nicknamed *il vecchio*. Coppi dragged his sport into the modern world, while Bartali was a throwback to the pre-war years. The writer Curzio Malaparte made the link to the religious faith of the 'old man': 'Bartali belongs to those who believe in tradition, its immutability; to those who accept dogma. He is a metaphysical being protected by saints. Coppi has no one up there to look after him. He is alone on his bike. Bartali prays as he pedals; Coppi, a rational, sceptical being, full of doubts, only believes in the motor he has been given: his body.' As Malaparte noted, Coppi was a sceptic, questioning every side of his profession in the search for perfection. Bartali's approach, on the other hand, was that of a believer, no matter how outdated or wrongheaded he might be. Fiorenzo Magni told me: 'Coppi was amazingly organised, which mattered a lot then, when you had to do so many things for yourself. Bartali was more of a fatalist, who assumed it would all turn out all right.'

Bartali relied on peasant remedies, some learned from his mother, but all harking back to the witchdoctor notions peddled by the *soigneurs* since cycling began: salt, olive oil and vinegar baths, hot compresses of vinegar and salt applied with a well-wrung cloth, local application of tobacco from cut-off cigarette butts, and rubs with grape juice because he had noticed that vineyard workers did this to relieve pain. He liked a glass of liqueur distilled by his father, and believed he had to protect himself from magnetic fields. To that end, he travelled with a compass so that he could align his bed north–south, and every night when he arrived in his hotel room he would shift the furniture accordingly.

Physically and mentally, Coppi was fragile while Bartali was hard as nails: 'the man of iron' in contrast with the rival whose brittle bones were compared to glass. Coppi could handle bad weather or bad luck, but only if he was on form and his mindset was perfect. He needed constant moral support from his team-mates, Cavanna, the management. Sandrino Carrea told me: 'Coppi would get demoralised and say he had lost if some guy was two minutes ahead on the road, even if there were still 100 kilometres to go. [In that situation] Bartali would say, "We can do it, we can do it", even if there were only five kilometres to go. If Coppi had had the grit of Bartali or Magni, he would have won even more.' Bartali, on the other hand, appeared impervious to heat and cold. 'He was never tired, he never felt the weather,' Fiorenzo Magni told me. He rarely wore a racing cape and, as Pugnaloni's story shows, he could get by on a few hours' sleep. Given the number of crashes and punctures Bartali suffered, disproportionate even for those times, it is just as well that bad luck did not undermine his self-belief.

Stomach troubles beset Coppi from time to time, but the digestive system of the 'old man' was a legend in itself. 'He could have eaten stones if he wanted,' recalled his domestique Giovanni Corrieri. He reputedly drank up to twenty-eight *espressi* a day, which might explain why he never needed to try amphetamine. He swore he never doped, and as Coppi cynically remarked, 'If Gino says it, it must be true.' He would break eggs on his bars, letting the white fall to the ground and eating only the yolk. He would get through five or six in a stage. In his bottle would be watered down egg custard or sugar and water.

These were pre-war remedies, and Bartali never moved towards modern cycling as Coppi did. Nor did he have the same ascetic lifestyle. The story goes that once Coppi was dining at one of the finest restaurants in the Rome area. He got up and left early. 'Don't you like the food?' asked the owner. 'I like it too much,' was the answer. Bartali saw things differently, as the night out before Milan–San Remo showed. Coppi would be in bed at 9.30, whereas in a twin hotel room Bartali might talk at his room-mate until 3 a.m., and the victim would plead with him to shut up or at least go somewhere else so that he could rest. Whereas Coppi was completely abstinent and while the *gregari* might enjoy a glass of wine at dinner,

Gino had a bottle. 'If I had drunk just part of the wine Gino has, I'd be dead,' joked Coppi. And that was not all. 'Gino smoked, and he smoked a lot, especially after the war when he was at his strongest,' says Alfredo Martini, who was asked in the 1952 Tour to go and beg Gino's favourite brand, Nazionale, off fans at l'Alpe d'Huez.

On their bikes, they relied on different attributes. As Ettore Milano told me: 'Coppi had class, Gino had power.' Alfredo Martini is a little more nuanced: Bartali had stamina but Coppi had speed. Bartali's racing style was based on *grinta*, guts and strength. He used his stamina and sheer physical power, particularly in bad weather, to wear the opposition down with repeated attacks. Coppi, on the other hand, would wait until he could sense the right moment to make the single move that would get him clear of the pack. Once away, his ability to ride solo would ensure he could not be caught.

Tactically, Coppi was far more astute. He had to be, because Bartali was faster in a sprint finish. Coppi would watch and wait while *il pio* would waste energy with fruitless early moves in a race. Giovanni Corrieri was always frustrated with his old boss's inability to learn from his mistakes or to act on the advice of his team-mates. 'Perhaps Fausto would only jump once, but if you gave him two metres [lead] it was all over . . . I told Gino so many times: stop jumping, just watch Fausto's wheel, because if he counter-attacks, you will never see him again. But the next day it would be business as usual. Fausto would just wait for the right moment for the fatal blow.' In terms of strategy, the long-term planning of his racing, Coppi was better organised, and he wanted to hire the best men to help him. There are no figures such as Cavanna or the legendary mechanic Pinella di Grande linked with Bartali, who often had mechanical problems when he raced.

Sometimes the tactics adopted by the pair were more

sophisticated than trips to the cinema. Bartali noticed that a vein behind Coppi's right knee would swell up when he was close to his physical limit. As early as the 1946 Giro he delegated one *gregario* specifically to sit behind his rival and watch for it, with orders to yell 'the vein, the vein' when the swelling appeared. It is said to have prompted the attack that won the older man the Giro della Rinascita. Coppi on the other hand, noticed that Bartali tended to cut the hairpin bends on a mountain climb if he wasn't going well. To counter Bartali's strength and repeated attacks, he also developed the classic tactic of riding steadily up the climbs, letting Bartali jump away time after time, reeling him in again and again with metronomic steadiness. It could happen up to ten times on a single mountain pass.

*   *   *

Opinions remain divided on just how close the pair were. 'I have eight or nine true friends and Fausto is the best,' said Bartali, who also said they were 'like brothers'. Coppi never described him in such terms – he was not that kind of man – but, tellingly, Bartali was the first person to whom he showed a photograph of his newly born son, Faustino. Martini repeats that they were friends off the bike, but not close friends because their characters were so different. As Rino Negri said: 'Like all timid men, Coppi kept his opinions and convictions to himself. Gino, like all Tuscans, loved to talk like a river in flood.' For example, at the dinner table, there was not a lot of banter between them. Giovanni Corrieri saw it like this: 'They were rivals but didn't really hate each other. They feared each other athletically but had mutual respect.'

The relationship was clearly a knowing one, with its own conventions, such as refusing to refer publicly to each other by name, using instead epithets such as 'that one there, the other'. They took pleasure, most of the time, in annoying each other as a matter of form. Bartali, Coppi commented, would often laugh at him to annoy him; Coppi clearly loved to play Bartali at his own game, spying and dis-information. He told Rino Negri: 'I knew what he was up to when he sent people to me to assess my state of mind. I split up his informants into two categories; when I wanted him to find something out quickly I sent [one], when I wanted him to feel something was suspicious I sent [the other].' The objective was to gain the psychological whiphand: on one occasion, while climbing the Pordoi Pass, one of the Giro's toughest mountains, Coppi said 'ciao' to his rival as he left him behind, making sure that Bartali could hear. 'I don't believe he ever swore, but that time I wondered . . .' It is the kind of gamesmanship that comes naturally to sportsmen with lively minds, the cycling equivalent of sledging in cricket, or the things muttered between rugby's front rows as they pack down in a scrum.

There are those, however, who testify that the rivalry was 'absolute, tremendous'. Ubaldo Pugnaloni told me that Bianchi's domestiques would always be terrified if a race went down a particularly bad stretch of road. Their concern was that Coppi might puncture, in which event 'all hell would break loose' as Bartali's Legnano tried to take advantage. They would then have to try to help Coppi regain the speeding pack.

Even so, there was considerable complicity between the pair and their teams. Coppi and Corrieri had a particularly close friendship. Both Bartali and Coppi clearly understood the financial value of the rivalry. They must have been aware that headlines would come from every word they said to the press, every action in a race that was witnessed by the jour-nalists. Sometimes the complicity went beyond mere theatre. The duo had a secret pact in the 1946 Giro to combine forces

in the Dolomites against their younger rival, Ortelli. Coppi
would have preferred not to lose to Bartali, but if he were to
do so, it was better for his image, and his financial interests,
if he were to finish second to his great rival than to come
fifth to an unknown. If Ortelli emerged as a rival, that would
threaten both of them. The thinking seems convoluted, yet it
has its own logic.

Sometimes, the lengths they went to seem puerile. In one
Giro d'Italia Coppi became tired of hearing the fans chanting
'GI-NO', 'GI-NO' at Bartali. The crowds could easily spot his
rival, as he was wearing the red, green and white Italian
national champion's jersey, so Coppi ordered a team-mate,
Donato Piazza, to put on the jersey he had earned for becoming
Italian track champion and ride at the front of the bunch.
The upshot was that Piazza took the applause, not Bartali.
The downside was that Piazza was only permitted to wear the
jersey in track events, not road races such as the Giro, and
he was breaking the rules. But Coppi was happy to pay the
fines.

The relationship reached its nadir at the 1948 world championships in Valkenburg, Holland, held a month after Bartali
looked to have gained the advantage over the younger man
with his Tour de France win. It was now late August, and
Coppi had won nothing major since March. Victory for Bartali
in Holland would mean the ascendancy of *il vecchio* was
absolute; additionally, as ever, there were rumours that Bianchi
were losing patience with their leader. But in Holland the
rivalry had a new twist: the world championships were
contested by national teams. That meant the pair were joint
leaders of the Italian squad, and expected to combine forces
to represent their country. Instead, they watched each other,
neither willing to put in an effort that might have given the
other an advantage. They simply let the race go away from
them, amid a cacophony of whistling from the Italian fans

who had made the journey north to see one of their heroes take the gold medal. 'Wherever you go I'll go,' said Coppi, and he was as good as his word, even following Bartali into the changing rooms.

The disgust of the entire country was shared by the Italian cycling federation, which banned both men for two months for what was euphemistically called 'a lack of willingness to compete'. The ban was quickly rescinded: Coppi won the Giro d'Emilia and Giro di Lombardia, both in typical lone escapes, on 10 and 24 October respectively, to take some consolation from a year that had gone Bartali's way. (It had also seen him lose his world pursuit title to the Dutchman Gerrit Schulte.) The Lombardy win was typically dominant; he escaped well before the climb to the Madonna del Ghisallo, broke his own record time for the ascent, and stayed out in front for over eighty kilometres to win by almost five minutes, his third consecutive win in the Classic. The conditions were atro- cious: he finished covered in mud and was immediately wrapped up in a leather overcoat.

The Valkenburg debacle had far-reaching effects. Bartali would never be world champion. He and his great rival would never truly trust each other. In all its pettiness and negativity, the episode would come to define the dark side of their rivalry. Most importantly, however, Valkenburg haunted the Italian cycling authorities and the national team manager, Alfredo Binda. They would be a laughing stock if this were allowed to happen again. Putting 'two cockerels in the same hencoop', as the Italian saying has it, was not to be undertaken lightly but, as Coppi prepared to ride his first Tour de France, also contested by national teams, it had to be done.

CHAPTER 8

SUMMER LIGHTNING

Among the millions of fans obsessed with Fausto Coppi by the summer of 1948 was a provincial doctor in a small town north-east of Milan. Doctor Enrico Locatelli and his young wife Giulia were known locally as 'the ideal couple' or 'the inseparables'. They never quarrelled. They would spend evenings together in their sitting room, where she would crochet while he read *La Gazzetta dello Sport*, searching the pink paper for any article that mentioned his idol, whose photograph could be seen all round the house. If the paper did not have a piece on Coppi, he would throw it down and go to bed. As for Giulia, she had no idea why anyone should be so interested in any sport of any kind. Cycling held no attraction for her, just yet.

Almost every region of Italy had its own Giro – a one-day event that was organised by the local paper and which would usually draw the greats of the day. Such local classics have since declined in importance, virtually to the point of anonymity. Nowadays the Tre Valli Varesine, the Three Valleys of Varese, just north of Milan, would barely get a few paragraphs in *La Gazzetta dello Sport*, but in the late 1940s it was another key episode in the Bartali–Coppi soap opera. The race itself, held on 8 August 1948, resulted in the usual *polemica* between Bartali and Coppi. Victory went to the latter, with 'the other one' claiming he had ridden dishonestly. It was an important step in the escalation of mutual distrust between the two men during the build-up to the world championships. It was, however, far less significant than one apparently minor event on the periphery of the race.

As far as Dr Locatelli was concerned, what mattered was that the race was held not far away from the village of Varano Borghi, where he had set up his practice when he and Giulia moved north in late 1945, not long after their wedding. Locatelli's wife had no particular desire to accompany her husband when he told her they were to go and obtain Coppi's autograph at the Tre Valli Varesine. Giulia went along, but with a different thought in her mind: here was a way of escaping the small village where they lived, for an afternoon at least. Just as Gustave Flaubert's Emma Bovary found that life with her doctor husband in the French provinces was slow, so Giulia was chafing at the bit. Doctor Locatelli was a busy man, devoted to his work. Even though Milan was just an hour away, Varano Borghi felt cut off from the mainstream, and she spent many hours with her two-year-old daughter Loretta, whose name was always shortened to Lolli.

Giulia subsequently produced two subtly different versions of how she and Coppi met. According to one account, she and her husband went to approach Coppi at the *punzonatura*, the ritual of the evening before the race when the *campioni* would register and have their bikes checked. The Locatellis arrived late in Varese, as did Coppi. In the traffic jam approaching the race's headquarters, the doctor and his wife were stuck in a line of traffic behind a large grey Lancia Aprilia bearing an Alessandria registration plate. It was the doctor who recognised Coppi in the car; the couple followed it through a yelling throng of fans, some grabbing the car, some climbing on to it. At the *punzonatura*, the police made a vain attempt to force the crowd back from the car so that the doors could be opened. And when they did open she saw him get out: a tall, slender, reserved man, aloof and somehow detached amidst the chaos, dressed in a dark-brown suit with a blue tie.

In a second version, produced thirty years later, she was

more downbeat about her first impression: 'To tell the truth, he made no impression on me as a man. I thought he was ugly, with that enormous chest and his long pointed nose.' Both accounts tally in one way: she met Coppi at his hotel and asked for an autograph, although one version has this happening the evening before the race, the other the evening after the finish. At his hotel, Giulia caught him as he went up the stairs. He did not even bother to look at her; give a piece of paper to the porter, he said, and I will sign it. 'You are being unkind,' she replied; she would have an autographed photograph or nothing. 'This time he looked at me and went red in the face with embarrassment. He murmured shyly, "Yes, yes, of course."'

Coppi turned, and called to his brother Serse to get the bag of photos from the car. To whom should he dedicate the picture: '*Signorina* . . .' *Signora*, she corrected him. When visited by the journalist Jean-Paul Ollivier in the 1980s, Giulia Locatelli still had a postcard of a young Coppi in the Italian national champion's green, red and white jersey. It was a symbol of the way she had dragged Coppi from indifference to acquiescence, a foretaste of the power she would eventually exert over him. She may have sensed an opportunity when this celebrity, the idol of the baying crowd, had been bent to her will in that single encounter on the stairs. She would return again and again to see him race. 'I became obsessed with Coppi,' she confessed.

As well as the veneer of celebrity, the smart suit and the big car and the hordes of fans, what was there about Coppi himself that might attract a woman? The most telling comment I could elicit came from the wife of one of his team-mates: '*Era squisito*', he was refined. What did she mean by that? 'Delicate in his manners, courteous in the way he spoke, almost feminine.' Another woman mentioned that he had long, delicate hands. It is hard to get further from the old cliché of the cycling champion as an uneducated peasant or manual worker.

Coppi's son Faustino recalls Giulia's view of her lover: 'She would say "He was a gentleman" even though he came from a peasant family. He had a certain courtesy, a way of behaving. They lived together for several years and there wasn't once when he didn't get up when she arrived at the dinner table.' After their affair went public, Giulia explained the attraction like this: 'Coppi is not a common man, and in a certain sense he is very unlike people who earn a living from sport. He has the style of an artist, you could say a musician, he moves delicately, dresses with taste. He is at home in any company.'

Coppi was a man in search of certainty: that was reflected in the people who influenced him, powerful minds such as Cavanna, his brother Serse, Bartali. In that context, it was understandable that he might eventually succumb to a strong-minded woman. Giulia's initial interest in Coppi went hand in hand with that of her husband, and together the couple visited more and more bike races, always seeking out the champion. For the moment, Giulia Locatelli looked like any other impassioned autograph hunter.

*   *   *

Coppi had plenty to distract him in the next few months besides his one-year-old daughter Marina. He was more restrained in his track racing, and that restful winter ushered in the best spell of his career. The big issue derived from the Valkenburg debacle, however. In a few months, Italy would have to choose the national team for the Tour de France, which was contested by squads from each country rather than the sponsored outfits that rode the rest of the season's races. Alfredo Binda and the heads of Italian cycling had to decide which of the two stars should lead the national team. Should they go for the defending champion, Bartali, or his bitter rival? Could they leave either one out without drawing virulent protests from the fans and media? If they put both men in the team, how could they work together?

The two men had at least restored amicable relations when Coppi visited Bartali in Tuscany at Christmas 1948, but it fell to Binda to get them to the start of the Tour in the same team. The Italian manager was a man of stature: as the *campionissimo* of the 1920s, he had at one time been so dominant in the Giro that the organisers paid him to keep away. He had also won the first world professional road race championship in 1926. Here was no lightweight, but a man who could talk to Coppi and Bartali on equal terms. A summit meeting was called in early March 1949 at the town of Chiavari, east of Genoa on the Mediterranean coast, with all the senior figures in Italian cycling present, and a written agreement under which the pair agreed to cooperate was drawn up under Binda's guidance on 14 March.

Bartali said publicly that he would work with his rival, but Coppi showed astonishing form as the 1949 season progressed. Just five days after the agreement was signed the younger man opened a four-minute gap in thirty kilometres to win Milan–San Remo. Three weeks later he scored a narrow win in the 'best of three' pursuit decider against Schulte in front of a 20,000 crowd at the Vigorelli. He then headed to Belgium and northern France, coming close to victory in the Flèche Wallonne Classic and engineering a victory for his brother Serse in Paris–Roubaix, which, he said, gave him more joy than if he had won himself. Back in Italy, as the Giro neared, he won the Giro di Romagna, with Bartali ten minutes behind.

That year's Giro took place amid massive public interest. The 'third man' of Italian cycling, Fiorenzo Magni, had won the 1948 race, while Bartali had taken the Tour de France and 'saved the republic'. So Coppi needed to re-assert himself in his home Tour. The hype was immense, but only Coppi lived up to it, with two deadly blows on two great mountain stages. For the rest of the three weeks he and Bartali observed each other closely, amid rumours that Bartali might have been poisoned by a malevolent Sicilian. The race was remarkable for one other thing: the despatches of the writer and poet Dino Buzzati in *Corriere della Sera*, some of the most lyrical reports cycling has ever prompted.

The emotion was not generated only by the racing: 4 May had seen the Superga air crash, in which the entire squad of the dominant Turin football team, *il Grande Torino*, had been wiped out. Coppi and Bartali had been friends of the players, with whom they had turned out in benefit matches, and Coppi began the Giro with an FC Turin badge on his Bianchi jersey. The memory of the war was also still close: the race returned to Trieste, now part of Italy, to scenes of rejoicing, tears and seas of Italian flags, and it travelled past the flattened town of Cassino, where, wrote Buzzati, 'there were no lovely girls at the windows – the windows were missing. Even the walls were missing.'

Coppi swooped on the main stage in the Dolomites, riding away from Bartali when the 'iron man' punctured on the Pordoi Pass and opening a gap of seven minutes by the finish in Bolzano. That prompted Buzzati to write the following, about the *campionissimo* in flight: 'Look at Coppi, is he climbing? No. He is just forging onwards as if the road were as flat as a pool table. From a distance, you might say he is out for a blissful stroll. Close-to, you can see his face becoming more and more lined, his upper lip contracting like a rat caught in a trap . . . [he is] hermetically sealed in his own suffering.'

As the crow flies, just sixty kilometres separates the towns of Cuneo and Pinerolo in Italy's western Alps. But for 10 June 1949, the new Giro organiser, Vincenzo Torriani – whose name would be inseparable from the event until the 1990s – had devised a massive loop of 254 kilometres into France and back for the race's eighteenth stage. It took in five climbs: the Maddalena – known to the French as the Col de Varche – the French passes of the Vars and the Izoard, with its scree-slopes and Death Valley-style rock pillars, the ascent to the Franco-Italian border at Montgenevre and the long drag past the ski resort of Sestriere before the descent to Pinerolo. With 4,200 metres of climbing in total over the five passes, it was one of the toughest courses for any mountain stage in any Giro.

At the stage start, Coppi was a few seconds behind the race's overall leader, Adolfo Leoni, the sprinter who had been the mover behind the rebirth of cycling in post-war Italy. The stage had been preceded by the predictable verbal exchanges with Bartali: 'Tell that one I'll drop him.' 'Tell the other one he won't see my back wheel for long.' Bartali said Coppi would attack on the first three cols, 'I'll catch him on the fourth and drop him on the fifth'; Coppi riposted that Bartali 'will have to have a good look at my back wheel at the start because that's the only time he'll see it'.

It was good knockabout stuff, but it was irrelevant once the stage had started. Coppi went clear on the Varche, amid late spring snow in the high meadows, in pursuit of another Italian, Primo Volpi. There was a massive 192 kilometres to go, but he simply rode further and further ahead, dodging around massive potholes in the tarmac, until, at the finish, he was indisputably the Giro winner, with Bartali floundering in his wake, twelve minutes behind. To escape so far from the end of the stage, with some five hours' riding through the mountains ahead, in the day's rain and cold, was a massive gamble, a colossal state-ment of confidence in his own ability. Those present recall that he was almost angry afterwards. 'That loony Volpi made me completely kill myself,' he said to Mario Ricci.

Buzzati produced his most effusive piece yet, reflecting that here, surely, the older champion, Bartali – twelve minutes behind and almost twenty-four minutes back in the overall standings – had been killed off by his younger rival. Buzzati observed the muddied face of the 'iron man', his open lips, his expression of suffering and wrote: 'Thirty years ago I learned [at school] that Achilles killed Hector. Is this too glorious, too solemn a comparison? No. What would be the point in calling these "classical studies" if the fragments that remain in our minds were not an integral part of our lives? Fausto Coppi does not have Achilles' glacial cruelty . . . but Bartali is living through the same drama as Hector: the tragedy of a man vanquished by the Gods. Bartali has fought a superhuman power and he could only lose: his opponent is the malevolent power of old age.'

Less elaborate, but a better illustration of the massive time gaps Coppi opened up on that stage, was a tale told by the French journalist Pierre Chany. He described following Coppi before deciding to stop for lunch. As Coppi disappeared up the road, he and his colleagues had a starter, a main course and coffee. Bartali came past as they left the restaurant. It seems unlikely, unless the waiter was extraordinarily quick on his feet, but it makes the point.

*   *   *

Coppi's dominance in the Giro left the Italian national cycling federation and the trainer of the national team, Alfredo Binda, with a nasty conundrum. The consensus reached at Chiavari broke down after Coppi's victory in the Giro. Coppi's backers, underpinned by the financial muscle of Bianchi, demanded that Bartali remain at home. Speaking to *La Gazzetta dello Sport*, Coppi made his case: he had always felt his rival was not a team man, that he did not play by the rules, and that they should not race together. The prospect of Bartali leading another team in the Tour, the mix and match 'international' squad, was raised, but quickly dropped. The national standing of the pair was such that the Italian president Alcide De Gasperi was moved to declare publicly that they had to unite on behalf of Italy. This was hardly surprising given his friendship with Bartali; more remarkably, the communist leader Palmiro Togliatti said publicly that he agreed with De Gasperi.

Binda, Coppi and Bartali met again in the central Italian town of Osimo that June, and Binda laid down the law. If the pair left the room without coming to an agreement, he told them, Italy would never forgive them and their images would be mud. He proposed the following deal: they would each take their own *gregari* with them and would agree to help each other until the Tour reached the mountains, at which point they could ride their own races and it would become clear which was the stronger.

The Italian team manager had a gut feeling that neither man wanted a repeat of the Valkenburg farce, because they feared what it would do to their reputations. However, he made sure that he retained control of the team. He would have the power he needed to restrain either man if he started to put self-interest above the common weal. He had the ultimate right to select the team, while allowing Bartali and Coppi to bring some of their own team-mates. He kept the power to throw anyone off the race if they disobeyed his orders, and he established that he would be the one who told the *gregari* what to do. The written agreement was finally signed at the Hotel Andreola in Milan, just two weeks before the Tour started on 30 June in Paris.

*   *   *

The cover of *Miroir-Sprint* magazine's tribute to Coppi's life and career shows the *campionissimo* as he is seen by cyclists across Europe: with the pensive look of a man haunted by personal tragedy

The five Coppi children with Fausto
(top right) and Serse (front centre)

Fausto and friends after a hunting trip

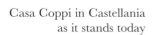

Casa Coppi in Castellania
as it stands today

1946 - Gli aquilotti della gran marca nazionale "BIANCHI"

Canavesi   De Stefanis   Leoni   Coppi F.   Coppi S.   Barrisone   Servadei   Pugnaloni   Simoni

Bianchi's first post-war team line-up in 1946, including the Coppi brothers
and Ubaldo Pugnaloni

Early team postcard of Fausto from the 1940s

Coppi is perfection on two wheels as he crushes the field in the La Rochelle time trial in the 1949 Tour de France

Elegance off the bike as the French fans track his every move

The gallery of fans applauds Coppi in the Alps in the 1949 Tour de France

Celebration after victory: the Nancy time trial clinches his double of
Giro and Tour in the same year

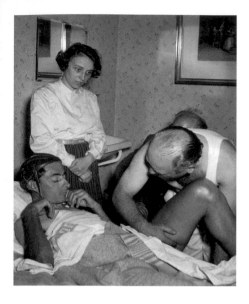

Biagio Cavanna massages
Coppi as the cyclist's wife,
Bruna, looks on

With his mother Angiolina
in Castellania

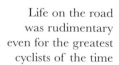

Life on the road
was rudimentary
even for the greatest
cyclists of the time

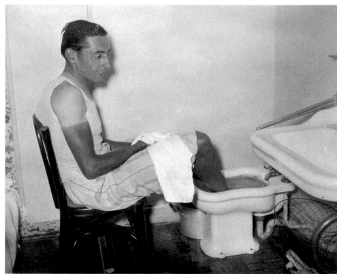

The relationships that defined a career: *above*: Serse kisses Fausto after the younger Coppi wins the 1949 Paris–Roubaix; *right*: Gino Bartali on the right and the *campionissimo* are not at their ease before a Tour de France start, *below*: relations are 'normalised' when Bartali, in overalls, appears at the Giro after his retirement

One of the legendary 'bottle' photographs: in this 1949 image,
Coppi is passing the drink to Bartali

After Bartali had won the 1948 Tour, taking seven stage wins along the way, Coppi had told his *gregario* Ettore Milano that if he didn't win the 1949 Tour he would give up – he was sick, he said, of hearing people talking about Bartali's win on the radio. In the event, he came within an ace of ignominious failure. Just five days after the race began, he was standing by a roadside in the depths of Normandy, holding a broken bike and asking plaintively if he could go home. It was the greatest crisis of his career, with his vulnerable side brutally exposed.

Coppi had begun his Tour with a tour of his own, a trip around the sights of Paris on his bike. By stage five, which ran over 293 kilometres from Rouen to St Malo in blazing heat, the Italians were not showing well; both Coppi and Bartali were eighteen minutes behind the race leader, the Frenchman Jacques Marinelli. But on that day, Binda ordered his Italians to go on the attack, and Coppi worked his way into what looked like the stage-winning escape. Best of all, he left Bartali well behind him, in a tactical fix: the older man could not set up a chase, because he could not ride against his own team mate.

As the race passed through the village of Mouen, with 160 kilometres remaining to the finish and the lead over the peloton already ten minutes, disaster struck. Marinelli reached for a bottle that was being held out to him by a spectator, wobbled and fell, taking Coppi with him and entangling their bikes. The Italian's machine was a broken wreck: forks twisted, tyre forced off the back wheel, front wheel broken, the chain in the spokes. That should have mattered little: showing considerable foresight, Binda had asked the Tour organisers to allow him a second team car to provide service in the event of his riders having mechanical problems, on the grounds that he had two leaders, who might be in different places on the road.

So there was a car behind Coppi, and in it was his Bianchi *directeur sportif*, Tragella, who was on the Tour as Binda's assistant. But Binda's foresight counted for nothing: the only spare bike Tragella had was too small. Coppi's spare was with Binda, who had stopped at the feeding zone in order to ensure Bartali got his lunch. No less than seven minutes had passed by the time Binda caught up, to find Coppi and Tragella standing by the roadside, looking, as he put it, 'like two dogs that have been beaten with sticks'. Coppi was certain that his race was over.

It was down to Binda and the other Italians to keep Coppi going. But merely getting him started again required Binda to use all his persuasive powers. Initially he tried compulsion, warning Coppi that if he stopped without permission, he would be fined. That failed and the manager resorted to white lies, telling Coppi that he himself had retired from races in this kind of situation, and had always regretted it. This was fantasy, but the situation was desperate: Coppi would not respond. Eventually, like a parent negotiating with a toddler, Binda told him that if he rode as far as the finish, he could go home the following morning, if he still wanted to.

Binda's next step was to make Bartali wait; he knew that Coppi would be stimulated by the idea that Bartali might win if he went home. Initially Bartali pedalled alongside, 'alternating persuasion and insults', he recalled. 'It was like talking to a wall. Then I got angry. "I'm going home", Fausto said. And I replied, "My fine boy, how are you going to look to your fans? You're giving up. Goodbye glory, goodbye cash, no one will take you seriously any more. You wanted me to stay at home for this Tour and what do you do, you give up on the fifth stage?"'

There were a total of eighteen Italians in the race, split into two teams: the national team itself (who wore jerseys in the red, green and white of Italy rather than the sky blue of today) and the *cadetti*, a team of younger riders. One of the latter, Alfredo Martini, remembers the afternoon well. He told me that once Coppi was with the bunch again, he told the Italians not to bother chasing the leaders, although they tried several times. The race, Coppi said, was over as far as he was concerned. 'He said' – and Martini suddenly lapses into the throaty Ligurian patois, half French, half Italian – 'I might as well be at home under an umbrella with a cold beer.'

Coppi was not even willing to stick with the peloton, and when he drifted off the back Binda asked another Italian, Mario Ricci, to wait and escort him to the finish. There was more psychology here. Ricci was an old friend of Coppi's from his Legnano days and was also the best-placed Italian overall. Asking him to give up his own chances was a way of making Coppi aware that his status in the team was not being challenged. But even as he rode, Coppi continued to repeat that the Tour was a madhouse, and he was going home. At the finish on the St Malo outdoor cycling track, he had the body language of a man defeated: drooping shoulders, ponderous footsteps. He was almost nineteen minutes behind the stage winner, Ferdi Kübler, and a massive thirty-seven behind Marinelli, and the Italian team's next job was to persuade him to stay in the race overnight.

It took a concerted effort, led by Binda. The manager's memoirs, *La Testa e I Garun*, include a photograph from that evening: Binda is standing next to Coppi's bed, in his white cap with an Italian tricolour on the side, goggles around his neck (the team cars are open-top jeeps, the roads are very dusty), his arms spread out in a gesture of supplication. Coppi lies on the bed with his arms spread like a wounded bird, his mind clearly elsewhere. Fiorenzo Magni was among those who did not believe Coppi now stood a chance. It was, says Ettore Milano, a chaotic evening in the team hotel just outside St Malo: some of the team in tears, pleas and curses flying through the air.

Milano told me: 'We said to him, "Look, mate, we are at war here, we will go on to the end. We don't want to be disrespectful, [pulling out] is not just like being cheated on by your wife, it's like having your balls cut off." What could we do but joke? We all made him go on. We got round him and made him continue in the race.' Milano also pointed out to Coppi that he was marrying shortly – Cavanna's daughter – and needed money. If Coppi went home, he would have no wedding. Binda again played his man well, persuading Coppi to postpone his departure for a few days: he knew that the next day's stage was relatively easy, the day after that was a rest day, and that in turn was followed by a time trial which 'he, the king of racing against the watch, was capable of winning on one leg'. It was a familiar picture: Coppi needing to be influenced by stronger minds at a turning point.

With hindsight, the *campionissimo* acknowledged that his behaviour was not rational. To his critics, he said, 'You try, just once, sitting on the roadside with an unusable bike, with the impression of being terribly alone, and with the knowledge that your rivals are all against you.' There was, inevitably, intense speculation over the reasons for his crisis of confidence. Partly, it was put down to the rivalry with Bartali. Coppi told team-mates that in his view Binda and Bartali were in league and the reason his bike was not on the van was because Binda wanted Bartali to win. Binda, ironically, said later that Bartali never forgave him for persuading Coppi to remain in the race, because it deprived him of a second Tour win.

There was another explanation: Coppi had trouble adapting to the Tour. This was not the schematised, controlled racing of Italy, where the *gregari* looked after things until the *campioni* took over. 'Coppi's morale fell to bits because he realised that the Tour wasn't like the Giro,' says Raphael Geminiani, a friend and rival, and later a team-mate. 'In the Giro there was a kind of arrangement between the riders that you wouldn't really race until the feeding station, whereas in France we would attack as soon as the start flag was dropped. Controlling the race was much harder, because everyone went from the gun, everyone was a danger, breaks could get a huge amount of time; it was more chaotic.'

For foreigners like the Italian team in France, there was also massive uncertainty involved in racing away from home terrain. The route would be unknown territory, as maps were in short supply and the break in racing because of the war meant that the riders had little experience to draw on. Given the importance of gearing for climbs, pacing yourself and knowing where the roads were bad, this was a serious handicap to riders from abroad. There was also Coppi's innate need for reassurance, the background of potential double-dealing involving Bartali, and the sudden transition from dominance – ten minutes ahead of the great rival on the road, a massive statement being made – to complete powerlessness.

The crisis en route to St Malo looks bizarre on the face of it, but it is actually understandable given the circumstances and Coppi's character. Indeed, it could be argued that it marked a turning point. Beforehand, Coppi had finished first in only one major road race outside Italy, the previous year's Het Volk Classic, where the judges disqualified him for being given a wheel by a fellow competitor – another example of the difficulty of racing abroad. The dominant victories that followed, in the next couple of weeks and the next five years, suggested that getting back into the 1949 Tour in fact made him a more formidable competitor.

*   *   *

What came after St Malo was stage racing at its finest: a dramatic comeback as Coppi ate into that thirty-seven-minute deficit, against a background of constant intrigue, gossip and speculation about double-dealing. As Binda expected, Coppi won the time trial, down France's west coast from Les Sables d'Olonne to La Rochelle. He regained eight minutes, inspiring the Tour de France organiser, Jacques Goddet, to write a eulogy in *L'Equipe* in which he compared the purity of Coppi's pedalling style to the lucidity of Dante's Italian in *The Divine Comedy*. The sniping with Bartali remained constant, however. After the stage to San Sebastian, Coppi accused the older man of a treacherous attempt to get away from the field, and Binda had to intervene. In the Pyrenees it was Bartali who claimed he had been betrayed when Coppi attacked after he crashed on the climb of the Col de l'Aubisque. That one was defused when Coppi explained that he had not been aware that Bartali had a problem. Neither trusted the other; both were waiting to find out just who was the best.

With the Pyrenees behind him, Coppi had reduced the deficit on Marinelli to just over thirteen minutes. The two days' racing through the Alps were to decide the winner. The epic stage from Cannes to Briançon, over the snowy Col d'Izoard, began with a 4 a.m. start, before which Bartali went to Mass, and closed with *il pio* in the yellow jersey. Along the way, the stage saw a major imbroglio when Tragella was not in evidence at a feed station when he was supposed to be giving Bartali his bag of rations. According to most accounts, Tragella simply hid, because he could not bear to help Bartali; ironically, it was his protégé Coppi who realised this was un-acceptable behaviour and gave his rival his bag.

On the Izoard, according to Binda's version of events, the two men staged a near repeat of the Valkenburg farce. They were both clearly stronger than the rest of the field on the climb, escaped together and gained a big lead, but then slowed to tourist pace, each apparently afraid that the other would benefit. Again, it fell to Binda to resolve matters, not a rapid process. The manager began by reminding them of their deal, then pointed out their responsibility to the national colours. Finally he warned that as repeat offenders they would face heavy fines if they disobeyed him and disgraced themselves. He talked of the shame they would feel in front of their families, wives, children. Gradually, they speeded up, and remained in front of the field. On the climb, Coppi slid in the mud and fell into the ditch; Bartali waited. On the descent, it was Bartali who punctured and Coppi who waited, enabling his rival to win the stage and pull on the yellow jersey at Briançon, on his thirty-fifth birthday.

Again the image of unity is undermined by the partisans: Cavanna said later that Coppi heard Binda telling Bartali that evening, 'No one will take the jersey from you now.' If that is the case, Binda was either wildly inaccurate in his reading of the race or he was trying to reassure Coppi's great rival; the younger man was only one minute and twenty-two seconds behind, with a time trial stage still to come, and he had looked the stronger as they climbed the Izoard. The following day, en route to the Italian town of Aosta, Coppi was again the strongest, forcing a selection in the field on the Col d'Iseran, the highest point in the Tour at 2,800 metres, then leading Bartali away on the Grand St Bernard. The pair began the descent together, but Bartali punctured, then, having changed the tyre, he crashed, leaving Coppi with a dilemma: should he wait? Initially, he slowed down, in the hope that Bartali would catch up, but eventually Binda told him to go on. The Italian manager had to tell him twice, first sending a motorcyclist with a message, then driving up to him. The outcome was inevitable: at the finish Coppi had almost five minutes' lead, and the yellow jersey.

To this day, *Bartaliani* insist that Binda told their man he had not given Coppi the order to leave his team-mate, the race leader. The Dutch writer Benjo Maso speculated that Bartali knew he had lost, and was lucky to puncture because he was able to portray himself as an unfortunate loser. Certainly, Bartali milked the situation afterwards, saying: 'When my tyre went flat my first thought was: Italy! The most important thing was that an Italian should win in Italy. So I told Fausto to go on as fast as he could.' Later, however, he accused the Italian cycling federation of working for a Coppi win, under pressure from the powerful Bianchi bicycle company.

As it turned out, Coppi's physical superiority was clear from the results of the two time trial stages: in the second, from Colmar to Nancy, over 137 kilometres, Bartali was over seven minutes slower. This was, probably, the moment when the rivalry ceased to matter in sporting terms: there was no question that Coppi was the stronger. His overall victory left no room for doubt: Bartali was ten minutes and fifty-two seconds behind him, while Marinelli, in third place, was twenty-five minutes and thirteen seconds back, having lost over an hour since St Malo.

There was, however, far more to Coppi's victory: no cyclist had ever managed the double of wins in the Giro d'Italia and the Tour de France in the same year, and only six others were to match the feat in the next sixty years. They are numbered among the very greatest road racers in the history of the sport: Jacques Anquetil, Eddy Merckx, Bernard Hinault, Miguel Indurain, Stephen Roche, Marco Pantani. Coppi, Anquetil, Merckx, Hinault and Indurain are at the top of cycling's tree because all managed it twice in their careers; Merckx, the greatest of them all, did it three times. Lance Armstrong, so dominant in the Tour in the early twenty-first century, never attempted it even in his heyday.

Coppi's friend Raphael Geminiani cannot think of any sporting achievement to compare with winning the two great stage races. 'There is no parallel. The Giro is more than twenty days' racing, the Tour another twenty or twenty-two. So there are over forty days of competition when you are obliged to perform at the highest level if you want to win both. If you have an off-day you may lose everything. The double requires strength of character, an ability to perform on the key days. Only the greats of cycling have it in them.'

From a twenty-first-century perspective, this first double remains a colossal achievement, because the demands the sport made on the athlete at the end of the 1940s were far greater than today, and there were many more things that could go wrong in a three-week race, as Coppi had found out when he hit the deck at Mouen on stage five of the Tour. Races were run on roads that in places were hardly surfaced, on bikes which were unreliable, with team back-up that was primitive. To overcome these obstacles took vast strength of character, for Alfredo Binda and the whole of the Italian team as well as for Coppi.

Coppi was already a huge star in France, and the Tour win made 'Fosto', as they called him, almost as popular there as he was at home. Jean Bobet tells the tale of a track meeting at Rennes in the early 1950s, pitting him and his brother, the future Tour winner Louison, against the Coppi brothers. They drew a record 9,061 entries, with more than 2,000 turned away. At Paris's Vél d'Hiv the fans would start queuing in the morning to get tickets for evening meetings with Coppi. As the Tour de France's official historian, Jacques Augendre, says, 'Our country quickly fell under his spell. It's no exaggeration to say that he contributed to the reconciliation between France and Italy after the war.' (The *Bartaliani*, naturally, would point to their man's win in the Tour in 1948, and his reception by the French president Vincent Auriol.)

Those international triumphs helped Italy itself regain its pride after the years of defeat and exclusion. Uniquely among Italian national teams, the Tour de France squads of those years were *tricolori* not *azzurri*, wearing the national colours of green, red and white rather than the usual light blue. This merely added to the sense that Italy's cyclists were flying the flag. There was no denying the symbolism of Italians crossing the Alps in those colours to the applause of French crowds, and 'conquering' France just eight years after Mussolini's disastrous invasion attempt.

Coppi and Bartali were reconciled as well: not long after the race, the pair visited the Ursus tyre company, a sponsor of Coppi's, where the Tour winner received a bonus of 500,000 lire which he shared with his great rival. A week later, they went together to the cyclists' chapel on the Madonna del Ghisallo, on a high hill overlooking Lake Como north of Milan, and presented the parish priest with a yellow jersey. Coppi donated a bike; Bartali's was, apparently, lost in Portugal.

*   *   *

Among the fans who now flocked to watch Coppi wherever he went in Italy were the doctor from Varese and his dark-haired, striking, strong-minded wife. In her attitude to cycling, Giulia Locatelli bore no resemblance to the woman who, a year earlier, had been indifferent to her husband's passion. Her obsession had outstripped that of Dr Locatelli. She was now the one who went out to get the newspapers, which she would scan for mentions of Coppi. Giulia's passion raised eyebrows in the little village near Varese. She was pursued in the street by children shouting *Viva Bartali*.

At races, she showed the same urge to get close to the champion which had marked their first meeting. She would demand more of him than the average fan, grabbing his hand when they met. She would lie outrageously to gain access to areas restricted to the cyclists and their entourages. 'I was the fan of the house, a maniac, more obsessed than my husband. From then on, our Sundays were filled with cycling, races, cyclists, Coppi above all. We would go together, or I would go with friends, to anywhere where there was a race, a track meeting, an award ceremony. It didn't matter what as long as there was a chance of meeting Coppi.'

CHAPTER 9

EXTINCTION OF THE WORTHY BRUTE

To help me find Sandrino Carrea's house, his wife Anna sello-taped a copy of *La Gazzetta dello Sport* to their gate, which opens onto the main road that runs through the valley below Castellania. The pink paper flapped on the ironwork, which was big, wide and attractive for a relatively small house. Its size is down to Coppi. At the time Carrea was building the house, he and his team leader often passed the site as they trained. 'You should make that wider,' recommended the Bianchi leader. Carrea was hardly going to ignore him: as one of the *campionissimo's* best domestiques, he had spent his working life obeying the great man's orders, so he duly enlarged the entrance.

After all, both the gate and the house had come to him thanks to his master. Carrea still has the item that was, in effect, the down payment on his home. It is kept in a clear plastic bag, and he takes it out to show me. It's made of coarsely woven wool, dyed yellow, and has the initials HD in stylised lettering on one breast. It's a yellow jersey from the 1952 Tour de France and it was Carrea's for a single day. He pulled it on in Lausanne, having infiltrated a lucky break with Coppi's wholehearted approval. Even so, he feared that Coppi might feel he had delusions of grandeur and send him home. 'That would have ruined me.'

It was hot that night in Lausanne. Alfredo Martini left the window of his hotel room open and he overheard Coppi saying to Carrea, 'Don't get to like that jersey too much, Sandrino, it will be mine tomorrow.' Carrea duly relinquished the *maillot jaune* to his leader the next day, but even so he became, briefly, a celebrity. He earned a dozen track-racing contracts and a trip to Algeria to race with Raphael Geminiani. His share of the prize money from Coppi's win in the 1952 Tour was two million lire. He doubled it by riding appearance races, criss-crossing Europe, sleeping with his bag of contract cash under his pillow, and he built the house when he came back.

Carrea is now in his eighties, but still going strong. He calls the dog to order, and potters out into the garden to pull vegetables for dinner. That evening everything on the table, it seems, is Sandrino's own produce: wine from the grapes that grow up the hill, sausage from the pigs, his own apples and chicken, rocket salad. He still loves to go hunting in his patch of ground up the hillside behind the house. Anna wishes he would slow down, but Carrea will not stop.

It is not in his make-up, any more than he ever dreamt of shirking when he worked for Coppi. By then Carrea had survived a spell in Buchenwald and two death marches; in 1945 he was working as a mason when he was brought into cycling by Coppi's brother Serse, who introduced him to Cavanna. The sage felt his neck and hands; the callouses convinced him that Carrea had potential and he was sent on a training ride with Coppi and his team-mates. Later, with Ettore Milano and Serse, Carrea was one of a three-man elite within the elite that was the Bianchi team.

While Serse and Milano were Fausto's confidants off the bike, Carrea came into his own on the road: he was the strong man who would wind up the pace to stretch Coppi's rivals before the leader put in the killer attack. '*Vai piano, Andreino,*' Coppi would yell as Carrea strung the field out. 'If you don't slow down, you're going home this evening.' Carrea would drive even harder; the warning was their coded signal to him to increase the tempo. Carrea was the epitome of the team worker who denies himself all glory to serve his leader. He later received the 'golden water bottle' after being voted 'domestique of the century'.

*   *   *

The relationship between domestique/*gregario* and team leader has no parallel in any other sport. It calls for such self-denial on the part of the team worker that it is clear why Carrea's lucky break appealed so much to the public. I ask Carrea why he did not want to win races for himself in spite of his obvious physical ability – he barely understands the question. The reasoning was fair enough in a time of poverty: it was better to have assured earnings by serving another than take the risk of riding for yourself. This was after all a time when merely having a bike was a step up socially, and a *gregario* could earn four times the wage of a manual worker.

Being a *gregario* gave a cyclist the chance to travel, often with expenses paid – the *campione* would pick up the tab for training camps, for example – as well as a certain status. Milano and Carrea were not just *gregari*, but Coppi's *gregari*. Once Coppi had attained legendary status, by the early 1950s, the prospect of merely being in the same team as Coppi was 'like touching the sky'. Alongside a star such as Coppi a cyclist could double his money; when that kind of reward was available, why take the risk of leadership?

The duties performed by the worker bees were many and various. The most important was filling and fetching water bottles.* In those days, feeding from team cars was not permitted, so the job involved stopping now and again by the road at public fountains and bars and having to regain the pack

---

* Hence the French nickname *porteurs d'eau* – water carriers.

each time. 'We knew every water fountain in Italy,' says Milano. Raiding bars and shops for drinks was common: the *gregari* would nonchalantly tell the counter staff *'paga la Gazzetta'* – the Giro sponsor *Gazzetta dello Sport* would pay. Domestiques would race laden with food: *panini* with raw steak or ham, jam sandwiches, oranges, bananas, three or four bottles. They would help Coppi regain the bunch if he punctured, although *gregari* recall that at times Coppi was physically so superior that he would lead the chase with a string of them clinging on for grim death. There were other 'domestic' duties: a *gregario* would be sent out in the evening to buy expensive cologne for Coppi's massage. On occasion, a *gregario* would be sent to search Bartali's room to see if there were any syringes to be found.

The one thing that mattered was conserving the strength of the *campione*. That started with room allocation: *gregari* would take the top floor rooms if the hotel had no lift. Pushing the leader early in a race was routine stuff. Jean Bobet recalls being taken to the back of the bunch by Hugo Koblet in the Giro di Lombardia: Koblet wanted to show him something. 'Fausto was freewheeling, with Milano on his left, Carrea on his right, pushing him.' Sometimes the *gregari* would organise themselves on a climb – one every ten metres, like a human chain – to push the leader from one to the next. It was against the rules, but they made sure the *commissaires* (race referees) couldn't see. They would push him if he was ill during a stage, or if he needed the toilet, because if he pulled off into the hedge his rivals might attack. Four *gregari* might have to help when the *campione* answered nature's call: two to push, one to find newspaper, a fourth to collect water for washing if necessary.

Under Coppi, the relationship between *gregario* and *campione* developed to its most sophisticated form. One team rider had to be present in every escape to give the squad control of the race. 'Coppi started from the principle that having riders behind is useless so he needed riders in front,'

says Fiorenzo Magni. 'That way, when he attacked, he had
support ahead of him; one or two riders who could pull a bit,
help for fifty kilometres perhaps, then he would leave them.'
They would also give moral support or offer up a wheel if he
punctured or had mechanical trouble. These are the fundamental tenets of cycle racing as a team. Others had raced
this way but Coppi adopted the idea more wholeheartedly
and systematically than had been the case in the past.

Each worker had his allotted job: Michele Gismondi had
to stay in the front until midday, chasing down targeted
riders – men who were known to attack in the first half of a
race – then simply get to the finish as best he could. Luigi
Casola was the 'banker', who would do the rounds in the
bunch at the start of the event and buy off other riders to
race against Bartali. Milano was delegated to assist Coppi on
the flat, along with Serse; Carrea would make the tempo in
the hills. Their job was simple: to soften up the opposition
physically and mentally before Coppi attacked. The theory,
Milano told me, was that Coppi was better suited to racing
in the highest mountains, over 2,000 metres, than his opponents,
even Bartali, and he could simply ride away. 'The opposition
would be half dead already and he could go away so power-
fully. It was down to him to decide when, but it was not a
matter of deciding, he could feel the moment.'

Reading Marco Pastonesi's *Gli Angeli di Coppi*, an anthology
of tales from his *gregari*, it is not so much the many tales of
self-sacrifice that hit home as the degree of deference among
the domestiques. Many of the men Pastonesi interviewed seem
extraordinarily anxious about whether or not they are meant
to use the formal or the informal 'you' when talking to Coppi.
They seem overwhelmed when they are permitted to use *tu*.

However unassuming Coppi might seem when off his bike,
whatever crises of confidence he might have when on it, there
could be no stepping out of line: the *campione* could make

or break a team-mate. Hence Carrea's distress at winning the yellow jersey. Coppi – like the other *campioni* – had the connections to pull strings to get a masseur off his military service, or to prevent a rider who had made him look foolish from getting track racing contracts. More obviously, the income of the *gregari* was linked directly to the winnings of the *campione*: Coppi had his own retainer from Bianchi, but his winnings and the team's start money were shared communally between the squad, including the back-up staff.

As a 'head' of the peloton, with friends and influence throughout the sport, Coppi's power extended beyond his own team: if a *gregario* in another squad was asked to close a gap, for example, he usually did it. If lesser men wanted to escape or go for an intermediate prize, they would ask permission and explain to Coppi, Bartali and the other 'heads' what they were up to. Sometimes, the *campione* might feel like doling out a favour and his *gregari* would work on another's behalf. Ubaldo Pugnaloni recalled that one occasion, in the 1949 Giro, when he was riding for another team, he asked Coppi for permission to go for a sprint in his home town of Ancona. He was astonished to see the entire Bianchi squad leading him out.

The hierarchy of *gregari* and *campioni* was rigidly structured, which meant that Bianchi was no place for a rider of ambition. Pugnaloni recalls losing a Giro dell'Emilia because the team car was following Coppi and he could not receive assistance at a key moment. On another occasion, he was racing in Milan–San Remo and Coppi stopped because he had conjunctivitis and the mud thrown up from the road was inflaming his eyes. The entire Bianchi team were told to stop as well, including Pugnaloni, who was in contention for a place in the first half-dozen. 'I want to go on', he said. 'You can go to San Remo', he was told, 'but your suitcase will be in Milan'. The van carrying the luggage was turning around as well. He is damning: 'more than a *gregario*, you were a lackey'.

Coppi's rigid grip on Bianchi, his insecurity, his superstition, gave rise to the notion that champions are set apart, that they should be spoiled, their every whim indulged. This would have suited those who managed the great man: while Tragella needed his team to have a rigid structure with devoted *gregari*, Biagio Cavanna knew the value of mystique, apartness. That was the way the *soigneurs* worked. The impression had to be given that the *campione* and his intimates were out of the ordinary. Raphael Geminiani is explicit: 'When Coppi arrived at the hotel it was as if an alarm had sounded: he had to have his room ready, there had to be silence, all the curtains had to be drawn because he believed he recovered better in the dark. We had to whisper, not talk, which was also for Cavanna because he could feel the muscles better if there was no noise to distract him. Coppi would come to the dinner table for twenty minutes' (here Gem' makes noises, *toc, toc, toc*, to simulate rapid, mechanical eating) 'then up and off to his room to lie down'.

Sometimes the demands went beyond professionalism, beyond control freakery, into the realms of pure caprice. After stage finishes in the Giro and Tour, Ettore Milano recalls a 'crazy' search for white wine vinegar, because Coppi did not want red wine vinegar in the salt, vinegar and water mix used to massage him. On hot days, Coppi might ask for a bottle of cold water, but it had to be in a thermos wrapped in cotton tied with a ribbon to keep the hot air out, and flavoured with mint cordial.

Coppi created an impression on others as well as his *gregari*. Jacques Goddet felt that he was the man who transformed cycling champions from peasants into men of the world. For Goddet, the cosmopolitan, multilingual Coppi – 'fluent in French, working on his English' – was a pioneer, who 'created the prototype of a champion who was a gentleman and a businessman. He was capable of showing up at an embassy or a salon, and was at his ease on a stage or in front of the terrible inquisition of the press machine. He was capable as well of talking through a contract and throwing himself into businesses that were very different from his experience on the road.' By the end of his career, Coppi was negotiating his sponsorship deals and building his own bikes. The peasant boy who had walked in order to save half a lira on his bus fare went a long way in the space of fifteen years.

*   *   *

Coppi hit his sporting peak between the end of 1948 and spring 1950, a period in which he was rarely beaten in any major race. The double of Giro and Tour was the highlight, but there were also two crushing Classic wins outside Italy in the spring of 1950 – the Flèche Wallonne and Paris–Roubaix – a brace of wins in the Giro di Lombardia, a Milan–San Remo, and back-to-back victories in the world track pursuit title. Physically, Coppi was the strongest in the world, as his performance in defeat at the 1949 world road race championship in Copenhagen showed. There were no hills where he could escape alone, as was his habit. So he simply rode as fast as he could, for as long as he could. By the finish only two men were able to hold his wheel, one of whom, the one-day specialist Rik Van Steenbergen, won the sprint.

The result was a bronze medal, but there was consolation in taking the pursuit title on the Ordrupp velodrome, and there were other victories, such as a seventy-five-mile lone escape to win the Giro del Veneto, a result which clinched the Italian road race championship (awarded over a series of races during the season). The year ended with a fourth win in the Giro di Lombardia, at record speed after a lone escape from the Madonna del Ghisallo; the season had included fourteen major wins. Coppi's status as the dominant force in world cycling was confirmed when he received the Challenge Desgrange-Colombo, the newly introduced year-long award which rewarded the most consistent competitor in major international races. The trophy had been in the bag by the end of July.

Coppi's dominance over this eighteen-month period did not happen by chance. He himself was relatively modest when he listed what it took to win. 'It looks simple, and it is. There is nothing mysterious about living a healthy life, training methodically, watching your health and having a masseur available who knows well what to do and who can make all the fatigue disappear after every training session.' What is striking, however, is the approach Coppi took in achieving all of this.

'Coppi invented cycling,' Raphael Geminiani told me. 'The war caused cycling to revert to a primitive state: the roads were bad, the bikes were heavy, equipment was poor and not properly maintained, back-up was lousy, nutrition old-fashioned. Coppi was the first to modernise cycling, with the help of the Italian manufacturers: Bianchi bikes were beautiful, marvellous things, but there were also the jerseys, socks, gloves, sunglasses.' 'For a rather haphazard and very rough and ready form of cycling, Coppi substituted in fifteen years another sport conceived on an industrial scale,' wrote Pierre Chany.

Since the war, Coppi and the Bianchi team had perfected the way a squad raced, with the help of the selfless *gregari* and the bike company's financial power. This was to be a blueprint for future greats. The Bianchi way was emulated by Louison Bobet and Jacques Anquetil – winners of eight Tours between them between 1953 and 1964 – and also by the Red Guard of Rik Van Looy, who dominated one-day racing in the late 1950s and 1960s. The same team principles were applied by Eddy Merckx, Bernard Hinault, Miguel Indurain and Lance Armstrong, to name but the best. This was, however, just one area in which Coppi was laying down the foundations on which professional cyclists and their teams would build an entire sport.

This was a period when cyclists had to evolve their own ways of doing things. 'You had to work things out, listen, to compensate for the fact that no one told you anything,' says Martini, tapping his head. Coppi was a rapid learner, a man who left absolutely nothing to chance. He explored any area which might lead to any improvement, always looking to broaden his experience, with a desire to know things 'fino in fondo' (Martini) – from beginning to end – and an unwillingness to accept received ideas. His approach went far beyond merely riding his bike.

Other cyclists – the Pelissier brothers, Alfredo Binda, Antonin Magne, Georges Speicher – had investigated diet, but Coppi was the first to apply himself rigidly to diet as a way of improving his performance. Contemporary descriptions of what he ate would not look unfamiliar to any top athlete today, including yoghurt, grilled meat, fresh fruit, salad in abundance, herbal teas, soups. He experimented with the vegetarian diets of the American Gayelord Hauser, Greta Garbo's lover, the idol of American bodybuilders in the 1930s and 1940s, and author of the 1936 bestseller Eat and Grow Beautiful. The notion of an Italian peasant's son, whose education ended early, looking to Hollywood for inspiration truly reflects an open mind, a desire to try anything.

He cut down on meat, and experimented with molasses, yeast, honey and wheatgerm, alongside detoxing – one of Hauser's diets was a seven-day detox using vegetable soup. This was a complete contrast to the methods that had gone before, such as the 'Binda zabaione' – twenty egg yolks shaken in a bottle. Such experimentation would have been radical in normal times, but this was the late 1940s, when Italy was still experiencing post-war food shortages and wheatgerm was not the easiest item to buy at the local grocer's.

With its emphasis on lightly cooked food and more raw vegetables than in the past, the Coppi diet became influential outside Italy. For example, it features in a British cycling training book of the 1950s, *Scientific Training for Cycling*, by Dr C. R. Woodard. Coppi also changed the way cyclists ate during a race. 'Before, everyone said that the more a rider ate, the better he would go,' Raphael Geminiani told me. The conventional wisdom was that riders should take the start with a large rare steak in their stomachs, begin eating 100 kilometres into a race, and then eat heavily. Instead, Coppi began using carbohydrate. 'Coppi demonstrated that with a light stomach at the start you would go better. He would eat little and often – a bit of rice cake, some brioche and jam.' Thus, Coppi might sometimes start a race having had only a cup of tea and two bits of toast for breakfast, and would begin eating fifty kilometres from the start. Cycling was not entirely receptive to these new ways. Carrea once tried a mouthful of the mix of fruit pulp, grains and orange juice in his master's bottle: he spat it out because he felt it was *'una schifezza'* – filthy muck. Cavanna felt threatened, naturally, and his immediate reaction to his protégé's interest in Hauser and his methods was that Coppi should give it all up and eat only pure, genuine fillet of veal.

While they might not always have agreed over diet, Cavanna and Coppi brought radical ideas to training. When Coppi was out on the road with the little group of the blind *soigneur's* protégés, they never stopped. Two at a time they would go to a roadside fountain for water while the others would accelerate to make it difficult for them to catch up. In the final hours, they would simulate racing. When Coppi wanted a workout, they would be made to set a blistering pace up a particular hill. Geminiani underlines: 'Before Coppi, the belief was you trained for 150 kilometres at 24 kilometres per hour and it would do you good. Coppi followed the example of athletics and brought in interval training: 130 kilometres at a high pace, or 130 kilometres in the morning, 100 kilometres in the evening, flat out. That gave him the top-end speed in a race, which was enough for him to leave the others behind. He didn't get that from training at 25kph.' Coppi was also an early adherent of motor-paced training and would time himself up particular climbs to check his form.

He was one of the first *campioni* to take a strategic overview of a three-week stage race rather than taking things as they came. He would plan to *'fare il vuoto'* – open a huge gap – on two or three major stages, and then control the remaining stages. For a one-day event, he was prepared to inspect the final kilometres up to twenty times over.

Similarly, Coppi left nothing to chance in his choice of back-up staff. When he moved from Legnano to Bianchi, part of the deal was that he took with him the mechanic Pinella di Grande. With his Brylcreemed hair, big-pocketed overalls and checked shirt, the mechanic was legendarily laid back, a vital asset at a time when many more wheel changes had to be made in races than is the case today. Coppi said of the mechanic that he was so unflappable that he wondered whether he actually understood how important a given situation was. Di Grande was a perfectionist himself, who would yell at the domestiques if they punctured their expensive tyres. One of his tricks was to get a piece of specially shaped hardwood such as oak and hammer it up the steering column so that if, as sometimes happened, the steel fractured due to the pounding on the poor roads of the time, the wood would hold the bike together.

Bianchi's team managers, Zambrini and Tragella, were adept at the deals which greased the wheels of competition. When foreign *campioni*, such as Louison Bobet, came to race in Italy, they were permitted to ride for Italian teams. Bianchi snapped up the best as useful allies for Coppi. They would use Bianchi's economic muscle on Coppi's behalf more directly as well. For example, Vito Ortelli, probably the best Italian cyclist of the post-war years after Bartali, Coppi and Magni, was offered 100,000 lire to work for Coppi in the 1947 Giro. Ortelli was also paid 20,000 lire to give Coppi an easy ride through to the final of the Italian pursuit championship in 1946. Unfortunately, Ortelli's team didn't bother telling him about the deal.

And, of course, Cavanna was still a ubiquitous presence, still massaging Coppi, still haranguing him and the whole team over every subject under the sun. He had a massive influence on Bianchi's recruitment through his amateur squad, which ended up acting as a feeder club for Coppi's Bianchi. Sponsored by SIOF, a local chemical company, they used second-hand tubular tyres and hand-me-down bikes from the Bianchi mechanics. The result of this production line that took local riders from this corner of Piedmont and turned them into domestiques to serve the great man was a close-knit unit. The fact that they were largely Ligurians like Coppi, mainly from the Novi/Alessandria area, was an important factor at a time when people had dialect as a first language, Italian as their second. Simply being able to communicate on more than a basic level would do wonders for team spirit, while if they talked *dialetto* in a race, the opposition might not understand what they were saying.

Raphael Geminiani, a relative latecomer to Bianchi, believed that Cavanna played a vital wider role at the team, sitting at the dinner table, listening to the riders talk and assessing their state of mind and their needs. More than the introverted Coppi, he was the man who worked on the team's morale, encouraged them each day. But there was inevitably a conflict with the team manager, Tragella, who could not stand having Cavanna in the team car shouting at Coppi and made the blind masseur stay in the hotel instead.

Details were important at Bianchi, and that didn't apply

only to their leader, who lost his confidence if he felt he had lost control of things. Coppi was a stickler for punctuality, and insisted on clean handlebar tape for every stage of a major race – an old morale-boosting trick. At Bianchi, much was made of personal presentation. The *gregari* would be sent back to their rooms to shave if they came down in the mornings with stubbly chins, and if they didn't have clean socks and jerseys they would be made to change them. A team manager would go and check their rooms when they left the hotel: if they were not in good order, they would be made to go upstairs and tidy them.

Equipment mattered, too. It was a vital imponderable at a time of bad roads and slow wheel changes and variable quality control. If Coppi considered that his tyre sponsor was not providing what he wanted, he would obtain special tyres and persuade contacts to smuggle them to the team – though sometimes the sponsors would get wise and change them all back again. He experimented with shortened frames, giving a more dynamic ride. The Castelli clothing company made him special warm winter jerseys. He rode higher gears than the *gregari*, who cursed if they were given a 'Coppi wheel' when they punctured. His position on the bike changed enough after the war to imply that he had sought to become as aerodynamic as possible: his back becomes stretched out on the bike parallel to the ground, where before it is rounded. His bars are wider, so his arms are more comfortably extended, without the elbows flapping.

His drive for perfection was mirrored by that of the Italian cycle industry: in the Coppi years the Italians made multi-speed gears and the double chainring ubiquitous. Italy was where the best tubular tyres were produced by companies such as Vittoria, Pirelli and D'Alessandro. The Columbus tubing company produced lighter steel tubes. It was an era when followers of the sport were continually seduced by the technological advances coming out of Italy – 'Each year saw a new marvel, be it a kind of tyre or a Campagnolo derailleur, the kind of thing we could only dream of in France,' recalls Jean Bobet. Half a century on, northern Italy is still the hub of the world cycle industry. It would be an exaggeration to claim that Coppi alone drove this growth, but the process was partly inspired by the presence of a dominant figure, driven by a need for technical perfection.

There were other things Coppi was unwilling to leave to chance. He worked out, together with Cavanna, that he should avoid crowded places such as dance halls and theatres where there was a greater chance that he might pick up infections. He had to stay in the open air. Hence his love of hunting, although long sessions were needed on stationary rollers to get his legs used to cycling again after hours wandering with his gun and his dogs.

In those days before doping was prohibited, drugs of any kind were worth investigating. Coppi was overt about his use of stimulants, which were not banned until five years after his death. His comment to the radio reporter Mario Ferretti that he only used drugs 'when necessary' is now widely quoted, with the caveat that it was 'almost always' necessary. It is a philosophy, understandable back then, unforgivable now, which conditioned the way most professional cyclists saw the issue for the next half-century. He explained to Rino Negri: 'I'm a professional. If I could discover a medicine which didn't damage my heart and nervous system I wouldn't hesitate to use it to win, and often. I'd be crazy with joy if I was the chemist who found it.'

For his hour record he took five tablets of simpamine, a mild form of amphetamine which Cavanna utilised to give his protégés a boost while they were out training before the war; Coppi was adamant, however, that he would have gone far faster if he had used one of the stronger forms of amphetamine which had become available after the war. Cavanna spoke with professional pride about his ability to make *intrugli*, ('brews') – mixes of caffeine, alcohol and amphetamine, to be taken at an appropriate moment in a race. Then there was *la bomba*, a bottle containing seven or eight espresso coffees, sugar, peptocola and two or three mild amphetamine pills.

There are plenty of instances of doping involving Coppi, enough to underline that amphetamines of various kinds were ubiquitous at the time. He gave two white pills (to be taken with food just before the finish) to another cyclist, Gianni Malabrocca, to help him win a stage in the Giro in 1946. In Marco Pastonesi's *Coppi ma Serse*, fellow professional Renzo Zanazzi tells of entering a hotel room to see Serse and Fausto on their single beds with a tray of pills on the cupboard between them. 'We are working out what colours we are going to take tomorrow.'

Raphael Geminiani emphasises: 'There is someone avant-garde in every field, and Coppi was the avant-garde of cycling. First he got to know himself, how far he could go physically, then everything else followed that. Every cyclist since has been inspired by him. Nothing fundamental has been invented since Coppi.' The Tour organiser Jacques Goddet wrote after Coppi's death that 'the worthy brute who merely pedals is an extinct species. Cycling has become a sport of intelligence, care and technical expertise. Thanks to Coppi.' Louison Bobet, the first man to win the Tour de France three times, felt his way of working had been transformed after riding the 1948 Giro with Coppi. He said: 'Now I know how to do my profession.'

*   *   *

The 1950 Paris–Roubaix and Flèche Wallonne saw Coppi at his finest. The two Classics had completely different charac-teristics: Roubaix a long, flat slog with lengthy sections of cobbled roads; Flèche a shorter but tougher slog over the Ardennes hills. Of the two, Coppi's victory in Paris–Roubaix came to be seen as a turning point, a demonstration of the way he had transformed cycling since the war.

He had been outwitted – to his intense annoyance – by Gino Bartali in Milan–San Remo in mid-March, but conversely a few weeks later Roubaix went entirely to plan in spite of foul weather, wind and rain. Early on, he was sheltered from the wind by Carrea, Oreste Conte and Fiorenzo Crippa, and Carrea and Serse pushed him time after time, unseen by the race referees, who were keeping dry in their cars. When a crash happened, it was Ettore Milano who led Coppi from the back of the peloton to the front to keep out of trouble. Meanwhile, Conte was seen to have his pockets full of race food: tarts, rice cakes, honey sandwiches – 'enough to withstand a siege', Pierre Chany noted.

The food was passed to Coppi just before the feeding station in Arras. Here, as the peloton collected food bags from support staff, most of the riders had to slow down. Coppi did not have to pick up a bag and attacked in pursuit of an earlier escape. There was chaos as the other favourites tried to launch a chase. Within a few kilometres, Coppi was in the lead, with only the Frenchman Maurice Diot, one of the earlier break-aways, for company. They shared the pacemaking, until Diot refused to collaborate, on the grounds that his team-mate Van Steenbergen (he of the previous year's world championship) was leading the chase behind.

Chany takes up the story: 'Fausto moved instantly right up to the edge of the pavement and left Diot with no shelter. He accelerated once to get the measure of Diot, a second acceleration shook the robust Maurice, a third attack stunned him. Coppi's race was over and the demonstration began.' In the final forty-five kilometres, 'on roads that were barely fit to ride on', Coppi opened a three-minute gap on the

Frenchman and nine minutes on Van Steenbergen. Whatever Diot achieved on his bike is now forgotten, apart from the words he said on finishing that race. 'I've won!' 'What about Coppi?' 'Coppi is in a different race. I feel I have won.'

Coppi's win in Flèche Wallonne was even more crushing: at roughly half-distance, he repeated the attack at the feed station that had worked so well en route to Roubaix and again raced alone until he caught up with an early escape on one of the climbs. He then took out his water bottle, drank a little, sprayed the back of his neck, took out an orange and ate it, while two of the earlier escapees tried desperately to hold his pace. Having cooled down and had a bite to eat, he turned to the other two and suggested that they should begin riding harder, as the peloton might catch up. Their reaction was to stop and get off their bikes in disgust. Coppi simply rode alone to the finish in Charleroi; the next man was five minutes behind.

On his day Coppi was completely unstoppable. Alfredo Martini explained to me: 'Staying on his wheel seemed an easy thing at the beginning, you would feel good. But then, every kilometre that you did was like someone putting a brick on your back, one at a time, inexorably. Until ten bricks, you could take it, but with the eleventh . . . you collapsed and off he went.' Other cyclists described how on a mountain climb he would change up his gears as the climb progressed, continually increasing his speed to a point where the opposition had no answer.

Fiorenzo Magni, the 'third man' of Italian cycling at the time, says that Coppi was uncatchable: 'I remember one race, he was flat out, I was flat out a few yards behind him, I just couldn't get to him. And when he went away, say on the Ghisallo to win the Giro di Lombardia, he would open a three-minute gap over the best guys, who would be chasing: Bartali, me, Kübler, Louison Bobet. He was a locomotive.' In a Giro del Veneto not long after the war, Coppi broke away early on; Magni led the chase, enlisting the rest of the field to help, yelling at them and forcing the pace. The gap increased, and when it got to five minutes in spite of his best efforts, Magni stopped, got off his bike, picked it up and threw it in the ditch.

Coppi's run of form and luck was not destined to last, and on 2 June 1950 it came to an abrupt end as the Giro d'Italia tackled its first mountain stage in the Dolomites. The crash stemmed from a mere trifle. As the field tackled a small climb near the town of Primolano, Coppi moved past a rider named Armando Peverelli, who a year earlier had crashed into a rockface during the Tour de France, losing the sight in his left eye. Coppi came past on Peverelli's blind side; unseeing, the other man moved, catching Coppi's front wheel, and he fell. The first to get to him was the Giro director, Giuseppe Ambrosini, who tried to lift him back onto his bike. There was no sign of any bleeding, although the right side of his shorts was torn, but putting any weight on his right leg, or simply moving it, left Coppi in unbearable pain.

Coppi was taken to the Santa Chiara hospital in Trento, where he received flowers that afternoon from the winner of that Giro stage, none other than Gino Bartali. He had broken his pelvis in three places – which makes those attempts to get him back in the saddle seem all the more ludicrous – and would not race again until September. That very same evening, he was visited in room 20 by Dr Enrico Locatelli and his wife Giulia, who had come from their home in Varese to watch the stage. The news of Coppi's crash was broadcast to the crowds at the roadside by the race announcer's car; immediately, Giulia decided to visit her idol in his hospital bed, in spite of her husband's remonstrations that only the family would be allowed into the room.

At the hospital door she showed the same determination

that had taken her into riders' quarters at races across northern Italy. The duty doctor insisted that she could not enter. She made him call Coppi and tell him Dr Locatelli and his wife were there. By now, clearly, Coppi knew who they were, as they were duly summoned upstairs. Coppi, Giulia recalled, was pale, sweaty, unable to smile because of the pain. He tried to sit up as they entered, but fell back at once. Few words were exchanged. Coppi showed Dr Locatelli the plaster cast and the location of the fractures; the doctor reassured their hero that he would be well looked after.

It was almost two years since Fausto and Giulia had first set eyes on each other, and it would be several more before their relationship went further. There are accounts of a correspondence after Coppi was transferred to Roncegno, a village outside Trento, to convalesce in the cooler air of the mountains. Her letters would arrive at his hotel, the Hôtel des Thermes, where he was staying with his wife Bruna and their daughter, Marina; his were sent to a *poste restante* address in Varese. This side of the friendship was something that should be kept from her husband. However, none of these letters have been published, and in 1979 Giulia produced what she stated was the first letter Coppi ever sent her – dated September 1953. Giulia herself gave diverging accounts of what happened next, but one thing is certain: she fell pregnant later in 1950, and gave birth to a son, Maurizio, to follow her daughter Lolli. This, plus an attack of typhoid fever – probably in the summer of 1950 – would explain why she and Coppi did not have another significant meeting until 1952.

CHAPTER 10

LOSS OF THE LUCKY CHARM

'The man drags constant worry in his wake and it is his most cruel adversary' – Jacques Goddet, after Coppi's 1949 Tour win

The crash near the Turin velodrome on 29 June 1951 seemed relatively minor. According to one eyewitness, a local amateur named Nino Defilippis, a few of the cyclists in the Giro di Piemonte one-day race misjudged a bend, one of them put his front wheel down a tramline, and down they went. Serse Coppi was among the fallers; he skidded across the road and banged his head on the pavement. 'We picked him up,' Defilippis told me. 'He said he was fine, so we rode into the finish with him. He signed the finish sheet and then we showed him the way to his hotel, because we were local and knew the roads. We said goodbye. Not long afterwards he died.'

Serse Coppi went to his hotel room and washed, taking the rare step of using the vinegar bath that had been prepared for his elder brother, because he did not feel well. When Fausto arrived with another *gregario*, Giovannino Chiesa, Serse complained of a headache. 'The pain was on the left side of his head, so we lifted his hair and had a look,' said Chiesa. 'There was no blood. There was a small mark, like the scratch a child might make on its mother's face.'

Serse's decline was shockingly rapid, the attempts to save his life increasingly desperate. The riders called for an ice pack; by the time it had arrived he was asleep, but, according to Chiesa's account, he was not sleeping properly. The riders grew afraid. A doctor was called. As he lay there, Serse was rolling his eyes, extending his toes as if he had cramp, tensing his body. His face had darkened. They called an ambulance; as he was taken to hospital, Coppi and Chiesa moved his head to stop his tongue dropping down his throat. He had stopped breathing. An operation for cerebral haemorrhage was delayed because there was no blood or plasma in the hospital and it was a Sunday. He died before he reached the operating table.

He was buried quickly: Fausto had to start the Tour de France in four days' time. The impact was terrible. The *mamma* of the Coppi family, Angiolina, never fully recovered. It was the same for Fausto. He had persuaded Serse to race so that they could be together as they had been in the village. He had got Serse a place at Bianchi so he could have him at his side. Serse had been riding the race to prepare to support him in the Tour. Now he had just watched him die, suddenly and horribly after a desperate battle to save his life. The guilt must have been immense. Like his war service, this was something Fausto never discussed.

There is a consensus among those who knew Fausto that the death of his brother was a turning point in his life. Milano, Carrea, Piero Coppi, Martini and Pugnaloni are unanimous: after this, nothing was quite the same. To his contemporaries, the disintegration of Fausto's marriage, his disastrous divorce, his long, painful decline, even his premature death, all seemed to stem from this initially banal crash on a tramline in Turin.

*　　*　　*

When Sandrino Carrea talks about Serse, he doesn't use words to begin with. He throws his arms wide and makes a noise somewhere between a pack of hounds scenting blood and a steam engine's safety valve under high pressure. The sound is obscure but the meaning is clear: Serse was a character, a big character. The scene with Carrea is repeated, in various ways, whenever one of the Coppi brothers' associates discusses Coppi junior.

Ironically, in view of Serse's relative lack of talent as a cyclist, his personality made far more impression on those around him than that of his brother. Fausto's contemporaries tend to remember him in general terms: 'a gentleman', 'a wonderful person'. Asked to pin down precisely why Fausto was so nice, they um and ah. Detailed anecdotes are hard to find. Serse, on the other hand, was the sort of larger-than-life figure who leaves many crystal-clear memories behind him, partly because he was not obscured by the aura that envelops his god-like elder brother.

There is no reverence when Serse is discussed, but there is plenty of laughter. It was Serse who took the lead when the village boys' games took them into forbidden territory: an orchard to steal apples, football in a hayfield. Later, when they went shooting together, the obsessive Fausto would go for partridge; Serse would shoot towards the road to scare the passers-by and laugh fit to burst. That summed up the relationship: Fausto wanted Serse at his side; Serse simply wanted to play.

They were divided during the war when – and here memories become dim, leaving a sense of something hidden – Serse chose to fight for the fascist rump, the Repubblica di Salò. Post-war the younger brother emerged to persuade Fausto that he should continue racing, living with him for a few months in Rome as the Germans were driven northwards and the professional cyclists began competing amidst the rubble. He did so wearing Fausto's pink jersey from the 1940 Giro, a little ragged and very baggy by now, and he was not above pretending to be his brother. Immediately after the war

Serse won a major race, Milan–Varzi, ahead of his older brother, and thus earned his place in the Bianchi team alongside Fausto in 1946.

In his cousin Piero Coppi's view, Serse had some of the qualities needed by a *campione* – the charisma, the personality, powerful legs – but he didn't have the necessary application. Like his elder brother, Serse went to visit Biagio Cavanna and was told of the conditions that he imposed on his pupils: in bed at ten o'clock, up at six in the morning, taking turns to collect the freshly drawn milk, plus the training. He didn't come back. His only major win came in Paris–Roubaix in 1949 – a victory shared with France's André Mahé, who was leading but was sent off course at the finish. Mahé pointed out that Fausto gave Serse a hand-sling as he bridged to the break and then instructed his brother to protest when the judges initially awarded the Frenchman first place.

Serse was 'an uglier, smilier version of Fausto', according to Orio Vergani. He was nicknamed *'oreggiat''*, because of his sticking-out ears, but there was enough of a resemblance for autograph hunters such as Giulia Locatelli to confuse them. Serse had a rounder face, more marked with laughter lines, and a pointy chin. Dino Buzzati wrote, somewhat unfairly, that he was 'an ironic imitation' of his brother: the same features, but a tenth of the talent and the style of 'a duck, a giraffe, an accordion'. A photo of the two of them on their bikes in the Giro in 1951 illustrates the contrast perfectly. Fausto looks utterly relaxed and at one with his machine, head perfectly poised, arms slightly bent. Under his crinkly grin, Serse's chin is lower than his shoulders – slightly broader than his brother's – while he has magnificent leg muscles but the uncomfortable look of a man to whom cycling does not come naturally. He leaned to the right as he rode his bike. 'An ugly little guy, *un po' gobbo*' – a bit of a hunchback – 'with no neck and his head sunk between his shoulders,' says an ex-pro of the time.

Four years younger than the *campionissimo*, Serse became one of Fausto's *gregari*, and, as a popular personality, would do the rounds in the bunch when a threatening breakaway developed, persuading the other teams to join Bianchi in pursuit. Any help he gave on the road was, however, merely the visible element of a far deeper relationship of co-dependence. He described himself as Fausto's '*gregario* of the mind': it was his presence that mattered. He shared his brother's hotel room and rode 'in the shadow of Fausto's shadow' (Mario Ferretti). As Buzzati put it: 'Fausto cannot do without Serse and feels lost if he doesn't know that behind him, in the group of backmarkers, Serse is slogging faithfully away . . .' And, indeed, before taking flight on a mountain, his elder brother would say kindly, 'We'll wait at the [stage] finish.' 'We would say goodbye and off [the back of the bunch] Serse would go,' recalls Carrea.

The relationship was complicated: Fausto was his brother's boss, but Serse knew he had the psychological whiphand; his elder sibling needed him. Perhaps the monastic Fausto lived vicariously through Serse, who did the frivolous things he did not permit himself to do. So it was that the elder brother would give detailed instructions for their next day's training, but Serse would go out dancing. While Fausto went to bed early and avoided crowded places, Serse smoked, played boule, hung out in bars, chased women, played practical jokes and loved to party. He would go out dancing and 'come home with the morning papers', as Carrea put it. He had a simple and apparently effi-cacious policy with the opposite sex; an ugly woman was '*meno sfruttata*', underutilised. 'He was not overgifted for cycling, but for love, yes,' recalls another contemporary who had showered with him: '[he had] equipment that made you envious.' His conquests were rumoured to include celebrated actresses. Together with Bianchi's other playboy, Luigi Casola, he would disappear in search of adventure on the rest days of the Giro.

Serse's nocturnal lifestyle meant he had trouble keeping up with Fausto when they trained, which was daily, in theory at least. After his marriage to Bruna, Fausto was living in Sestri Ponente, while Serse remained with their mother in Castellania. They would ride in opposite directions down the same road to meet for training in the mornings; Fausto would know by where they met just what time Serse had got to bed the previous evening. Serse would ask the other *gregari* to phone up Fausto and provide his alibis. Milano recalls covering for him: '*Dov'è quello là?*' he shouts, mimicking Fausto's Piemontese accent, then he tells how he would spin some tale to satisfy their leader. But there was, says Carrea, no jealousy, no arguments.

Serse was not the first or the last brother to make a living in cycling on the back of his elder sibling. In the 1990s, Stephen Roche and Laurence Roche formed a brief double act, while the five-times Tour winner Miguel Indurain took his younger brother Prudencio with him to the Tour; as Serse did for Fausto, Prudencio signed autographs on Miguel's behalf. The German Jan Ullrich employed his brother Stefan as a mechanic. Other cycling champions have had their joker figures, as important for boosting morale as for their cycling skills, for example Sean Kelly and an obscure Belgian called Ronan 'Ronnie' Onghena. It was Serse, along with Casola, who kept morale high at Bianchi: they threw him in the sea on a rest day in one Giro.

Out training before one race, Alfredo Martini was struck by the way they would complete each other's sentences. Fausto was reliant on Serse for psychological support in his lowest moments. The light-hearted Serse acted as a buffer against his inner doubts: it was Serse who kept Fausto racing as the war ended, who made Fausto continue in the 1947 Giro after he, Serse, had gone home due to a crash. 'A father figure' was Orio Vergani's view of the younger brother, while Buzzati described Serse as 'Fausto's lucky charm, his guardian spirit, a sort of living talisman – a little like the magic lamp without which Aladdin would have remained forever a beggar. It is Serse who really wins because without him Fausto would have fallen apart a hundred times. Neither is capable of living without the other.'

*   *   *

As in the face of other crises, such as the death of his father, Fausto's immediate reaction was that he wanted to quit cycling. There was, however, no time to reflect. The previous year had been disastrous by his standards thanks to his broken pelvis. The vast plaster enveloping his left leg and most of his upper body while the broken bones mended had been removed after forty days; he had convalesced for two months, then begun racing again that September, with no time to gain any meaningful results. The Giro di Lombardia was as close as he got; he was not strong enough to escape on his own, yet made it into the race-winning escape, only to lose any chance in the finish sprint when he and the other leaders caught a slower group as they lapped the Vigorelli.

The start of 1951 had been wrecked by another crash, when his front tyre slipped as he sprinted on the soaking wet velodrome where Milan–Turin finished. A broken collarbone meant a further month without racing and no time to prepare properly for the Giro d'Italia. There, with Fiorenzo Magni rampant, he still managed to win a time trial and a major mountain stage and finish fourth overall.

As they had during the 1949 crisis at St Malo, Coppi's confidants rallied round to persuade him to stay in cycling and to start the Tour. Bartali was one of the main influences, with particular power because he had been in precisely the same situation fifteen years earlier. He too had wanted to quit cycling, to join the clergy, after his brother Giulio had hit a car as he descended a mountain in an amateur race. Although, like Serse, Giulio Bartali had died as a result of a medical error, both deaths typified the dangers cyclists ran in those days due to poor tyres, abysmal road surfaces and a lack of head protection. Such deaths were by no means uncommon.

Not surprisingly, Cavanna was persuasive as well, rationalising the situation thus: 'It is a disaster but it could have happened to anyone and it could have happened in another way.' Another team-mate, Luigi Casola, told Coppi he would go to the Tour in Serse's place – although he actually went in his car, as he was not selected. In the end it came down to hard cash: as Carrea puts it, they were paid to go – 500,000 francs – so they went. 'If we hadn't earned it, someone else would have.' The lengthy spells Coppi had missed through injury in the previous eighteen months meant that it was in everyone's economic interests that he rode the Tour.

Physically, in theory, Coppi was capable of riding the Tour and doing well. He had, after all, just ridden himself into good enough form to win that mountain stage in the Giro. But when he arrived at the Tour, he had not slept for three nights. One eyewitness said he had the look of an automaton. Not surprisingly, he eventually cracked, in dire heat on the relatively flat stage from Carcassonne to Montpellier. Coppi had raced well enough through the Pyrenees to be lying fourth overall behind the eventual winner, Hugo Koblet. He was well placed until the final 100 kilometres of the stage, but he began vomiting and found himself completely devoid of strength. He rapidly lost sixteen minutes on the leaders, notably Koblet and a bevy of French riders led by Raphael Geminiani. Half a dozen of the Italian *gregari* rallied by Carrea, Martini, Milano and Luciano Pezzi did their best to help him limit his losses, but to no avail. Pezzi, who died in 1998, gave his version of the battle to Jean-Paul Ollivier twenty years earlier:

'He was leaning over his bars with an indefinable grimace on his face. His empty eyes were fixed on the road. He was trans-fixed, as if he had been stunned. He couldn't speak, couldn't answer our questions. There was no reaction.' Coppi only came to life when Pezzi grabbed a bottle of wine from a spectator and poured it over his head.

It was a classic cycling calvary: the champion suffering in agony, zigzagging along the road, surrounded by his loyal servants. Ironically, given his earlier wish to quit the sport, Coppi would not contemplate getting off his bike. The battle for survival depended on whether they could get him to the finish within the day's time limit, calculated as a percentage of the winner's time. The normal margin was 10 per cent, but Coppi stood no chance of finishing in time. However, an obscure rule stated that if more than a tenth of the field were outside the 10 per cent limit, it could be extended to 15 or 20 per cent. It was Pezzi who worked out that if the group containing Coppi finished together, they would all be safe. But one Spanish cyclist, who did not understand the rule, kept trying to leave them behind, hoping to regain some time and finish within the 10 per cent limit. The *gregari* had to grab his saddle and slow him down each time he sped ahead, to ensure the group kept to the right number.

Coppi remained in the race, although there is some debate as to whether the organisers would have wanted him to go home even if he had been outside the 15 per cent time limit. As Carrea says: 'There were newspaper sales of 300,000 a day [in France] at stake; without Coppi there was no interest in Italy. It was in their interests that Coppi should be there.' It was a battle against the odds that strengthened his hold on the hearts of the French and Italian public, although the race referees were implacable. They fined three of his domestiques, Pezzi, Milano and Biagoni, 200 francs each for pushing their captain, while Coppi was fined a total of 600 francs for three offences: allowing himself to be pushed by each of the trio on various occasions.

The illness was probably caused by the cumulative effect of the strain of the three weeks since Serse's death; it was only temporary and Coppi recovered rapidly, scoring a familiar lone victory in the Alpine stage to Briançon and riding well enough to finish tenth overall behind Koblet. The Italians went home with 800,000 lire between them. Honour, and their bank balances, had been saved. However, the rest of Coppi's season was blank, apart from a win in the Grand Prix of Lugano time trial and the usual string of 'victories' in exhibition events across France and Italy. The world championship was a target, particularly as it was held that year on Italian soil, at Varese. But he did not even make it to the start due to a bout of illness.

There was speculation in the Italian press that the illness was an excuse as he had realised that he would not have the strength to beat Koblet, but Coppi was adamant this was not the case: 'I would have been very stupid not to have seized the chance of competing in a world championship on a course which suited me, in front of my fans, at a time when the fatigue of the Tour was only a memory.' Whatever the debates, to salvage his season there remained only the Giro di Lombardia, which he had won four times in the past five years. Try as he might, he could not shake off a small select group including Bartali, Magni and Bobet, and in the final sprint on the Vigorelli velodrome it was the Frenchman who triumphed, a bitter end to a bitter season.

*   *   *

Coppi's closest associates, such as Sandrino Carrea and Ettore Milano, still have not come to terms with Serse's death, more than fifty years on. For Milano, the tragedy still has a dream-like unreality about it, with the twist that in his view Serse predicted his own end, on the way to the race. Milano recalls that he and Livio drove with Serse to the race start, and as they arrived at the railway bridge in the nearby town of Alessandria, Serse said, 'I'm not going home again.' He had bought a new suit, and he apparently said, 'Put these clothes on me when I'm dead.' These were throwaway statements: Serse was going to stay with a semi-steady girlfriend in Turin, so of course he wasn't coming back. His crack about the clothes was typically flippant. They only took on any meaning after the event.

Fausto himself also felt that Serse had had a presentiment of his death. He had, he said, listened all the night before the race to a dog barking, 'as if it wanted to bring me bad luck'. His mother said that after packing his suitcase Serse had been unwilling to leave the family home. She had, of course, warned him to take care, but that was because he was as lunatic a driver as any professional cyclist. For Sandrino Carrea, the death points to what he sees as a curse on the entire family, 'exterminated by misfortune' from the father downwards.

More important and more clear-cut, however, was the effect on Coppi's relationship with his wife, Bruna. In that sense the death was definitely a curse. To start with, Coppi changed, becoming even more pensive and withdrawn. It was, says Piero Coppi, as if 'something inside him had died'. 'He never laughed after Serse's death,' Carrea told me. 'Before, Serse would play the fool for him. After Serse's death we all felt it was in our interests to stick close to him, look after him, make him smile.'

Ettore Milano was specially assigned to look after Coppi, and that was not without its strains: Alfredo Martini asserts that Milano's devotion became 'almost pathological', beyond the call of duty. He worried more about his master's health than his own. 'Between them relations were so close that I believe without Milano at the races Fausto felt disorientated,' says Martini. 'Coppi confided everything in him.' It was Milano who took over Serse's role as room-mate, not with total success at first. 'I shared with him after Serse died, he didn't like to sleep alone. The first time I did, I got to the room, put on a poker face and went straight to sleep. He said *porca miseria*, you've come here to keep me company and you've just nodded straight off.' It was also noticed that Coppi became more nervous. After a nasty accident to a fellow cyclist in the Giro, one eyewitness recalls him announcing that he was giving up cycling.

Bruna Coppi became ever more convinced that her husband should stop racing, because the dangers were too great. Raphael Geminiani was explicit: '[Bruna] didn't like cycling. She made Fausto put on a crash hat, obliged him to wear elbow pads. Everyone said to him, "Come on, stop this nonsense."' Magni concurs: 'She said the things a mother would say.' And Coppi's mother said the same as his wife: Angiolina Coppi had been scared about Fausto racing from the very start, and his father had had to persuade her to let him compete. Now she felt that losing one son prematurely was enough, and, like Bruna, she pleaded with Fausto to give up competing. It is said that as she stood in front of Serse's body she yelled 'Give me that bike and I will break it with my own two hands.'

In one sense, Bruna's fears were understandable. During their marriage, Coppi had had only two serious crashes, and they had come in the last two years, together with Serse's tragic death. Later, Coppi acquired the reputation of being a particularly accident-prone cyclist, and this is certainly true of the latter part of his career. Including the broken pelvis in 1950, Coppi had six major crashes in ten seasons. The 1950 and 1951 accidents deprived him of vital racing – without them, could he, perhaps, have won the Tour three times, or even four? Biagio Cavanna, for one, felt that Coppi was not particularly unlucky. As the *soigneur* saw it, he had no more crashes than the average cyclist, but took more harm when he fell heavily because he had less muscle to cushion the bones.

Such rationalisations would have meant little to Bruna, a woman who never had a particular taste for the limelight and found Coppi's celebrity hard to cope with. Was there a subtext when Coppi – or rather his ghostwriter – wrote in his 1950 autobiography *Le Drame de Ma Vie* that 'the important thing is to find a wife who understands the life a cyclist is forced to live'? His was, unfortunately, not a life that was easy to empathise with; being a professional cyclist's wife has never been straightforward. To this day, cyclists' marriages seem to break down at an alarming rate, but maintaining a marriage must have been particularly hard half a century and more ago. Marina recalls that she and Bruna experienced Coppi's victories, defeats and crashes only through the radio, in the same way as the rest of the Italian population. There were occasional phone calls as well, such as the one during the 1949 Tour de France when she told her father, 'Keep the pink jersey, Daddy'. 'She hasn't quite got the hang of her colours yet,' smiled her father as he told the tale.

The long trips to get to races meant, for example, that a four-week Tour could turn into a six-week trip, at a time when communications were rudimentary. Adriana Bartali remembers going to the cinema to see how her husband was getting on in his races, working out his health by looking at his picture in the newspapers, and having to book telephone calls for eight o'clock. Coppi rarely spared himself: in the winter of 1949, for example, he undertook a marathon trip together with Serse, racing in Tunisia, then driving across North Africa to race in Casablanca, Tangiers and Algeciras before crossing back to Spain and driving most of the way to Paris. It was hardly necessary, but the money was there to be earned.

Moreover, Coppi's life bore no relation to that of a shop-keeper's daughter in provincial Italy. The transition from poverty-stricken prisoner of war to cycling star had happened virtually overnight. How on earth could Bruna have understood all that her husband was experiencing, and how could she have imagined the addictive qualities of the glamour, the adrenaline and the acclaim? She was not a woman who enjoyed the public gaze.

However, the notion that Bruna did not attend bike races is a myth: one of the most touching images of her and her husband is from the 1946 Giro d'Italia, where they are looking into one another's eyes, behind a bike. There is another picture of her kissing Fausto after the 1946 Giro di Lombardia. The affection looks deep and mutual. Exceptionally, Bruna was permitted to visit the Tour de France in both 1949 and 1951 – in the latter year on compassionate grounds. She was also at the 1952 Giro and Tour. When she did attend races, however, she made a point of remaining in the background. She would not sit among the guests of honour. Instead, she sat on the steps, to remain unseen. 'There were places but I never took them. I stayed on the steps so that any expressions I had of worry in a crash or joy in a victory could not be noticed.'

She travelled to criteriums and track races with Coppi, Fiorenzo Magni and his wife, and Magni recalls one revealing episode in Paris. 'The wives went shopping. Bruna kept saying, "How beautiful this blouse is, how lovely this cardigan is" and my wife said, "Why don't you buy them?" Bruna said, "No, think how much work it took to pay for them. I mustn't spend the money."' She was, says Magni, 'too Genovese' – in Italy the Genovese are thought unwilling to spend money – 'but it was not tightfistedness, rather a modest mindset. That's the heart of the problem. Bruna stayed the same, and he changed. He learned about the world, he travelled, she wanted to remain a housewife, go to the hairdresser's once a fortnight not once a week, have one set of best clothes not two. That [mindset] is not something you change, that's for life.'

As Italy's biggest sports star, her husband was no longer only hers. No matter how much affection he bore her, or how much he loved little Marina, his life was dictated by other things. Biagio Cavanna had a simple take on the marriage: Fausto was Bruna's husband when he was at home, but belonged to the people of Italy, to his sponsor, to his team-mates when he was away. Cavanna's son-in-law, Ettore Milano, felt the same way: 'Bruna didn't understand like the wives of Gino [Bartali] and [Fiorenzo] Magni understood,' he told me. 'When they were at home each was a husband, when they were away, no. Due to her ignorance of cycling, Bruna didn't figure that out, and that was her fault. You can't clip a man's wings.' Nino Defilippis, who came to know the couple as their marriage crumbled, has a more subtle view: Bruna married a man who turned into someone else: 'Bruna was a country miss,' he told me. 'When Coppi married her he wasn't the Coppi that he eventually became. His wife married Coppi the ordinary man not Coppi the *campione*. Coppi became Coppi, she remained the same and couldn't adapt.'

The marriage of a reticent, frequently absent husband and a shy woman made for a mutual lack of communication. The story is told of Coppi's visit to England in the early 1950s, when a microphone was thrust under his nose at a function and he was asked a question in English. He answered, in perfect English; he had learned the language in the prisoner-of-war camp. Bruna was incredulous, a little angry: her husband had never told her.

Moreover, Bruna did not get on with the strongest character involved with Coppi, Biagio Cavanna. The masseur felt she interfered too much in her husband's business. After Coppi's death, he recalled: 'You would hear her saying all the time, "Don't go here, don't do this, do that, I don't want this, this won't do." Coppi would listen, because that was his character, then he would do what he wanted.' According to Cavanna, the continual disagreements got to Coppi, particularly the public ones. 'I followed the evolution of Coppi's feelings for his wife day by day,' recalled Cavanna, 'and in the long term the character of the woman wore him out.' Ettore Milano concurs: 'Neither [Bruna nor Giulia] managed to fundamentally understand and respect Coppi as a man.'

As is customary in cycling, Coppi would reveal his thoughts to the masseur while he was having his legs done. Cavanna would then relay his sentiments to Bruna – no doubt merely increasing her stress and annoyance. 'I told her fifty times that she was wearing him out and she would lose him. It got to a point where he was keeping his family merely because they were there. When Giulia Occhini arrived on the horizon, Fausto Coppi's love for his wife was over. Coppi was neither awkward nor timid with women; they simply weren't a problem for him. He was a sentimental man who merely wanted to feel satisfied sentimentally. One woman was enough for him.'

It is unclear how Coppi's relationship with Giulia Locatelli developed in 1951 and 1952, but at some point she took the step of inviting him to the home she and her husband shared; he came several times, she recalled, because he had a relation doing military service at a nearby aerodrome and so had a ready excuse. Conveniently, he had now moved northwards over the Apennines from Sestri to the large, opulent villa in Novi Ligure which is now Marina's home. It was probably an hour closer to where Giulia lived, but that was coincidence. It was just down the hill from Castellania, Biagio Cavanna was on hand, and so too was Coppi's newly acquired hunting ground, an estate to the east of Novi, towards Asti, at the town of Incisa Scappaccino.

Once or twice, team-mates came with him to see Giulia. 'We became friends. Friends. I never thought I would fall in love with him. I am the child of a broken marriage and I wanted my children to grow up in an affectionate environment.' But Bruna never accompanied Coppi on these visits. It is unclear why Coppi let the friendship develop, but he was not a man to confront issues that involved offending those close to him, with whom he had emotional ties. Nino Defilippis says he was 'scared of making mistakes, *di fare brutta figura*, a countryman's character'. He was also a man with innate respect for women. He always addressed his mother in formal language, and Giulia Locatelli was struck by his good manners. Perhaps he simply floated along, vaguely attracted to one woman, profoundly attached to the other, because resolving the situation would have involved embarrassment.

There is a consensus among those who were close to Coppi that his relationship with Giulia Locatelli would not have happened if his brother had not died. Ettore Milano is explicit: 'Serse was more subtle, more awake, better at reading people, less worried about offending anyone – he would have advised Coppi. He would have told her where to go. But Fausto didn't have the strength of character, didn't have the authority. He wasn't capable of it.' This may be wishful thinking, linking the death of one much-loved brother with the catastrophic private life of the other, but it has the ring of truth about it: in the absence of his father, Coppi was dependent on Serse for honest advice. The more worldly younger brother might well have encouraged him to keep the affair secret to keep his family together, might have felt that Giulia Locatelli was a dangerous influence from the start. Knowing Serse, he would probably have slept with her while his elder brother was still plucking up the courage to say *buon giorno*.

A man alone: Coppi on the attack in the Alps en route to the second Tour and Giro double in 1952

Giulia Locatelli, on the right in the dark top, joins Coppi on the world championship podium in 1953

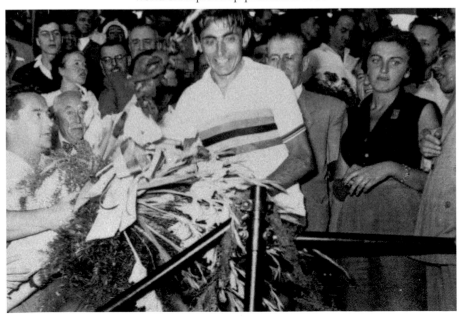

The wife and the mistress:
above: Coppi and Bruna
celebrate his victory in the
1946 Giro di Lombardia;
right: looking for the way
with Giulia Occhini

MARINA

IL NE LES A
JAMAIS
SÉPARÉS
DANS SON CŒUR

FAUSTINO

The children: Marina and Faustino as depicted in the pages of *Miroir-Sprint*

Close to the end of Coppi's career, the applause of the *tifosi* seems more respectful than passionate as the champion's powers fade away

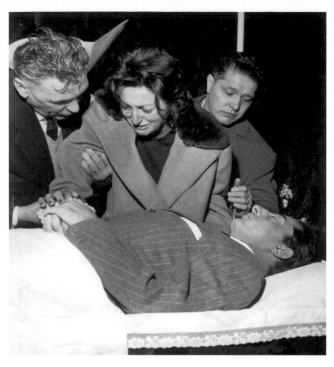

As the *campionissimo*'s body lies in state, Giulia Occhini has to be restrained by friends, *left*, while the fans, *below*, are stricken by grief

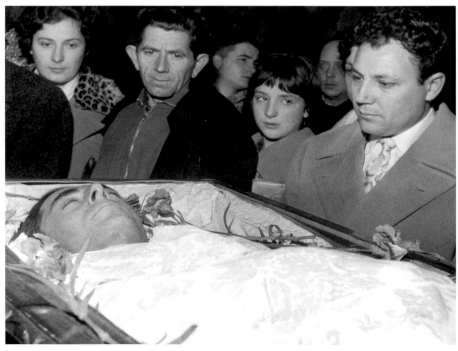

Coppi lives on in caricature, on idealised magazine covers, and in a display in the Bianchi bicycle factory that includes his world championship-winning bike

LA DOMENICA DEL CORRIERE

Supplemento settimanale illustrato del nuovo CORRIERE DELLA SERA - Abbonamenti : Italia, anno L.1400, sem. L. 750 - Estero, anno L. 2000, sem. L.1050

Anno 55 - N. 23   7 Giugno 1953   L. 30.

Il campionissimo sullo Stelvio. Lungo le rampe del famoso passo alpino Fausto Coppi sbaraglia tutti gli avversari e conquista la "maglia rosa", nel 36° Giro ciclistico d'Italia. (Disegno di Walter Molino)

The massive crowds outside the cemetery in Castellania as Coppi's coffin
is carried in by friends and fellow cyclists

CHAPTER 11

A MAN ALONE

'He is alone, alone on his bike. He is a man' – Curzio Malaparte, *Coppi e Bartali*

For most Italians of a certain age, it takes only three words to evoke Coppi's image and achievements. *Un uomo solo*. A man alone. The phrase was coined in 1949 by the radio journalist Mario Ferretti when Coppi staged his longest solo escape to crush the Giro d'Italia field on the Cuneo to Pinerolo leg. '*Un uomo solo è al comando, la sua maglia è biancoceleste, il suo nome è Fausto Coppi.*' One man alone is in the lead, his jersey is white and light blue, his name is Fausto Coppi. He remains the greatest of cycling's escape artists. Rino Negri estimates that he raced 3,000 kilometres alone, to win only fifty-eight races. His philosophy was simple: 'Either I don't escape, or if I do, it is when I cannot be caught.' In a pamphlet comparing Italy's two great cycling champions, the writer Curzio Malaparte felt that Coppi's habit of winning on his own reflected the cyclist's belief in his own strength rather than in any divine power. 'He has no one in heaven to protect him. He only believes in the motor that has been given to him, his body.'

Coppi was often asked what was the 'ecstatic moment' in a race. He would always answer 'when you cross the line first'. Then he would reconsider; it was when he had weeded out all but the very strongest cyclists in the field, and realised that even these riders were weakening as he rode. In other words, the moment when his physical superiority became obvious and he could be certain that victory would not escape him.

Fiorenzo Magni believes Coppi's racing style was in part due to his turbulent marriage. He asked Coppi why he would escape so far from the finish, when he could achieve the same result by waiting until the last hill. '"I like riding alone", he told me. It was a taste, a matter of satisfaction.' Magni says: 'Coppi's massive efforts in a race were an indirect way of taking revenge. He was never happy at home and when he broke away he was throwing out the dynamite he had inside.' Coppi was certainly a man in search of solitude: he once told the Giro organiser Vincenzo Torriani that his dream was to buy a home in the highest block of flats in Milan and live by himself.

That reflects the popular notion of Coppi as a man alone in his racing and alone in his personal life after the death of Serse: increasingly estranged from his wife, unable to find complete happiness with his mistress and eventually betrayed – as he saw it – by a society that had bestowed on him the status of a national icon. It all fits the idea of this particular cyclist as a tragic hero, but the reality is more complex and uncertain.

*   *   *

For Coppi, 1951 was a poor year: for the first time since the war, he ended a season without a truly important victory in a one-day Classic or a major stage race. He was now thirty-two, and while his old rival Bartali was still racing, a new young generation of cyclists had emerged, led by the Swiss Hugo Koblet, the 'pédaleur de charme' who had so dominated the 1951 Tour, and the Frenchman Louison Bobet. The murmurs that perhaps the campionissimo's time was past were inevitable. The initial post-war euphoria had dissipated and there were other things on people's minds: the Cold War was beginning, the Soviets and Americans were experimenting with ever more powerful nuclear weapons, the McCarthy witch-hunts were underway, the first steps were being taken towards the creation of the European Union.

By the time the 1952 Giro d'Italia came around, it was more than two years since Coppi had won anything significant. The start of the season had been promising but no more than that. His young Bianchi team-mate Loretto Petrucci had won Milan–San Remo. In Paris–Roubaix he had clearly been the strongest rider in the field even though he had been beaten by Rik Van Steenbergen, a superior sprinter who knew that all he had to do was hang on until the finish. But Coppi had said the previous autumn that he had a plan: he would 'not put his neck out' between March and May, to save his strength for the double: Giro and Tour.

The *campionissimo*'s decision was vindicated on the fifth day of the Giro when he won the mountain time trial stage near Rome. With a field that could hardly have been stronger, including Koblet, the 1950 Tour winner Ferdi Kübler and the double Giro winner Fiorenzo Magni, not to mention Bartali, an early win was critical for his confidence. Better still, by the time the race entered the Dolomites he was in the pink jersey, thanks to a crash which had delayed the leader, Giancarlo Astrua. Best of all, he had a strong rider alongside him at Bianchi to share the pressure and worry the opposition. Coppi's team had hired the young Frenchman Raphael Geminiani, who was given an open brief: he was to attack on every climb, so that Coppi's rivals would waste their energy chasing him down.

The value of having Geminiani in the team became clear on the stage from Venice to Bolzano, over three major mountain passes. In a display of classic team tactics, the Frenchman was sent ahead of the field early on and his captain caught him up later in the stage, once he had got rid of the peloton. That meant Coppi had Geminiani's support until he felt he needed to deliver the *coup de grâce*. On the final climb, the

dirt-tracked Pordoi Pass, the Frenchman rode his heart out
for the first five kilometres; once he had cracked, Coppi took
off for the stage win, which gained him five minutes and won
him the Giro. On the final massive mountain stage at the
Swiss end of the Dolomites, over the Saint Bernard and
Simplon passes, there remained only the relatively minor
matter of ensuring that his young team-mate led over the
climbs, so that he could be paid for his earlier efforts with
victory in the King of the Mountains trophy. For Coppi, it
was not merely a matter of rewarding Geminiani, however:
it was a chance to deprive Bartali of a prize which might
distract attention from his own overall win.

The 1952 Tour was preceded by the same *polemica* and
diplomatic wrangling as the 1949 race. Coppi initially insisted
that Bartali should not ride – he said he would go on holiday
by the sea if Bartali were selected – even though *il vecchio*
had come fifth in the Giro. Forgetting their double act in
the Alps during his Tour win, Coppi complained that Bartali
had ridden a negative race in 1949 and 1951, waiting for
him to falter. What Coppi did not say, but probably thought,
was that Bartali had finished in eighth place in the 1951
Tour to Coppi's tenth and might thus have the right to say
he should be leader.

The Italian cycling federation president, Adriano Rodoni,
responded to the impasse by refusing to send an Italian team
to the Tour. It was a bluff, of course, calculated to make
Bartali and Coppi see sense. *La Gazzetta dello Sport*, no doubt
aware of the importance for its circulation of Coppi's presence in the Tour, organised a summit meeting at Recanati
with Coppi, Bartali, Magni, Binda and Rodoni. There Binda
forged an agreement to form what was one of the strongest
ever Italian teams in the Tour, led jointly by Coppi, Bartali
and Magni, with the pick of their domestiques. According to
Rino Negri, the paper itself paid the riders to race the Tour

that year. It was money well spent: when Coppi and Bartali were performing, circulation rose to between 700,000 and 800,000 copies.

The old rivalry with Bartali dominated the early part of the Tour, which started in Brittany and circumnavigated the country clockwise. Four days in, after the stage across northern France to Roubaix, Coppi was sitting at the dinner table when he said to Binda: 'When will he stop spying on me? When will I stop feeling his eyes stabbing me in the back?' He threw his fork into his plate of rice and stalked off. The rumour swiftly ran round the town that he had gone home – this was, after all, the time when the entire Tour caravan would fit in a single town. Nearby, a little group of journalists were having dinner; Coppi came into their restaurant, sat down and, over a large beer, explained his reasons for walking out: 'You know, when I feel Bartali in the bunch, looking at me, waiting for me to show a sign of weakness, it's true, I want to throw everything over and go back to my little house in Sestri. I've just had a bellyful of it.'

He did not go home, but it was an inauspicious start to one of the most dominant Tour wins in the race's 105-year history, one of those rare occasions when a great champion is in perfect form and potential key opponents – in this case Kübler, Koblet and Bobet – are missing. The day after his fit of temper, which happened to be the anniversary of Serse's death, Coppi made his first statement, attacking alone on the climb to the finish in the Belgian town of Namur. He finished second on the stage behind a rider who had escaped earlier on, but, most critically, was two minutes ahead of Bartali. 'That's good, there will be no controversy. *Il Fiorentino* [the Florentine] will have to help you now,' said Cavanna as he massaged him that evening. 'I don't want his help,' grumbled the *campionissimo*. 'Play the game,' advised Cavanna. 'If he helps you without thinking twice – and indeed especially if he does think twice – accept his help. Then he'll know you aren't worried, and that's all that matters.'

Early in the race, Coppi's team-mate Fiorenzo Magni and the Frenchman Nello Laurédi had swapped the yellow jersey between them; but it became clear that Coppi was head and shoulders above the rest seven days in, when he took a conclusive victory in the sixty-kilometre time trial from Metz to Nancy, in spite of a farcical incident when he punctured and the Italian team mechanic, Umberto Marnati, rushed from the team car with a back wheel, even though Coppi was waving his front wheel in the air. Not surprisingly, the Italy leader was beside himself. 'Get me a gun so I can shoot this useless idiot,' he shouted. But the race was in his pocket. By the end of the stage, Bartali was almost seven minutes behind, and none of the other possible winners was any closer.

With Magni and Bartali sworn to act in Coppi's interests, and limited opposition compared, for example, to that year's Giro, the Italian team was dominant. First Magni, then Sandrino Carrea, briefly pulled on the yellow jersey as 'caretakers'. Carrea's day of glory came in Lausanne just as the Tour entered the Alps. He had had so few expectations that he was back in his hotel by the time it was discovered that he had become race leader. The police had to be sent to fetch him. Coppi immediately relieved him of the yellow jersey on the climb to l'Alpe d'Huez. On this first ascent of what has become the Tour's most celebrated summit finish, only one rider could hold him for a while: the Frenchman Jean Robic, winner of the 1947 Tour. With four miles left to the top of the Alpe, Coppi was 'inexorable and unequalled in his mechanical suppleness', wrote the Tour director, Jacques Goddet. He raised the pace once, then, without turning round, Coppi sensed the little Frenchman was at his limit and accelerated again, creating a definitive gap.

Later he said he knew Robic had gone; he could no longer

hear him breathing. Nowadays, on the Alpe, that would be unimaginable. Since the 1970s, this has become the Tour's most popular stage finish, with hundreds of thousands of fans of every nationality flocking to line the twenty-one hairpins three and four deep. It is also, now, a thrusting hub of the French ski industry, hundreds of chalets perched on a ridge high above the Romanche valley. Before 1952, summit finishes were a rarity in the Tour – the 1952 race introduced the idea with three stages ending on mountain tops – and the Alpe's hairpins had barely a fan on them, let alone the throngs of today, while the resort consisted of a single building. Coppi chose a room at the back of the one hotel, the Christina, to avoid the noise that he knew the *tifosi* would make outside as they celebrated.

With Carrea lying second and Magni third, the Italians had a stranglehold on the race. After a rest day at the Alpe, they returned briefly to home soil, to a second mountain-top stage finish, at the Sestriere ski resort, over four major passes including the Croix de Fer and, most significantly, the Galibier, at 2,645 metres the highest and hardest *col* regularly climbed by the Tour. This was where Coppi clinched the Tour, escaping alone yet again. The next rider, the Spaniard Bernardo Ruiz, was seven minutes adrift.

Orio Vergani described the delirious scenes in *Corriere della Sera*: 'From the Montgenèvre customs post to here, for about twenty kilometres, there was not even a thin gap in the sea of people. On the climb to Sestriere, the shoulders of the hills were turned into limitless stands as in a natural amphitheatre. [At the finish] Coppi had more trouble getting away from the crowd than he had had escaping his adversaries on today's climbs. Fifty *carabinieri* were barely enough to get him out of this bedlam. Crazy women offer him packets of sweets, unknown people kiss, hug, shake and squeeze their Fausto. It's not a triumph. It's an orgy. The Tour de France is becoming a personal exhibition for one phenomenal talent.'

Any talk of Bartali stabbing Coppi in the back was long gone. He had finished ten minutes behind in Sestriere and confirmation that *il vecchio* knew his place came on the stage to Monaco, when he and Coppi were the only Italians in a lead group of forty. Coppi punctured; his old rival gave up his wheel. When the race climbed Mont Ventoux, high above Avignon, Coppi punctured again, and again Bartali stopped to help. In Perpignan came the ultimate tribute to Coppi's dominance: the organisers increased the prize money for second and third places by 500,000 and 250,000 old francs respectively. This was recognition that the Tour was as good as over, with eight stages still to be covered, and such a tribute has never been paid to any Tour winner since.

Two wonderful drawings by the French cartoonist Pellos illustrate Coppi's dominance in that Tour. One is entitled *'Tout est consommé'* – Coppi is at a table, his stomach bulging, with all his rivals looking hungry in one corner of the room, as Carrea, Magni and Bartali, dressed as servants, queue up behind the champion. The other, *'Ce qu'il faudrait pour qu'il ne gagne pas'*, shows, with Hanna-Barbera-esque cruelty, what it would take to stop the *campionissimo*: he is run over by a steamroller, seated on a mine, the road is strewn with tacks and mantraps, he is served arsenic, hit with a hammer by a grinning image of the Puy-de-Dôme, has vitriol poured over him and his *gregari* are tied to a tree.

The puncture put paid to Coppi's chances of increasing his lead on the Ventoux, but in the Pyrenees he was rampant again. Geminiani won the first stage – one suspects with Coppi's approval as they were team-mates at Bianchi – but the next day the *campionissimo* led alone over two passes, the Aubisque and the Tourmalet. He waited for the 'opposition' on the first, escaped on the second, waited again for what was left of the field, then finally broke away again a few kilometres from the stage finish in Pau. At the final summit finish of the race, the extinct volcano of the Puy-de-Dôme in the Massif Central, he was again unstoppable, overtaking the Dutchman Jan Nolten in the final 300 metres. At the finish in Paris the second-placed cyclist, Stan Ockers of Belgium, was twenty-eight minutes and seventeen seconds behind. No Tour has been won by a greater margin in the post-war years.

Coppi was still not confident in spite of his total control of the race and that massive lead. His room-mate Ettore Milano remembers a brief exchange before the penultimate stage of the Tour. 'The yellow jersey was on the bed and he said to me, "Will I wear it to Paris?" He had almost half an hour's lead but was still afraid something might happen, a dog might run out in front of him or something. He would not believe he had won until he crossed the line. He was always like that after Serse died.'

Coppi's doubts belied the reality of his second double. There could be no stronger statement of his continuing power after the disastrous season and a half that had preceded the Tour and Giro wins. As he acknowledged, he had come back from oblivion. 'Without saying it to my face I know that even my sincerest friends imagined that my various accidents had lessened my strength and that I didn't have the same physical means as in the past. At times, it was as if people were coming into my hospital room and saying, "What a shame your career has to end like this." They believed I was finished, but I knew nothing was wrong.'

*   *   *

At Sestriere, Bruna Coppi visited the Tour. Suitably made up and glamorously dressed, she was photographed in her husband's hotel room helping to apply cold compresses to his sunburnt forehead. The picture of marital bliss was not all it seemed, however, as Felix Lévitan testified in that year's *Miroir du Tour* magazine. *L'Equipe* photographer Armand Pilon spotted Bruna Coppi 'sitting timidly a little way away from the bed where her husband was lying and receiving homage from his friends'. Pilon asked to take her picture and was refused. 'Mrs Coppi hates photographs, and quite possibly, photographers,' wrote Levitan, before adding: 'Coppi got involved. One word gave way to another. A rather lively phrase gave way to a more curt one. All in Italian, but enough for Pilon to realise that he had been the cause of a domestic row. Mrs Coppi took out her handkerchief and Pilon fled, distraught at having reduced her to tears by insisting on the picture.' He apologised to Coppi the following morning; the *campionissimo* blamed his wife.

Not long after the Tour, Bruna's fears about the dangers of Coppi's profession were realised: her husband crashed again, at a track meeting in Perpignan. The diagnosis was a broken shoulder blade and a cracked collarbone; the doctors' verdict, forty days' rest. Once back on his bike, he kept racing late into the autumn, winning a ten-day stage race, the Grand Prix of the Mediterranean, which finished on 17 November.

That winter, Coppi made further visits to the Locatellis' house near Varese. 'I made three visits, no more, you can't say I was a friend [of the doctor's],' said Coppi later, adding that he came only to see Giulia. Later, she would publish photographs of them together at the house, the sort of pictures any fan might take to record the visit of a star.

Coppi also invited the doctor and his wife to accompany him to Milan to watch the Harlem Globetrotters in an exhibition basketball match. Being Coppi, he had free tickets. The doctor, as it happened, was busy that evening. Giulia and Fausto were accompanied by one of his colleagues and his fiancée; Dr Locatelli was to meet them at the end of the show. During the evening, they managed to extricate themselves from their chaperones. Quite what they talked about

Giulia was unable to remember later on, although she remembered Fausto as 'gauche and emotional'.

The start of 1953 was quiet: Coppi managed only a ninth place in Milan–San Remo, won for the second year running by Loretto Petrucci, who found, however, all of a sudden, that he was no longer flavour of the month at Bianchi. The young Tuscan had been hired to win races, but only when it suited his master. Coppi felt threatened by his second win; Bianchi's *gregari* raced against Petrucci. So too did other teams, under orders from the boss of the bunch. Suddenly, Petrucci had up to thirty men racing against him. He found he had no exhibition race contracts, and he quit cycling at just twenty-five.

Coppi's last great stage race victory was forged on the Stelvio Pass in the north-east corner of Italy, where it meets western Austria and eastern Switzerland. 'Scenically the finest of all the Alpine passes, a marvel of engineering skill,' wrote one Alpine motoring guidebook, which describes the forty-eight hairpins on the north side between Trafoi and the 2,758-metre high summit as probably the most imposing continuous hairpin sector in the Alps. From a distance, it looks as if a child has drawn a series of zigzags across the nearly vertical scree slopes. It seems hardly possible that a road can cling to the vertiginous mountainside. The eight-mile long pass has featured in the Giro several times since 1953, but it remains Coppi's climb: the site of his last great lone escape to win a major Tour, even as his love affair with Giulia gradually gained momentum.

Hugo Koblet, the Brylcreemed *pédaleur de charme*, was in the race lead, his victory seemingly assured at Coppi's expense in spite of a heavy crash on stage four, when he ran into a little girl at a feed zone and fell heavily on his head. He was briefly out cold, and rode the rest of the stage in a daze, clearly concussed. When a race leader is in such a state,

cycling etiquette dictates that he is supported by his rivals:
Coppi and Louison Bobet marshalled their teams at the front
of the bunch to enable the Swiss to get to the finish. Koblet
recovered to win the time trial four days later and arrived at
the Dolomites with almost two minutes' lead on Coppi. The
ageing champion had won a team time trial with the help of
his domestiques, but, to counter that, Koblet had escaped on
a descent to win the stage to Auronzo.

Coppi looked to have played his last card on the stage from
Auronzo to Bolzano, over the classic Dolomite triptych of the
Falzarego, Pordoi and Sella passes, swathed in thick, chilly
fog. Koblet attacked on the Pordoi, gaining two minutes' lead,
only for Coppi to overtake him on the Sella, the last mountain of the stage. By the summit, over 2,200 metres high,
Coppi had left the Swiss behind, but Koblet, perhaps the
most daring descender of the time, caught up again on the
hairpinned drop to Bolzano, where he let Coppi take the stage
win. It was, it seemed, the classic bargain: the race leader
lets his challenger have a compensatory victory. Indeed, Koblet
later claimed that Coppi had ceded him overall victory at the
finish. There remained only the stage over the Stelvio to
Bormio before the final run to the finish in Milan.

The intrigue and gamesmanship began even before the start
flag was dropped. Firstly, Cavanna asked Milano to check on
Koblet as he registered for the stage. The masseur wanted to
know if the Swiss had 'drunk a lot', in other words if he had
overdone the amphetamines. '*La bomba* gave you an influx of
strength in the race, but after the race it prevented you from
recovering completely, often forcing you to spend the night
without sleep. So my job was to work out from Koblet's eyes
if he slept or had just turned over and over all night. The
problem was that Hugo wore dark glasses.'

Milano had to think of something quickly, and he persuaded
a photographer to ask Koblet if he would take his glasses off

for a picture. 'To my immense pleasure, I noticed that Koblet had eyes that would scare you. At once I went to Fausto and said to him, "Look, Koblet has 'drunk' – his eyes are in the back of his head." 'Mine are too,' said Fausto, clearly not convinced. Milano also kept an eye on Koblet during the early part of the stage. 'Look how Koblet's sweating,' he said to his leader, only for Coppi to reply, 'I'm sweating too.' Another domestique was assigned to see if Koblet was swigging water – amphetamines make you thirsty – and indeed he was.

'It was the first time the Giro had been up the Stelvio,' recalled Nino Defilippis, who assisted Coppi even though he was riding for Legnano, Gino Bartali's squad. 'The mechanics hadn't been able to check out the climb, because of the snow; the road was only opened that night. About four or five kilometres up the climb, there were just me, Coppi, Koblet, Fornara, Carrea and Bartali left in the group. Coppi shouted to Carrea, "*Pappagallo* [parrot], what are you doing, don't go so hard."' This was the code for Carrea to put the hammer down. Soon afterwards, Defilippis asked a fan on the roadside how far it was to the top. The answer was two opened hands: ten kilometres. 'After Carrea was dropped, Coppi came to me and said, "*Cid* [kid – Defilippis turned pro at twenty], can you shake up the group?" I attacked and got 100 metres' lead, Koblet chased to get me back, which was an error, as he got to within fifty metres of me and couldn't go any harder. Then Coppi came past us both like a motorbike. Koblet made a mistake, as all he needed to do during the stage was stay with Coppi. Coppi thanked me afterwards, but Koblet wouldn't talk to me again.'

Coppi crossed the summit alone, a tiny figure in the narrow corridor that had been cut through the fifteen-foot-high snowdrifts. Giulia Locatelli had travelled that morning from Varese, leaving her husband at home to nurse a headache. With her she took the same chaperones as before, Locatelli's colleague and his fiancée. As she stood in her white Montgomery duffel coat among the knots of warmly clad fans in the snow at the roadside, Coppi recognised her and asked as he passed, 'Are you coming to the finish?'

By the end of the stage, Coppi had the Giro won: on the slippery twenty-two-kilometre descent Koblet's ability to read the road at speed had deserted him, as happens to even the best descenders when they are forced beyond their physical limit. He fell twice and punctured once, and would not speak to Coppi after the finish, convinced that a pact had been broken. At Coppi's hotel, Giulia Locatelli made her way through the crowds of fans and between the various body-guards on the doors; the mechanic would allow her and only her to enter the champion's room. It was there that she allowed him 'a winner's kiss, very innocent, the kiss of a child'. After dinner the pair sat at Giulia's table – fortuitously, her chap-erones had gone out to buy postcards – and spoke mainly, by her account, about Coppi's life.

At the finish of the Giro the next day in the Vigorelli velo-drome, in spite of the presence of Dr Locatelli, Coppi slipped a clandestine note into her hand as the fans crowded around. 'Our relationship began there,' she later recalled. 'I felt different and Fausto looked different to me. He gave me his hand. I felt something there, a piece of paper.' The message on the card was brief: 'Tomorrow, at four, at Tortona station.' She was collected by Coppi's *gregario* Giovannino Chiesa – the duties of the closest team-mates went far beyond fetching bottles of water – and she and Coppi had a brief meeting in a car parked at a motorway exit. Few words were exchanged, but it marked a turning point.

It was Coppi who initiated the final, decisive step from flirtation to adultery and scandal. In spite of financial incen-tives from *La Gazzetta* – which lost three weeks of massive sales – and attempts by industrialists to influence him through his friends, he decided not to defend his Tour title. He would miss the 1953 race to concentrate on preparation for the world championship, the one major title he had not won. But he did not stay away from the Tour. 'I'm going to see Bartali,' he told little Marina as he left for what purported to be a training camp with his Bianchi team-mates. Giulia was on holiday near Ancona when she received the phone call. It was brief: be at Tortona station tomorrow, bring your passport. She had to find a car, fast, and she knew where to go. Having retired from racing, Coppi's former *gregario* Ubaldo Pugnaloni was now running a driving school in the town. Pugnaloni also rented out cars: she took one to meet Coppi. She had apparently forgotten her passport: at the Montgenèvre customs post, he had to pretend to the officers that the beautiful brunette at his side was his wife.

They spent the night in a small hotel in the French village of Clavière, where Coppi had booked a room in advance. They drove the next day up onto the great scree slopes of the Col de l'Izoard, where he had escaped alone among the Death Valley rock pillars to win a stage of the 1951 Tour, and where he and Bartali had left the field behind in the 1949 race. They stood by the roadside like any other spectators, Coppi shouting to friends in the peloton, and taking photographs. Television footage of the pair on that day shows Coppi looking relaxed, happy. Then the press photographers arrived. On returning from the Alps five days later, Mrs Locatelli saw the pictures of herself and Coppi in newspapers in Pugnaloni's office. 'She didn't know what to do,' the old *gregario* remembers. 'I, for my part, didn't know that she had gone with Coppi, only that she had left her car with me. She asked me if I could do her an immense service and tell the doctor that she had gone to the Alps on a trip that was organised by me. What was I to say? Who could say no? I remember she went away with the doctor, and he thanked me for looking after his wife.

He thanked me just like that.' More than fifty years on you sense that Pugnaloni is not at ease at having provided the alibi for the lovers' excursion that precipitated the scandal.

*   *   *

The bike Coppi used to win that year's world championship is kept by the Bianchi company at their factory in Treviglio, east of Milan. It still bears his race number, 60. His feeding bottle, covered with cloth to keep the liquid cool, is held firmly in the bottle cage. Compared to today's fat-tubed carbon-fibre or aluminium machines, the bike looks archaic with its frame of slender, fragile steel. Even so, with its ten-speed Campagnolo gears, upright frame design and narrow tyres, it is recognisably modern compared to the bikes Coppi and company were riding just six or seven years before in the post-war years.

Cavanna had told Coppi that this would be his last chance to win the world championship. He had always been un-successful before: quite apart from the Valkenburg debacle in 1948, the courses were never selective enough for him to get away from the field. This year, however, the circuit included the tough, cobbled climb of the Crespera, tackled on each of the twenty laps. Given the problems he had had with the Italian team over the years, Coppi wanted *un'uomo di fiducia* – a totally reliable team-mate – and a second-year Bianchi *gregario*, Michele Gismondi, was the man chosen by Cavanna; the young professional had just emerged from the blind mage's 'nursery'. Getting Gismondi into the team needed almost as much work as actually preparing for the event: he recalls trav-elling from Paris to Rome to ride the selection race with Coppi acting as *his* personal *gregario*: getting the sandwiches, making sure he rested in his couchette.

Making sure Gismondi rode the race was merely part of

Cavanna and Coppi's meticulous preparation. To avoid fatigue, Coppi gave up all his criterium commitments for a month before Lugano, missing out on 53 million lire in potential earnings. He rode one race in France, the Bol d'Or des Monédières, because the circuit in the Dordogne was similar to that in Lugano. For a week before the race, Coppi and Gismondi trained together on the course, finding the easier sections where it would be possible to eat during the event. Both men put in long sessions with Cavanna's 'nursery', outings that included solo efforts and that extended into the afternoon heat, when the race at Lugano would be decided.

While Bianchi was Coppi's personal fiefdom, the same could not be said of the Italian national team, even now. Although he had at least managed to persuade Binda not to include Gino Bartali, there were those, he said, 'who would sell their souls to the devil to see him lose'. The evening before the professional event, the Italians should have been celebrating the victory of Riccardo Filippi in the amateur race, but instead there was a dispute over who would or would not help Coppi. Petrucci said he was there to win and accused Coppi of egotism. There was conflict about whether Gismondi was there for the team, or solely for Coppi: should he wait for another rider, Rossello, if he punctured, or should he devote himself entirely to Coppi? Gismondi is adamant that he and Coppi were largely on their own in the race: 'It should have been everyone for Coppi, and it seems that way because he won, but several guys in the team were riding for themselves.' In the event, it made little difference: Coppi left the field behind with eighty kilometres to go, gaining 200 metres' lead in no time, and then pulling inexorably away.

Only one man managed to hang on: the Belgian Germain Derycke, who was a better sprinter than Coppi. The Italian knew that if he did not get the Belgian off his back wheel, he might lose the title. On the final ascent of the Crespera,

Coppi tried everything: he zigzagged across the road so that the climb would be longer for the Belgian, whom he felt was on the verge of cracking. He tried to manoeuvre him in front, so that he could attack from behind, but Derycke remained glued to his wheel. 'I saw him pass with Derycke,' says Fiorenzo Magni, 'and I yelled, "Make him work." He looked at me as if to say, "Don't worry."' Finally, on the toughest part of the climb, as they accelerated out of a hairpin bend, he sprinted. That was the end of Derycke. In the ten kilometres that were left to the finish line, he lost a colossal six minutes. There was one pleasing irony as Coppi rode to victory: a Chianti company that was producing Bartali wine had bought many of the publicity hoardings around the circuit, so as Coppi stamped his authority on the race he did so with his rival's name as a backdrop.

Coppi did manage to raise one arm in celebration when he crossed the line – he never used the double-handed salute – but he had terrible cramp in his legs. When he told Cavanna, the answer was predictably terse: 'With what you've taken do you expect to feel as if you've been on mineral water?' He had been put on a course of strychnine a week before the race, and on the day he was given pure caffeine. That was not the only stimulus, says Gismondi: 'There were other things that spurred Coppi to win – the lady with the flowers.'

The Bianchi boss Aldo Zambrini had taken Giulia Locatelli to the finish line so that his man could see her as he rode. The cycling rumour mill had been grinding since photographs of the pair had been published after the Tour de France; Coppi, it was said, had missed the Tour so that he could be with his mistress. But there had followed a hiatus in the affair. Coppi had declared himself to Giulia; they were now lovers. He had told her, in their little hotel – she said – that they would spend the rest of their lives together. Giulia had returned home to find Dr Locatelli in bed with an ice bag and his suspicions, and the atmosphere in the little house in Varano Borghi was chilly.

The day before the race, a newsreel had shown Marina reading out a letter in which she asked her father to bring her home the rainbow jersey. However, it was Giulia with whom Coppi shared the glory on the podium, although not every newspaper that acquired the pictures of the two lovers knew who she was. One Swiss paper captioned the image 'Fausto Coppi and his wife Bruna'. On the front cover of *La Gazzetta dello Sport*, she is visible on the periphery. Coppi, tellingly, dedicated his victory to his mother and Marina. Not his wife.

While it is Giulia's presence in Lugano that has captured headlines since, Bruna was also at the race, and she apparently encountered Giulia in the Italian team hotel afterwards. To avoid a confrontation, Coppi did not go to the post-race dinner: he, Bruna, Cavanna and Gismondi drove straight home. 'Bruna felt that something was going to happen, there was a dinner afterwards but she couldn't wait to get out,' Gismondi told me. Instead, they had a sandwich in Varese, where Cavanna joked that Coppi had better get him some sparkling wine because they had done nothing to celebrate the fact that his protégés had won both the amateur and professional titles.

The drive home was triumphant: the Italian fans queuing at the border in clouds of smoke from the burned out clutches of their cars cheered their world champion as he passed. So many *tifosi* had crossed into Switzerland to watch Coppi that customs checks on the border were suspended so that they could get home; when they did so they were laden with chocolate and cigarettes on which duty had not been paid. When *La Gazzetta dello Sport's* Rino Negri arrived at his home in Milan on the Monday, his paper's presses were still running as a total of 630,000 copies were sold across Italy, double what would normally be considered a big sale.

The following weeks were packed with track appearances and circuit races. In early October, Coppi teamed up with the amateur world champion Filippi to take another stunning win, at record speed, in the Baracchi Trophy two-man team time trial. On his bike, Coppi seemed unstoppable but what was happening in his private life also had a momentum of its own. Giulia remained with her husband, and Coppi stayed with Bruna, but another daring step towards the inevitable was taken at the end of the year. Coppi took Giulia to visit his mother in Castellania. Given the place of *la mamma* in all Italian men's hearts, gaining Angiolina's approval was like a marriage blessing, while exposing his peasant roots showed how far Coppi was placing his trust in his beautiful and very middle-class mistress.

CHAPTER 12

THE OUTLAWS

'*Vélo* is an anagram of love' – Louis Nucera, *Mes Rayons de Soleil*

Just outside the town of Novi Ligure where farmers' fields are squeezed uneasily by a sprawl of factories and industrial estates stands a tall, elegant villa set among high cypress trees, a little way back from the main road. The handwritten label by the bell on the gate reads simply: Coppi.

The house has barely changed since Coppi and his lover Giulia Locatelli moved there in 1954. It is still the home of their son, also named Angelo-Fausto, usually known as Faustino, and his family, which includes a little Giulia. But everywhere the past can be felt. I park my car under a line of fir trees at the top of the drive: a little later in the house Faustino shows me photographs of his father, his face prematurely lined by age and stress, lying on a camp bed under those same trees with his leg in plaster, examining a hunting rifle in one picture, eating a bowl of pasta in another.

When I call Faustino to arrange the visit, I learn that the telephone number has not changed since the days of his father. The interior of the house is ornate, with chandeliers, elaborate plasterwork, fine wallpaper, decorative furniture, vertiginous ceilings: it is a massive step up from anything Castellania can offer, and from Casa Coppi, where Fausto's mother Angiolina used to keep her kindling in the fridge he had bought her.

The photographs leave no doubt as to the identity of the previous owner. There is a series of pictures of Coppi sitting on a sofa drinking wine with a journalist, others of Faustino driving a pedal car. Another shows Fausto putting Faustino on a bike, not long, surely, before the *campionissimo's* death. There is a series of pictures taken while Fausto and Giulia were on holiday on Elba, endearingly amateurish and unposed. One shows Giulia to the left, with the sea taking up the rest of the frame. She looks tired, her body a little floppy: you can envisage her scolding Fausto for not making it more flattering. Her picture of her lover shows him bending sideways, displaying all the thinness of his body, his clearly defined leg muscles. As Faustino Coppi admits, the house is home to 'a cult of the dead'. By any measure, his can hardly have been a normal childhood, among the photographs of his illustrious father and the trophies brought back from races around Europe, all retained by his grieving mother.

A few kilometres away is the house Coppi bought not long before leaving Bruna and Marina; his wife remained there until her death and it is now the home of their daughter. Bruna's old house is in the centre of the town, Giulia's on the outskirts, but the two villas have much in common. They are both large, ornate, tranquil and set back from the road. Both still have furniture that dates back to the 1950s. Neither has changed a great deal since Fausto Coppi left for the last time; both the 'Coppi houses' are living museums.

Visiting both houses in the space of a day was a curious experience. Coppi's son and daughter are both disconcertingly like their father, who is an opaque memory for both of them. Marina admits she has difficulty distinguishing between what she remembers and what she has been told, that gradually she has built up 'a mosaic' of memories. Faustino confesses that most of what he knows of his father comes through his mother. It was not until several years after the deaths of both their mothers that the pair became reacquainted, at a race organised in Novi in memory of their father in 2000. Faustino and Marina had abruptly stopped meeting after their father's death – when Marina was twelve and Faustino four – because their mothers could not abide one another. The two houses lie less than four miles apart but for forty years they were divided by a gulf that might as well have been the Adriatic.

*   *   *

Article 587 of the Italian penal code was explicit: 'An adulterous wife shall be punished by imprisonment for up to one year. Her accomplice in adultery shall be punished by the same punishment . . . the crime shall be punishable on complaint of the husband.' It remained on the statute book until 1968, part of a set of laws that now seem positively medieval. The phrasing makes it clear that a woman's guilt was considered greater than that of a man, reflecting the importance attached to maintaining well-defined paternity, which would eventually be a key element in the Coppi imbroglio.

The law was out of kilter with a nation where sexual mores were beginning to change – a fact recognised by judges, who rarely gave more than a three-month suspended prison sentence. In the mid-1950s, when an amendment was proposed, it was not a move to decriminalise adultery itself, but merely an attempt to make men and women equally guilty in the eyes of the law. A straw poll of celebrities – lawyers, actresses, opera singers, sportspeople – sought their opinions on the proposed change, but did not find any voices in favour of the idea that adultery should cease to be considered a crime.

There was another twist to the law on adultery. If Giulia's husband injured or killed either her or Coppi during a dispute about the breakup of his marriage, the law would take into account the fact that he had been cuckolded, his honour blemished. A reduced sentence might be given if it was proved that a crime was committed to avenge one's honour. This was the premise for the film *Divorzio all'Italiana* of 1961, in which the hero, depicted by Marcello Mastroianni, plans to murder his wife and use Article 587 to mitigate his prison sentence.

Coppi and Giulia had become 'marital outlaws'. The phrase was coined by Luigi Sansone, the Socialist deputy who opened the debate over adultery and divorce not long after the scandal involving the *campionissimo*. Sansone estimated that some four million Italians were *fuorilegge* due to the anomalies in divorce law that left parents and children with no legal status. Women were disadvantaged, having to live where their husbands specified, while children born outside marriage were second-class citizens. Legally, husbands retained authority over their wives' children, even if these were the progeny of another relationship. Coppi and Giulia's situation was not complex; Italian law would make it so.

In embarking on their affair, Coppi and Giulia Locatelli were not merely breaking the law. In addition, they were defying the Catholic Church, which viewed marriage as part of the sacrament. Under Mussolini, control of marriage had been handed back to the Church, with the reversal of a law on civil marriages as part of the Lateran Accords of 1929. The government of the day was a religious party: the Christian Democrats. Both Church and party would fight attempts to legalise divorce and adultery.

For the media, the maintenance of the family unit was socially important, whatever false façades that entailed. This was a time when magazines praised 'the most devoted wife of all Italy' portraying an ideal of submissive womanhood not far from that of the exemplary mothers so beloved of the fascists. The elected 'best Italian wife' for 1954, one Anna Grazia Cicognani, was lauded for her 'faith, abnegation, spirit of sacrifice and above all her gentleness of character and understanding'. It was a time of public prudery, when, as the historian Daniele Marchesini notes, the television content guidelines specified that marriage must be portrayed in a positive way, that adultery should be shown as a grave sin, that children born outside wedlock were to be shown 'with care' and illegal sexual relations had to be depicted as 'abnormal'.

Coppi was flouting the moral norms of his sport as well. The private lives of the stars – or what was seen of them in public – were expected to be exemplary. The popular, idealised view of Coppi was of a man with a small child and an adoring, modest wife who dedicated her life to supporting him in his sport. Bruna, and later also Marina, turned up at the occasional race to show the public why Coppi was racing: to provide for his women. Coppi himself had played up to this before Giulia became an important part of his life. His memoir *Le Drame de Ma Vie* ends: 'Every win is part of Marina's dowry, and that's why I put all my willpower towards winning if I can. When, later on, I take my little Marina to the church dressed in white, perhaps, curious onlookers will say, tenderly "That's little Marina, you know, the daughter of the old *campione*".'

'Cycling was a mysogenistic area of life,' says Jean Bobet. 'A team is like a bunch of boys on holiday together. If they talk about women it is not their wives they talk about. They see wives as noble beings, but they discuss the women they find along the way. I believe this ethos contributed to Fausto's secret love life.' There was, as Bobet hints, a distinct contrast between the public image and what actually went on. Turbulent love lives had always been part of cycling. For all the best efforts of men such as the Tour de France organiser Jacques Goddet and before him Henri Desgrange – who attempted to ban women from the Tour de France caravan – there were women aplenty on the cycling circuit.

Coppi cannot have lacked female attention as he plied his

trade on the velodromes of Europe in the winter. International stars such as Gina Lollobrigida and Maria Callas made a point of visiting him and Bartali at races. Clearly they believed that being pictured with either *campione* would enhance their celebrity status. Giulia Locatelli claimed, after Coppi's death, that his conquests before her included noted actresses of screen and stage. This is impossible to verify; he must have had opportunities but no one knows whether he acted on them. What was extraordinary about his entanglement with the doctor's wife was that some of its crucial moments took place in front of journalists and cameramen who could not believe their good fortune.

*   *   *

After the world championships of 1953, the affair continued. The week after the race and a few hours before the star was due to face the Australian Syd Patterson in a pursuit match, a *soigneur* entered Coppi's hotel room close to the Vigorelli track in Milan. He found the cyclist in bed with Giulia. The *soigneur* asked if there was a risk that Coppi might sap his strength before taking on Patterson, who was world champion at the discipline; Coppi replied that he was good enough to make love and then beat the Australian later.

Coppi's *gregari* played their role in keeping the affair secret. Giulia Locatelli would travel to Milan to meet Coppi, taking her daughter Lolli as cover. In Milan, the eight-year-old would be consigned either to Ettore Milano or Giovannino Chiesa. She would be taken to a film or a puppet show, while the couple spent time together.

Lolli, naturally, was under orders to keep her mouth shut, because Dr Locatelli had his suspicions: he was receiving letters that warned that something was going on. 'My husband wanted to make me swear that the contents of the anonymous letters he received did not correspond to reality,' said Giulia Locatelli. 'I swore, yes, on the heads of our children, and I was sincere when I shouted through my tears that only sporting fanaticism connected me to Coppi.' The doctor and his wife would spent entire nights arguing, and he would set off to see his patients at 7 a.m. without having slept. At some point late in 1953, Fausto and Giulia escaped on holiday for a week on Capri 'like man and wife', she said later. Also late that year, she discovered that she was pregnant – or so she claimed in 1978 – but had an early miscarriage. In the wider world, however, the affair had yet to make headlines, although the podium photograph at Lugano had in effect made it public. Still the affair remained an open secret. 'Everyone in cycling closed their eyes. It didn't create too much trouble,' says Fiorenzo Magni.

All that changed at the 1954 Giro, where, as the defending winner and the world champion, Coppi was the overwhelming favourite. He lived up to his status on the first stage in Palermo, a team time trial that he and his Bianchi team-mates won by four minutes from Koblet's Guerra squad. However, on the second day he effectively lost the race, suffering serious stomach trouble after eating oysters for dinner in a Sicilian hotel. His deficit was eleven minutes; at the end of stage six, where he failed to respond to an attack by the promising young Italian Carlo Clerici, he had lost a colossal thirty-nine minutes and had no chance of overall victory.

That would have been bad enough for his public image, but the state of his private life finally hit the headlines during the rest day on the shores of Lake Garda. Both 'la signora' – as the team called Giulia – and Bruna turned up, almost simultaneously. Doctor Locatelli had received an anonymous letter, recommending that he keep his wife at home. Giulia had promptly fled with Lolli, pretending that she was going to help a friend in Bergamo prepare for her wedding. Lolli would later describe phone calls along the way to the race, the sudden appearance of various members of Coppi's entourage and her mother saying at one point, 'When I have married Mr Coppi, he will be your father'.

The race caravan was awash with rumours: Coppi and his wife had had an intense argument, their angry voices echoing down the corridor of the Bianchi team hotel. The mystery ended when Giulia got in her car and followed the cyclist on a time trial stage, the forty-two kilometres from Gardone to Riva del Garda – something completely unheard of. Bianchi were staying in an out-of-the-way hotel where a room had been booked for an unnamed guest. One writer described a pretty girl of eight or nine trying to persuade the police to let her into the hotel, saying 'I must go to Uncle Fausto'. It was Lolli. A Bianchi domestique let her in; the journalist said he didn't know Coppi had a niece, and the rider replied she was 'the daughter of the woman on the third floor'.

Five days later, amid the chaos, Coppi won the race's toughest stage across the Dolomites to Bolzano in his old style, but he could do no better than finish second overall behind Clerici. Giulia was also in evidence in St Moritz – the day before the finish in Milan – and this was the day she acquired the name *La Dama Bianca*, the White Lady, thanks to her white Montgomery duffel coat, of the style made famous by the English general during the Second World War. The *gregario* Sandrino Carrea recalled: 'We finished the stage into St Moritz and there was this lady with a white coat. "Carrea, where is your hotel?" she said. I told her we were at the Poste. It was the first time I had seen her. And Fausto didn't come to eat with us.' 'Who is Fausto Coppi's lady in white?' asked Pierre Chany in *L'Equipe*.

A couple of relatively minor events on the race were immediately linked with Coppi's private life and turned into a scandal. On the leg into St Moritz the field staged what amounted to a strike, covering the two hundred mountainous kilometres in nine hours without any significant racing. 'Sheep on bikes' was how *La Stampa* described the riders. Coppi himself had a fight with a Swiss cyclist, Emilio Croci-Torti, as they pedalled along, reflecting the stress he was suffering. The blame for both events was put on Coppi's 'physical and moral crisis', amid rumours that he and Bruna were about to separate. A weekly magazine headlined its review of the race '*Il Giro degli scandali*': the report said that the stars of cycling were overpaid and the sport was decadent, violent – there had been a fight at a stage finish as well as the Croci-Torti incident – and drug-riddled. The writer pilloried the stars for abusing their power over the *gregari* by making the lesser lights race how they wished. The vitriolic tone had been set.

*   *   *

When the White Lady is mentioned to one of Coppi's circle the response does not vary a great deal. To start with, she is never referred to by name, but in various derogatory terms – as *quella signora, la dama* or, in the case of one former team-mate, *quella la* – that woman. There is usually one small anecdote, enough to make it clear she is not approved of, before the eyes are raised to the heavens, and the former cyclist says he cannot say more, for fear of offending her son, Faustino. The questioner is then referred to another member of the inner circle, who 'knows much more'. Needless to say, the response is identical when that other ex-cyclist is questioned. It is enough, however, to get the message across: feelings have not weakened over fifty years.

A quietly spoken man in his early fifties, Faustino Coppi is gently protective of his mother. Given the odium that has been heaped on her over the last half-century, he has good reason. Faustino describes Giulia Occhini as 'protective, gentle, but a very, very strong character. She always knew where she wanted to get to and got there. There were no half-measures with her. She said what she thought and people took it as being unpleasant. There are people who have laid the responsibility for his death on her. They have said she changed my father [but] he was a person who had a certain way of living, then became famous and that changed. I don't think it was so much marriage with my mother, but an evolution in his lifestyle.' He uses the word 'marriage' in spite of the fact that Fausto and Giulia were never to be united in a ceremony that was recognised in their home country.

Giulia Locatelli began attempting to get her point of view across in the press from the day the scandal broke in 1954. On 15 June she emerged from obscurity. 'Today we met the mysterious lady known as the White Lady' read the headline in *La Stampa*. The interview was as revealing for what it did not say, as for what it did. Giulia was accurately described as a 'decisive woman, very sure of herself', but she insisted, disingenuously, that 'between me and Coppi is nothing more than a sporting friendship'. 'My life is ruined', she told the reporters, adding that she hoped her husband would forgive her rather than throw her out of their house. It was a virtuoso performance: the link with Coppi was established but she gave nothing significant away.

In the years that followed, no version of Fausto's life was produced without a reaction from her; interviews and ghost-written articles appeared from time to time in which certain facts of the affair were subtly changed to present her in a better light: the date at which she and Coppi became lovers, the way her husband behaved during the affair, her own conduct, what happened when Fausto died less than six years after their life together began. As an attempt to rewrite history, it makes sense: this was the woman who was, as she put it, portrayed as 'Italy's biggest sinner'. She was not defending only herself but the lover who was put in the dock alongside her.

Giulia resented being labelled the White Lady: 'Don't I have the right to my own name, like every other woman?' The title probably depersonalised her, if the tone of the letters she says she received is anything to go by. One, signed 'a mother', suggested sarcastically that she should get rid of her children if they were all that was keeping her from happiness. After a photograph was taken of her wearing a fat bracelet covered in precious stones, she was accused of gold-digging. Over the years, she met the opprobrium head-on. The contrast with the self-effacing Bruna could not be greater.

She described herself as 'impulsive, and tending to repent what I've done when it's too late to go back'. Even Faustino admits she was opinionated. Given the position of women in Italian society at the time, a woman like Bruna was seen as the ideal. Sandrino Carrea describes Giulia as a woman who saw things in black and white, and had no hesitation when it came to making enemies: '[Her attitude was] you are either for me or against me. *Era una bestia così* – she was that sort of creature.'

Giulia, clearly, was not an easy person to be around. Another former team-mate of Coppi's says: 'She was the kind of pushy woman who made herself known, who liked to be talked about. It was embarrassing. It was hard to be with a woman like that, who believed she was important, who boasted that she was Coppi's girlfriend. Bruna was the complete opposite: modest, shy. If there was a party, she would stand in a dark bit of the room.' When the White Lady went clothes shopping, eyewitnesses recall that she would have every item brought down from the shelves, and then buy none of them, to their embarrassment – these things get noticed in small-town Italy. 'If she was buying ham, she would always taste the first sort she was given, then buy the second. She was a terror. The important thing [for her] was that she was no longer an Occhini, she was a Coppi.' The reporter in *La Stampa* was a little more polite: 'La signora Giulia has an impetuous temperament, and you can see that in a few moments by the way she drives. She drives fast, and doesn't stick to the rules of the road if they might slow her down. When she can, she runs red lights.'

Giulia Locatelli left her husband shortly after the Giro ended. As she later told it, when she got to Tortona to meet her Fausto, in a distraught state at being separated from her children, he was off racing in Turin. Welcome to the world of professional cycling. As for Coppi, he left Bruna and Marina with a heavy heart. 'I don't ask you to pardon me, but don't hate me,' he said. He had written a letter to Bruna earlier saying, 'Something atrocious is happening to me but I am obliged to go through with it. I am sorry if I am hurting you. I love this other woman, about whom people will say things that are worse than hanging, without ever knowing her. If someone tried to ruin our love, I would be capable of killing him.'

Popular cycling tradition held that sex weakened the male athlete. Coppi would have had this dinned into him by Biagio Cavanna from his youth. Managers such as Eberardo Pavesi would shake their heads and say their team's poor form was due to a recent spate of marriages or new girlfriends. 'For years, I was abstinent,' Coppi told Rino Negri. 'Then I tried, and won the Baracchi after a night of love.' His first win in the autumn two-up team time trial came in 1953, after his affair with Giulia began. Riccardo Filippi, world amateur champion in 1953, put it this way: 'As for women, I recall only huge sexual fasts.' As Fiorenzo Magni said: 'A married athlete owes a lot to his wife. "No" today because it's the Giro di Lombardia, "no" because it's Piedmont. And imagine the abstinence for the Giro d'Italia or the Tour.'

Given the abstinence that Coppi says was part of his cycling lifestyle, the affair with Giulia must have been a sexual awakening of sorts for him. Much is made of his mistress's sensual appeal: amid the disapproval, one former team-mate still waxes lyrical about the beauty of her hair and eyes, which distracted the Bianchi *gregari* when she turned up at races. Raphael Geminiani is one of the few who does not disapprove of her and he is emphatic about what she must have brought to Coppi: '*La Dame Blanche* – oh lalala. She was the kind of woman who can lead a great man by the nose and he will still be happy. She took Coppi in hand. The White Lady made him discover a new side of life: pleasure' – he makes the sensual implications of *le plaisir* obvious as he says the words – '*l'amour*, restaurants, clothes, soirées. She was flattered to have someone like Fausto; he was flattered by her attentions.'

As a man who shied away from confrontation, Coppi would probably have preferred the affair to be secret, if not necessarily brief, but he had set in motion a chain of events that he could not control. Some of those close to him say he was put in an impossible position once Giulia had walked out on her husband. 'With Giulia he ended up *incastrato*, taken by the balls,' said one. 'It could have been a romantic adventure like any other, but the fact that she left her husband and two children and went to live with him put him under an obligation to do all the things that men say in that situation but don't actually mean. He behaved like a man of honour. In inverted commas.'

*   *   *

The trail that led Fausto and Giulia to the villa on the Serravalle road was not an easy one; matters were not helped by a freak accident in which he was hit by a wheel which fell off a lorry while he was training. A cracked skull was diagnosed, a month off racing recommended. Finding somewhere to live was the urgent priority, however. The couple stayed in hotels initially but were pursued by the press and the fans. Before finally settling on Villa Carla, they inspected various houses but were not welcome as tenants. One owner, learning it was Coppi and his mistress who wanted to rent, refused point-blank. The owner of a secluded hilltop villa near Tortona asked them for a completely unreasonable amount.

In the summer of 1954 the villa outside Novi was the subject of a three-page article in *Oggi* magazine – Italy's equivalent of *Hello!*. The walls of one of the bedrooms were papered in white and Bianchi blue, with bedclothes to match. There was a room solely for Fausto's cycle clothing, a billiards room, a waiting room for visitors, two servants' rooms, a bar in the sitting room, rooms full of toys for the children and cupboards full of trophies. It was, in short, the perfect bourgeois residence for an upwardly mobile couple, with its hints of aristocracy – the high ceilings, the elegant archways, the statues on the mantelpieces. There was one false note: two rooms had been set aside for Marina in the initial hope that she might come to stay occasionally. That never happened, even before Coppi's death.

The trouble the couple had finding a place to live showed how public opinion had turned against Coppi after that Giro, but there were other signs. At a track meeting in Turin, on relatively local soil, he and Magni were greeted with whistles. He was also whistled when he visited Castellania with Giulia; he asked the whistler what was the matter and was told it was because he didn't win the Giro. Given the tone of the newspaper coverage, it was hardly surprising. 'No one in Tortona can forgive him for leaving his wife Bruna and daughter Marina for the White Lady,' wrote one journalist. 'It is all people talk about. Above all, because this was not a spur of the moment passion of the kind that happens in a bike race, but a situation that matured slowly under the eyes of his wife with three children caught up in it. Everyone believes that Bruna does not deserve this fate in the slightest . . . Her life has become hell.'

Coppi's marriage was major news: the Italian media of the time was obsessed with sex. In weekly magazines such as *Oggi*, every variant of domestic scandal was explored: bigamy, marriage between old men and young girls, countesses running away with their grooms, jealousy killings, marital murder, wives who threw themselves under trains. Such articles appeared alongside photographs of young girls talking to the Madonna, pieces about weeping statues and the Virgin of Lourdes curing disease, and discussion of the qualities of the ideal wife. There was obsessive reporting of the case of Wilma Montesi, a young girl murdered amid rumours of sexual scandal that went to the highest levels of the establishment.

The picture is that of a frenetic mingling of Catholicism and emerging sexual freedom. At the same time, a celebrity culture was emerging, with the reporting of every move made by figures such as Marilyn Monroe, Ingrid Bergman, Princess Margaret and Liz Taylor. The White Lady was included in *Oggi's* list of personalities from 'a troubled 1954', together with Gina Lollobrigida, Katharine Hepburn, Princess Maria Pia of Savoy and Alcide De Gasperi (who had merely died, without sexual scandal).

Coppi and his mistress actively courted the media at times – Giulia rather more than her reticent lover. The impending separation of the two couples was announced by the cyclist's lawyer to a horde of journalists outside a Milan hotel on 8 July. Inside, Coppi lay in bed, recovering from the skull fracture; his mistress was at his side. Bruna did not want the marriage to end, and the coverage was massively in favour of the slighted wife, apart from one frenetic point in late August when it was rumoured that Fausto had committed suicide by shooting himself with one of his hunting rifles. There was prurient speculation about Marina's state of mind and Bruna's fainting fits. There were reports of a letter written by Bruna to the Pope, and his answer. The Pontiff expressed the view that, if Fausto did not return home, the hand of God would descend on him.

The wrath of Jacques Goddet certainly did. In a vicious full-page article in his newspaper *L'Equipe* the Tour organiser pilloried Coppi: 'pitiful', 'cloistered in vanity', 'blinded by the opinion he has of himself', 'a poor *campionissimo*, afraid of suffering, of not dominating, of failing, of disappointing'. Goddet concluded: 'He is no longer able to withstand the very idea of competition, he is the cholera of professional cycling.' As editor of *L'Equipe*, Goddet was in a unique position to make his disapproval known, but he was using Coppi's affair as a pretext for his own interests. The Italian's decision to stay at home rather than ride the Tour in July 1954 and 1955 had meant that sales of *L'Equipe* suffered. In addition, Goddet was embroiled in a major battle with the Italian teams over Fiorenzo Magni's decision to bring in the first team sponsor from outside the sport, Nivea. Coppi had sided with Magni, and that was enough for Goddet.

In his defence, Coppi said that he was avoiding the Tour to save his strength as he got older. He modestly requested that his private life remain private and that he be judged by what he achieved on his bike. But competing had its difficulties, because of Giulia's presence. He managed two stage victories in the Tour of Switzerland on his comeback after the accident, but there was a major falling out with the Italian national team manager Alfredo Binda, who was unhappy when he realised that the White Lady had accompanied her Fausto to the race. A few months later, when Coppi defended his world title at Solingen, Denmark, Binda suffered another blow: he arrived at the town to discover that Giulia had appropriated his room in the team hotel because it was next to Fausto's. He declared her *persona non grata*.

Showing something like his old form, Coppi took sixth in that world championship, helping Michele Gismondi to fourth place. Even that did not improve matters when they returned to Italy. He and Giulia were living in relative seclusion in their elegant villa. Coppi had banned the press, but Giulia occasionally let them through the gate to give interviews in which she put whatever spin she could on the situation. Negotiations were under way for both of them formally to separate from their spouses. There were convoluted discussions over the separations, at times lasting into the night. Bruna would not give up the belief that she could get her man back; Dr Locatelli was intransigent over allowing his wife access to their children. Fausto, on the other hand, was looking for divorce: at the time, this had to be approved by the Holy See. Not surprisingly given Pope Pius's public expression of his disapproval, the marriage could not be annulled.

That, however, was merely the beginning of their tribulations. There were attempts to persuade Coppi to go back to his wife. Both his team-mate Michele Gismondi and another confidant, the journalist Rino Negri, told Coppi to return to Bruna. Negri received this answer: 'If you talk that way you have never loved. If anyone else was doing what I am no one would talk about it.' Gismondi was told: 'If you knew *la Giulia* like I do, you would do what I have done.' Coppi justifiably believed he had the right to a private life, but all of Italy wanted to know about the affair. Unfortunately for Coppi, the reaction was not limited to a few whistles from disillusioned fans, yells on the roadside that Coppi should go back to his wife, vitriolic newspaper articles and vicious anonymous letters. The backlash against the errant couple went far higher up the human food chain than angry *tifosi* and sensation-seeking journalists.

CHAPTER 13

IN THE DOCK

'I have betrayed no one' – Fausto Coppi, November 1954

At the chapel of the Madonna del Ghisallo, high above Lake Como, there is total silence. The morning's visitors to the spiritual centre of Italian cycling have yet to arrive. The Ghisallo is a Catholic chapel like no other, partly an exhibition of cycling artefacts, partly a shrine to the fallen of the open road. The position allotted to the green, red and white Italian national champions' jerseys speaks volumes about the strength of the holy alliance between the Catholic religion and cycling. They hang on the altar, watched over by an image of the Virgin Mary.

The status of this chapel within the two-wheeled world can be read from the *ex-voto* offerings. Hanging above the west door are twenty-two framed jerseys, rainbow-striped for the world championships, yellow for the Tour de France, pink for the Giro d'Italia. They have been donated by the greats of cycling: Bernard Hinault, Miguel Indurain, Giuseppe Saronni, Alfredo Binda, Gianni Bugno, Ercole Baldini, Marco Pantani, Mario Cipollini. High up on the wall are the bikes: the full gamut, from Gino Bartali's 1938 Tour-winning machine to a futuristic item used by Francesco Moser for an hour record.

On the grille that fences off the altar, the cyclists' prayer is hung:

O mother of the lord Jesus,
keep us pure and fervent in our souls,
brave and strong in our bodies,
keep us from danger in training as well as racing.
We ask you to make the bike an instrument of brother-
    hood and friendship which will serve to lift us closer
    to God.

Outside is the summit of one of the great climbs tackled since
1919 by the Giro di Lombardia: the hairpinned eight-
kilometre ascent from Bellagio, on the shores of Lake Como.
The bell is still rung here each October when 'the race of the
falling leaves' passes through. A local priest, Don Ermelindo
Vigano, was the driving force behind the cyclists' chapel,
inspired by the annual sight of the greats racing past his parish
church. The Madonna del Ghisallo was designated the cyclists'
patroness in 1949, just as cycling's popularity reached its
zenith. This was the year of Coppi's historic double of victories in the Giro d'Italia and Tour de France, when his rivalry
with Gino Bartali was at its height. Don Ermelindo and his
church were following happily in the slipstream of two
European heroes of colossal stature.

Thanks largely to Gino Bartali's muscular Catholicism, the
Church had invested its moral authority in the sport, prompted
by one of Bartali's biggest fans, Pope Pius XII. The Pontiff
blessed the Giro or received the field in the Vatican no less
than three times between 1945 and 1952. He received Coppi
twice and went to watch the cyclist in the Napoli–Foggia stage
of the 1952 Tour of the Mediterranean. He had lit a votive
lamp in the cyclists' chapel at Ghisallo, and had made the link
between religious striving and the effort of cycling clear in
September 1947 when, in a St Peter's Square speech, he cited
Bartali as a role model: 'It is the time for intense effort,' he
said. 'Look at Bartali . . . race as well in this ideal championship

to conquer a far nobler goal.' He drew parallels between the 'terrestrial contest and the eternal contest', both 'sublime races of the spirit' in which the participants should not give way to fatigue or weakness.

The importance of this particular sport to this particular religion can be seen in the papal photographs on the walls: Pius XII lighting the votive lamp that stands in the chapel, Paul VI visiting in 1973, John Paul II in 1979 and 1998. Professional cycling, dedicated to Mammon, and the Catholic God meet here in a happy marriage that has lasted sixty years.

The great statue outside depicts a cyclist raising his arm in triumph, while another writhes on the ground in despair. The synergy between the earthly and the spiritual is made plain in the message on the plinth: 'God created the bicycle as an instrument of effort and exaltation on the arduous road of life.' The sport had obvious attractions as a propaganda tool for the Catholic Church. It boasted a star, Gino Bartali, who was militant in his faith, an obvious role model. As a parable for the great earthly struggle, cycling was ideal as well. The image of struggle and sacrifice could be used to make a wider religious point. There was also the symbolism of the ascent of a mountain pass. The explicit association with what was then Europe's most popular sport was valuable, but for it to function the stars of the sport had to act as role models, 'pure and fervent in their souls' as well as brave and strong in their bodies.

*   *   *

In mid-July 1954 Coppi received a letter headed *Centro Sportivo Italiano* and signed by one Bartolo Paschetta, who acted as a link between the Vatican and the sporting world. Paschetta was one of the movers behind the nomination of the Madonna del Ghisallo as the patron saint of cyclists, and would have known Coppi well, as Coppi had donated jerseys and bikes to the chapel. Paschetta's letter is written on behalf of Pope Pius XII and implores Coppi to return to his wife.

In one sense, it is a masterpiece of Jesuitical evasion. The letter does not mention the terms 'separation', 'adultery' or 'affair'. Paschetta merely refers to 'the news published in the papers'. The Holy Father, he writes, 'is pained', and 'refuses to believe that it is true'. Paschetta hopes that 'soon I will be able to confirm to the Holy Father that the news in the papers is unfounded': in other words, Coppi had better return to Bruna, quickly. He advises Coppi to 'reflect deeply on the consequences of a hurried decision' and adds, menacingly, 'I would remind you that you cannot violate certain laws and duties with impunity.' His wish, and by implication the Pope's, is that 'with a clear conscience you will rebuild in peace and love two families threatened with destruction'. What matters is 'above all you must avoid public scandals which do no good to you, no good to her' – naturally Giulia is not mentioned by name, but one assumes the reference is to Coppi's mistress – 'and compromise your glorious past'. It is Coppi's duty to 'disappear from public life'. The letter was published in a Catholic paper before being delivered to Coppi, who hurled it away after reading the first lines.

The heart of the problem was that Coppi's affair was public. Unlike, for example, Enzo Ferrari, who maintained two households, one run by his wife, the other by his mistress, there was no compromise for Coppi. One suspects that Giulia Locatelli would not have permitted it.

As Paschetta's crude attempt to bring Coppi back into line showed, the enormous publicity given to the affair in the papers and news magazines meant that the chaos in Coppi's private life had a wider importance. The Church was under pressure as the country recovered from the massive social upheaval of the war and the rigidity of the fascist oppression that had preceded it. Society was gradually becoming more secular, moving out from under the aegis of the priests. There were strains and divisions within the Church, as its leaders tried to work out how to deal with the changing times. What amounted to the Italian 'establishment' – the Christian Democrats, the Roman Catholic Church – felt its authority was being challenged. Taking a stand over the Coppi case was one way to assert that authority.

Coppi's view was straightforward. He knew he was causing pain to Bruna, but, as he told Negri and Gismondi, he was in love. 'He didn't have the impression he was doing anything dishonest,' says Raphael Geminiani. However, Giulia's husband Enrico provided the opportunity for the authorities to intervene. On 28 August Giulia failed to turn up at a meeting fixed to discuss the couple's separation; she sent a note saying she was working as Coppi's private secretary and was too busy. Although it was presumably a pretext, the formalities had been carried out. Giulia had a contract of employment dated 1 August 1954, renewable on a two-yearly basis, according to which she was paid a monthly salary of 30,000 lire. The contract, published in Jean-Paul Ollivier's *La Gloire et les Larmes*, had her address as the villa, Coppi's as Castellania. Dr Locatelli was outraged – presumably because he could see that this was merely a cover story – and decided to make a formal claim against her for adultery.

He did so later that night at the police station in Novi, at about 1 a.m. To verify the act of adultery, the couple had to be caught *in flagrante*, and so two policemen accompanied the doctor and two friends through pouring rain to the villa, arriving at about 3 a.m. Popular Italian cliché has it that the *carabinieri* are less than entirely bright, and their pretext that they had come to investigate a minor theft was perfectly in keeping with their reputation. Given the hour and the weather, it was hardly surprising that the maid, Tilde Sartini, was not taken in, and she made them wait an hour before opening the door.

The couple knew a police visit was probably impending and had taken what steps they could to pre-empt discovery and justify Giulia's presence in the villa. There are persistent claims, never actually verified but reminiscent of a Feydeau farce, that a secret passage had been built to connect Fausto's bedroom with the guest room where Giulia slept, so that if the police turned up she could return quickly to her own bed.

Having established that Coppi and Giulia were indeed in the same house if not definitely the same bed – following a certain amount of discussion about which pillows were where and why – the policemen made the mistake of allowing Giulia and her husband to talk together in the garden. The 'talk' turned into a shouting match, in the course of which the doctor thrust at her a doll that Coppi had given to Lolli, saying that his daughter could accept no presents from 'a man like him'. The night's business ended with Giulia hurling herself at her husband. Amid the insults, the shouts and the accusations, the doctor threatened his errant wife with 'prison or a mental hospital'.

His threat was realised at 8 p.m. on 9 September, 1954, when Giulia was arrested. As adultery was not a particularly serious crime, there was no obvious reason for her to be taken into custody; however, a phrase buried deep in Italian law books stated that if an investigating judge feared a suspect might try to evade justice he or she could be detained. The argument, convoluted as it was, seemed to be that Giulia might flee the country. Legally, she had no fixed abode: she had left her home, but she could not formally be living with Coppi because they had no recognised relationship. Giulia believed she was merely being taken to the police station in Alessandria – the regional capital, thirteen kilo-metres from Novi – to discuss her passport. She only found out later that she was being taken to prison. Coppi discovered what was going on a few minutes afterwards; he followed the police van in his car to try to get a bag of clothes to her.

The White Lady spent four days in prison. It is often said

she was held alongside prostitutes, although the only contemporary account that I have found states that the two women
who shared her cell had been locked up for theft. The account
(*Oggi*, 23 September 1954) adds that she was well treated,
although, not surprisingly, she spent the four days in a state
of shock, emerging with no clear idea of where she was and
what was going on. She was released amid crowds of press
photographers and newsreel cameramen, who pursued the car
taking her home at high speed.

The motive for detaining Giulia was clearly coercive: before
she could be set free, Coppi had to go before the magistrate
who was investigating the case, *dottore* Augusto Mazzoni. It
was also an attempt to divide the couple, to put pressure on
them individually. The magistrate made no bones about the
reason for having her inside. She was told bluntly: agree to
return to your husband and you will be released.

The detention was also used to set the conditions under which
the pair would live until their trial. Both their passports were
confiscated. Giulia was deprived of the right to see her children
and placed under bail restrictions: she had to stay in one place,
to be agreed with the magistrate, and must ask permission before
travelling. This was partly to keep her away from Bruna – the
fact that she and Coppi had chosen to live a few miles from his
other family was viewed as highly tactless. Primarily, however,
the move was intended to keep her away from Coppi.

This was nonsense. The White Lady chose to do her 'house
arrest' in Ancona because she had holidayed there on several
occasions and had relations there. She would have to present
herself at the *questura*, the town hall, at ten o'clock every Sunday
morning for two years, or until her trial. Fausto went too, naturally. They stayed for two weeks at Ubaldo Pugnaloni's house.
'Two weeks of hell,' recalls Pugnaloni: early every morning the
police would come and knock on the door to make sure that
Giulia and Fausto were not sleeping together. Later that autumn,

Bianchi had a training camp near the city, and Coppi and the White Lady lived together on the top floor of the hotel.

The public process of demolishing Giulia Locatelli's character had already begun. While Bruna Coppi maintained a dignified silence, as, largely, did Fausto, the White Lady's husband had wanted to get his side of the story across and gave one large interview to *Oggi*, which appeared on the day Giulia was arrested. Locatelli accused his wife of behaving like 'a heroine in a love story', and attacked Coppi and her for behaviour which was, he said, 'an affront to the traditional beliefs and moral norms of our people'. He bitterly criticised Coppi for betraying their friendship, claiming the cyclist had taken advantage of his hospitality to seduce his wife, and he was adamant that Giulia had engineered a situation in which Coppi had no choice but to take her in rather than keep the relationship secret. The doctor said he could not stand her deception. 'She has defrauded me: she is capable of maintaining today that while she was living under my roof her relations with Coppi were purely platonic. However, the truth is different and is very bitter and there are a thousand pieces of evidence to prove it.'

The doctor maintained that his wife had led Coppi on so that she could move upwards socially. 'She despised our petit-bourgeois lifestyle, disliked my world, felt suffocated between the walls of the house and was looking for any pretext to put herself on display and draw public attention to herself. Coppi was the chance she had been looking for. At the heart of this is the "role" my wife wants to play at all costs.' He argued that, had Coppi successfully defended his world title, Giulia would have stopped being his 'secretary' in order to milk the public acclaim.

Reflecting public sentiment, the magazine *L'Europeo* simply ran the headline: '*Giulia e Fausto sempre più impopolari*'. It was not quite that straightforward, even while the couple were staying in Ancona, as Pugnaloni recalls. Coppi remained an idol. 'We would go to the cinema and people would try to stop us leaving so that they could touch Coppi. They would put matches in the locks of the car doors so that we couldn't open them and we would have to call for help, then they would make him sign autographs. Sometimes there was applause, sometimes, when the *Bartaliani* were there, there were whistles.' When the White Lady emerged in public, there were always whistles.

With Uncle Fausto the sea captain acting as intermediary, Coppi and Bruna formally separated on 23 September. In two agreements dated 1 and 5 August, he had already settled a sum of 50 million lire on her, more than six times his Bianchi retainer for that season, but not outrageous given that he was earning 500,000 lire for appearing at a single track meeting. Relief at resolving that major issue and the knowledge that Giulia was expecting his child may well have spurred him to his last, brief, spell of domination in Italian races.

His victory in the Coppa Bernocchi one-day race on 17 October lifted him to second overall in the rankings that decided the national championship. Two weeks later came his fifth and final victory in the Giro di Lombardia; he escaped in familiar style over the climb from Lake Como to the chapel of the Madonna del Ghisallo, but was reeled in by nine chasers. At the finish on the Vigorelli he had sufficient race craft to outwit them in the sprint. Four days after that he partnered his young team-mate Riccardo Filippi to take the Baracchi Trophy team time trial, from Bergamo to Milan.

They took two notable scalps. The team that finished second was prodigious: Coppi's old friend and former team-mate Louison Bobet had just won his third Tour de France in a row; he lined up with the country's youthful prodigy Jacques Anquetil, who would go on to win the Tour de France five times. Paying tribute to the Italians' influence on him, Anquetil made a point of visiting Coppi's old master Biagio Cavanna at his 'college' in Novi. The French duo were powerless as Coppi and Filippi smashed the event record. In contrast, the seemingly ageless Gino Bartali had reached his limits: he won nothing in 1954 and, while Coppi enjoyed a brief, competitive Indian summer, *il pio* was preparing for his final race, on 28 November. His retirement was official as of February 1955.

In an open letter to the magazine *Epoca* on 14 November 1954 – the cover feature – Coppi said he hoped his wins in the Giro di Lombardia and Baracchi Trophy had restored people's faith, but added bitterly, 'The way the fans have whistled has hurt me most of all, because I have betrayed no one. In the darker moments of my career people thought that I did not give a damn about the crowds and was just going to races to be there, devaluing the passion and the enthusiasm that brings thousands of people to the roadsides and hilltops. Now, however, I have found myself again, and the tightly packed crowds who cheer me on. I am happy and moved by it. I will never forget the corridor of people who spurred me on in the Baracchi.'

*   *   *

On 13 March 1955, the crowds of fans turned out in Alessandria for a different kind of trial: that of Fausto and Giulia. The fat police dossier was not used, in the end, to pursue Dr Enrico Locatelli's charge of adultery. Having initiated proceedings against his wayward wife, he withdrew his suit in February as part of a complex deal that included a formal separation from Giulia, who henceforth reverted to her maiden name of Occhini. Giulia was made to sign two documents: in the first she renounced access to her children because her adultery put her 'in a position of serious moral embarrassment' and stated that their meeting at that time would 'not be advisable for their peace of mind, which I do not wish to undermine'. The second was a letter admitting her misdeeds, which was to be read to her children on their eighteenth birthdays.

Having used the threat of the law to gain satisfaction, Dr Locatelli left the judges to it and asked not to appear in court. With the adultery plea dropped, Fausto and Giulia went on trial for abandoning their respective families and failing in their duties as parents. As with Giulia's imprisonment, the charges were nebulous – this particular law was usually used to pursue absent fathers who did not support their children. (It was clear that Coppi had given 50 million lire to Bruna, while Giulia had no means of providing financial support to her children.) The couple's maid, Tilde Sartini, joined Fausto and Giulia in court, on a charge of abetting them in their adultery, even though that offence was no longer the object of a legal plea. She was there simply because she took longer than might have been expected to open the door to the *carabinieri*.

Coppi continually made the case that the police investigation stemmed mainly from a prurient interest in him as a celebrity, rather than from any 'crime' on his part. 'How many Italians sleep with other men's women? I'm convinced that the trial is only happening because I'm involved and people want to be part of the story. What seemed a huge thing at one time no longer is, at least for many people. I repent nothing. If I was not called Coppi I would not be being tried.'

The immense detail of the dossier suggests he had a fair point. The list of interviewees included Giuseppe Coppi, Cavanna, the *campionissimo*'s team-mates at Bianchi, Binda, the policemen who raided the house, the nightwatchman at the villa, Giulia's daughter Lolli – all were asked for their views on the relationship between Fausto and Giulia. Hotel staff were found to testify that Coppi and the White Lady had spent the night in the same room.

Not surprisingly, the case received huge publicity despite its flimsy foundations. The investigating magistrate received hundreds of letters from fans. One, from a group in Sardinia, railed bitterly against Coppi because he had performed poorly in a race on the island and – obviously – it was all because of his affair. In the papers, opinion was divided.

Coppi was heard first because he was racing in Milan–Turin the next day. He appeared in court wearing a grey suit and a Loden coat (bizarrely, there was a rumour that he kept a picture of Pius XII with him throughout), wiping the sweat off his hands with a handkerchief as he stood there. He was asked if he was aware he had deserted his family, and attested gloomily that the facts spoke for themselves. He explained it had 'become impossible to live any longer with my wife. She kept on bombarding me with questions about whether there was another woman in my life. In the end I confessed I was having a relationship with Signora Locatelli and the situation became unbearable.'

The whole bitter picture of the breakdown is there in the court transcripts. The most intimate details of Coppi's private life were raked over in public. He was questioned about whether he had helped furnish his and Bruna's house – he answered no because the demands of a cyclist's career meant he was rarely there – and then was asked why in that case he had furnished the house he was now sharing with the White Lady. He admitted that Bruna would barely ever let him back to his old house to see Marina – 'twice, after massive arguments'. When Coppi was asked why he posted his wedding ring back to Bruna in an envelope which seemed to have been addressed by his mistress, he answered that it was retaliation: he had asked Bruna to send him his clothes and she sent them dirtied.

Giulia did not appear in court, on the grounds that her pregnancy meant she was not in a fit state of health. Instead, the court was read a letter from her and the transcripts of her police interviews. She had clearly – and understandably – stalled over any public admission of their relationship. 'There has never been anything between us. I do however hope to become [Coppi's] wife. Currently I am his secretary and am paid 30,000 lire a month.' The questioning was prurient, going into Coppi's gift of a bracelet and a car, which she claims he sold her, 'but that doesn't mean I am his lover'.

There were moments of bleak humour. Tilde Sartini was asked about Fausto and Giulia's life together in the villa in Novi. Giulia, she said, lived in a guest room; when the *carabinieri* came to search the house Sartini would warn Coppi, and the room would not be searched because it was locked. This reflects the popular Italian myth of brainless policemen: had it not occurred to them that the person they are looking for might be in the locked room? There was also the farcical question of the pillows: when the *carabinieri* raided the house, they found no pillows in Coppi's room and two in Giulia's. Sartini stated that it took an hour to bring her master to the door because he was sleeping so soundly. 'Without pillows?' asked the court president, knowingly. In Biagio Cavanna's testimony he told the police that he knew about the relationship. Signora Locatelli went to the races and was there when he gave Coppi massage afterwards, but there was nothing surprising in that: lots of women liked to be there during the evening ritual. 'What funny tastes these women have!' commented the president.

Coppi had specifically asked that his daughter Marina, aged seven, should not be made to appear, but both she and Occhini's daughter Lolli, nine, were publicly questioned. There was no particular reason for them to have been so as their testimony added relatively little to an already thin case. The two little girls spent the hours of waiting before their brief appearances playing together – they had already met before the trial. They breathed on the windows of the waiting room and in the steam they wrote words that they had learned at school.

The prosecution insisted that the girls' testimony was a key part in establishing the severity of the 'crime' of their parents in abandoning their respective marriages, but that is hardly borne out by the transcripts. Lolli appeared in a blue coat with blue ribbons in her hair: she was asked briefly about when she had last seen her mother, and about her mother's trips to Milan. Marina was asked why her father didn't sign her school report: 'He is not at home any more.' 'Are you unhappy that he is not there any more?' 'Yes.' 'Have you been to see his new house?' 'Twice, and there were nice toys, even a bike.' 'Did you like the room he has made ready for you? Do you want to live in that house?' 'No, I want to stay with Mummy.'

It was a pitiless moment in a pitiless process, in which Bruna was made to describe publicly her husband's desertion. That included an occasion after the separation at the time when Coppi had injured his head when she found him and Giulia together: she dared not be left alone with him for fear that she would be accused of damaging his health by making a scene. Coppi's uncle Giuseppe spoke of his fears that Bruna might commit suicide. She confessed, 'When we spoke about this relationship, I said to him, "Keep this woman as well, but don't leave us."'

Giulia Occhini's character was publicly demolished. The doctor, appearing against his will, maintained that she was mentally unstable, capable of threatening suicide and of making the wildest requests (he even claimed that she had asked him to kill Coppi for her). She was, he said, 'an un-restrained megalomaniac, unable to control herself'. Another witness, one of her maids, described her as a mother who had no interest in her children but would continually go out to enjoy herself.

In his summing up, the prosecuting judge was particularly vicious about Giulia, setting the tone for the way she has been seen in the subsequent half-century. 'The behaviour of this woman has been contemptible, before and after she left her home. When she was under movement restrictions in Ancona, she asked for permission to go to Varese to see her daughter; instead she went shooting with Coppi.' She had, he added, consigned her children to the maid when she left home. He was blunt: Giulia Occhini was a gold-digger. 'The lovely Giulia was lying in wait for Fausto Coppi, because he is not only a superstar on his bike but has a big bank account. The lady says herself that she liked the fine restaurants and luxury hotels that her husband would not pay for.'

Coppi was publicly pilloried, his character belittled in humiliating style. Playing to the gallery, the prosecuting judge described the cyclist as Giulia Locatelli's 'slave', 'a poor little man who managed to win so many races but collapsed miserably the first time he had to fight against his own desires'. Coppi was a social climber, a man out to conquer the world but who 'was conquered himself'. Coppi and Giulia had abandoned their families 'when the adulterous act had been consummated, causing immeasurable damage to those who they left behind them'.

He accused Coppi of being an emotional illiterate, of deluding himself that he could buy his way out of the situation. 'He should be under no illusions: money can buy him all the White Ladies he wants but it can't buy him the affection of his family. His wife married him when he was still unknown, kept faith with him in moments of near poverty. The "White Lady" on the other hand came to sit next to him when he was on a golden throne, to enjoy the fruits of his success. It would be interesting to know how much he spends on *la Occhini* and how much on his family.'

Although Giulia had obfuscated over the relationship, Coppi's defence was one of emotional honesty: rather than maintain the deception, the lawyers said, both Coppi and Giulia had followed their hearts. 'What was Coppi supposed

IN THE DOCK   217

to do,' asked his lawyer, 'keep both women, lie to his wife and his lover?' Coppi, said his lawyer, was a committed, fond parent who could not be heavily involved in running the home due to the demands of his profession. As a result, his wife and child did not suffer greatly from his departure. He was asked only to 'pedal, win and earn money. He pedalled, won, and earned. How can he have failed to give moral guidance to the household?' It was also claimed that Coppi had no choice but to live with the White Lady once her husband had thrown her out: 'he welcomed her, protected her, motivated by a senti-ment of knightly loyalty'. But Coppi as Parfit Gentil Knight was an embellishment of reality. 'His defence was muddled; it did not convince anyone,' was the view of Rino Negri, one of Coppi's stoutest defenders at other times.

The couple were not helped by a nasty moment on the second day, when the prosecution revealed that Coppi and Giulia had shared a hotel room (room 12, the hotel is not named) in Milan over the weekend between hearings and before Milan–Turin. 'They might at least have waited,' said the prosecuting magistrate, acidly. Coppi's lawyer termed it 'persecution', which seems reasonable enough. On the grounds that the couple had flouted the law even while their trial was in progress, the prosecutor called for three months in prison for Giulia, two for Coppi. This reflected a general feeling – widely held to this day – that guilt lay more with the White Lady than with Coppi, as the cyclist had 'been chosen, led on by the White Lady, who was much more cunning and astute'. 'There was no serious reason for either Coppi or Occhini to leave their homes. The decision of both parties was illicit and unjust.' The outcome was a compromise: sentences upheld but prison suspended. Coppi did not comment, but later made it known that the only consolation he could find was in the fact that no one ever saw him and Giulia together in the dock.

Coppi was not a man who was given to expressing his feelings in public. That lends an extra strength to the diatribe about the hypocrisy of Italy and the Italians that he produced for Rino Negri in his book *Parla Coppi*. 'In Italy, appearances are what count. In Italy, you have to know how to lie. In Italy, you have to be able to keep your mouth shut even if you don't like something. In Italy, there is envy of anyone who has come from nothing to make something of himself even if he has made huge sacrifices. In Italy they don't hesitate to throw you in the mud if you make a mistake that any man could make. When I needed understanding, I found doors closed in my face.'

CHAPTER 14

DECLINE AND FALLS

'For guys like you and me, life means riding a bike' –
Gino Bartali to Fausto Coppi, 1950

In early April, Coppi responded to the trial verdict with one of
his last great solo victories, in the Giro della Campania, with
Magni more than five minutes behind. He was now allowed to
travel abroad again, which meant he could ride Paris–Roubaix,
where he managed second place to Bobet. Giulia's passport was
returned to her on 22 March; her destination was another conti-
nent. She flew to Argentina with the wife of Pinella di Grande,
Coppi's faithful mechanic at Bianchi, to give moral support as
she prepared for the birth of her child. In Argentina at least,
the baby could be registered as the legal son of unmarried
parents. That meant that he would be viewed as her and Fausto's
child; however, it did not mean that Dr Locatelli would necessarily renounce his claim to paternity, as the child's conception
clearly pre-dated the legal separation. In theory Locatelli could
be the father.

Giulia booked her return journey on the steamer *Giulio
Cesare,* one of the finest transatlantic liners of the era, and
had the birth induced so that she could board on time. Faustino
was born on 13 May 1955, while Coppi was riding the Giro
d'Italia, and Giulia sent Coppi a telegram with the words,
'Daddy, I'm waiting for my first pink jersey. Fausto.' A few
days later a photograph came through the post: Coppi showed
it first to Gino Bartali, recently retired and following the Giro
as a summariser for Italian television. For a few kilometres,

as the peloton rode along, Coppi waved the picture at all and sundry, saying, 'Look, it's Faustino, the son of Fausto.' This personal triumph probably made up for the fact that, when the race visited Rome, Pius XII made an unprecedented move. As if to remind the world that Coppi was *persona non grata*, the Pontiff refused to bless the peloton as before, because it included a 'public sinner'.

Even though he was in his thirty-sixth year Coppi could still have won that Giro. Instead, the race went to Fiorenzo Magni, who made an epic attack on the penultimate day between Trento and San Pellegrino. The young climber Gastone Nencini had not managed to take an insurmountable lead in the Dolomites, although he emerged in the pink jersey. Early in the San Pellegrino stage, however, the race went along a stretch of *strada bianca*, one of the particularly rough, unsurfaced roads frequently encountered by cyclists. The weather was poor and the result was a spate of punctures: ninety-six in total in the four miles. Magni told me that he knew about the *strada bianca*, because such dangers were marked in the race guide. He had put on heavier tyres, as had Coppi. When Nencini, inevitably, punctured, the two older men surged ahead, and a dramatic four-hour pursuit ensued, at the end of which Coppi won the stage and Magni took the Giro, a mere thirteen seconds ahead of his old rival.

The return of Faustino and his mother from Argentina was dramatic, too, in a different way. The *Giulio Cesare* docked in Cannes, where the White Lady cut a glamorous figure as she came down the gangway in a blue outfit, wearing sunglasses; the infant was hidden in a large holdall held by a member of the crew. The crowd of press photographers was so large that it took a few well-aimed punches from Pinella di Grande before Giulia and Faustino were able to get to the Citroën Traction Avant Fausto had been lent by a friend, 'with all the precision and lightning speed of a gangster getaway',

as one paper put it. The getaway included driving the wrong way up a one-way street (thanks, no doubt, to the gendarme in the front seat), with carloads of journalists and photographers in pursuit. If Giulia had aspired to join the ranks of the Lorens and Lollobrigidas in the news magazines, that ambition had been achieved.

Fausto had got what he wanted: a son. To ensure their privacy, he rented an entire hotel for Giulia and Faustino on their first night back in Europe. As Giulia told it later, he kissed her, then took his son in his arms, carried him to his room, put him on a rug and knelt down to look at him. He stayed there for a long time. A large new car – a Lancia Aurelia – was waiting for her on her return, and a ring worth, she said, 42 million lire. He was not present when she received the gifts – 'as usual so that I wouldn't thank him'. But inevitably Coppi headed for Rome almost immediately to race on the track.

As with his previous family, his life consisted of 'racing, winning and earning money': lots of it, in a highly lucrative series of exhibition events around France that summer. Coppi estimated that, compared with his heyday, his strength had diminished by a third, but he still managed one final challenge: winning the Italian national championship, run on points over a series of five one-day races throughout 1955. He clinched the title with victories in the Giro dell'Apennino, three days after his thirty-sixth birthday, and the Tre Valli Varesine (run, uniquely, as a time trial). That was the event where, eight years and a few months earlier, he had first set eyes on his new love. The season was capped with a third successive win in the Baracchi Trophy with Filippi.

In spite of his success on the road, however, it was not a peaceful existence. There were threatening phone calls and anonymous letters attacking Fausto and Giulia and calling Faustino 'bastardo'. Coppi was still receiving abuse from the roadsides, shouts of 'Go back to Bruna', and 'Down with the White Lady'. He told *Tempo* magazine at the end of that year: 'I have wanted at times, so much, to put my brakes on and tell the people who are whistling or shouting insults why I'm not at the front. But they wouldn't understand.' The pressure told on them both: one evening Giulia told Fausto she was leaving, he gave her 'a violent slap', she ran away and, together with Ettore Milano, he had to restrain her.

*   *   *

The Giro di Lombardia is aptly nicknamed 'the race of the falling leaves'. It threads its way around Lake Como and through the mists of the north Italian flatlands as the dead leaves gently drop off the trees on the lakeside hills. While Milan–San Remo exudes the burgeoning optimism of spring, the Giro di Lombardia is the harbinger of winter. It is the classic most indelibly associated with the *campionissimo*: Fausto Coppi won the race five times, and suffered one famous defeat, in the 1956 edition.

Half a century on, Fiorenzo Magni still remembers that particular race with some embarrassment. 'I don't know if what I did was decisive,' he told me, but the consensus is that Magni played the key role in chasing Coppi down when his victory looked to be assured. The fading champion had escaped, as he so often had in the past, on the climb that led to the chapel of the Madonna del Ghisallo, high above the lake. On the run-in to the finish in Milan he and a young Italian named Diego Ronchini were riding ahead of a chasing group which included Magni and the other big names. The pair had a lead that looked healthy enough to keep them in front until they reached the Vigorelli velodrome.

That is, until the intervention of the White Lady. Although Magni had remained on good terms with Coppi, he and his wife had always been friendly with Coppi's wife Bruna; to this day, although he can understand Coppi's decision to leave her, he cannot condone it. As the car carrying Giulia Occhini overtook the line of cyclists she saw Magni in the chasing group and could not resist the temptation to point out that her man had put one over the Giro winner. Today, Magni is diplomacy itself. 'A few words out of turn,' he says, when asked what Giulia yelled at him out of the car window: 'Eh, Fiorenzo, my Fausto has got you!' He does not mention the gesture she made, but Sandrino Carrea recalls the episode: 'When she came near Magni she went like this' – and at this point he wallops his bicep with his hand as he mimics her obscene gesture; one raised fist, the other hand clenching the muscle – 'and Magni chased fit to kill himself.' The 'Lion of Flanders' is reported to have said that he would have chased Coppi down after that even if he had had to bust a gut all the way to Novi Ligure. Later he would say that the blow to his pride was a bigger spur than amphetamine: 'I sunk my teeth into the handlebars to the point where I lost any awareness of being alive.'

The result was inevitable, as the other riders in the group joined Magni in the chase: Coppi and Ronchini were swept up as the race entered Milan. The old champion, now thirty-seven, had one final ace up his sleeve: he knew the Vigorelli velodrome like the back of his hand, and as he sped down from the final banking the finish sprint looked to be his. That is, until a fast-moving, blond Frenchman named André Darrigade inched past in the final twenty metres to snatch the win by a tyre's width. Coppi was last seen weeping in a corner of the track, and left by a side door as the crowd chanted his name. What they had just seen amounted to his swansong.

He had trained like a man possessed for that race, his last chance to salvage something tangible from a disastrous season. It had begun with an attack of typhus fever, which had cost him his place with his former employers, Bianchi. The illness had meant he could not race early in the year, leaving him in breach of contract, and Bianchi were not inclined to make allowances for the man who had caused a national scandal the year before. While he was ill, he had been sacked. He had bounced back by finding a new sponsor, the Carpano aperitif company, and setting up his own team, riding Fausto Coppi bikes. But at the Giro he had crashed, dislocating his back: two more months off the bike followed. He was still good enough to be selected for the Italian team at the world championship, taking fifteenth, and followed that with victory in the GP Campari time trial at Lugano. But this was small beer compared to that lost win in Lombardy, where, to add salt to the wound, the winner, Darrigade, was a rider he had hired himself to race for Bianchi, to support him in Italian events. Ronchini, his companion in the escape, was a Bianchi rider, a former team-mate. It was Coppi's old mechanic, Pinella di Grande, who had no choice but to tell Ronchini to stop collaborating in the break.

*   *   *

The final three seasons of Coppi's life, 1957–9, saw the inevitable decline. He remained a living legend, but it was a half-life: he won minor appearance races and his physical strength diminished with each year. The 1957 season saw his last disastrous crash, in Sardinia in early March. That left him with a broken femur, and was followed by five months off the bike before his last win in the Baracchi Trophy, when he went through all the agonies of hell to keep up with his young partner, Ercole Baldini. The slow fade-out was marked by a sprinkling of wins in such uninspiring venues as Calvisano on the Lombardy plains, Namur in Wallonia, and a six-day track race in Buenos Aires.

He still rode huge numbers of appearance events. His team-mate Michele Gismondi recalls riding three track meetings a day with Coppi when logistics permitted. Gismondi would deal with the bikes, Coppi with the cash. In between, there were ignominious outings in major events. At the 1958 Giro Coppi finished only thirty-second and was heard to ask the field to slow down on a relatively innocuous climb. He fought desperately merely to finish forty-fourth in the 1959 Paris–Roubaix, and made a disastrous start in the 1959 Vuelta a España, where he lasted only fifteen stages, finishing well behind the stage winner each time the going got tough. Not wanting to show him up by actually being seen to push him, the *gregari* would pretend to lean on his back.

The demands were high and he had his ways of dealing with them, as his friend Nino Defilippis told me in the most chilling of terms. 'We were at the Vél d'Hiv in Paris with Darrigade, Bobet, Anquetil, for a ten-day track meeting. He said, "Nino, will you inject me?" I said, "No problem" because I knew how to do injections, he didn't. He gave me the little flask, which probably had two pills of stenamina or simpamine in it. I said, "Fausto, why are you doing some-thing like this for a track meeting?" He said, "Most of the people have come here to see me. I can't allow myself to look bad." My answer was, "Well, if I'm going to have to keep up with you, I'd better have some, too."' Coppi only had one needle, so they shared it, two-thirds of the flask for the young pretender and a third for the man who had been the greatest cyclist in the world, now reduced to charging up to save face.

The fading champion retained his glamour among the syringes and sacks of lire. The British professional cyclist Tony Hewson described meeting Coppi at a criterium in France in the late 1950s. 'An unassuming black car edged its way into the square and two men got out . . . Suddenly there was a groundswell of sound like a rustling prayer – *"Il campionissimo"* and people hurried from everywhere. I didn't know what to expect: something fabulous, justifying his fame: a luxury sports car, police escort, army of minders, fanfare, choir of angels! There was nothing, just these two men and a modest black car with the crowd swarming around them. Yet so powerful was the Coppi mystique that this humble presentation seemed merely to enhance his glamour.'

It was during these years of decline that Coppi made two legendary appearances in London, racing at the Herne Hill velodrome in what are still called simply 'the Fausto Coppi meetings' by fans of a certain age. For the first meeting, on 14 September, 1958, Coppi was paid £300 – half his usual fee – and the 12,000 crowd paid £1 10s each, twelve times the usual entry price. The great concrete bowl has not been full since. The afternoon's entertainment, with an Italy v England format, began with a Catholic cardinal blessing the crowd, and included a 'tea break' in which the professionals rode slowly around the track, stopping to sign autographs.

Herne Hill came shortly after a rare high point for Coppi: the 1958 world road race championship, held in the French city of Reims. He had to fight hard merely to qualify for the Italian team, led by Ercole Baldini, his partner in the Baracchi time trial the previous autumn. Baldini had succeeded Anquetil as the holder of the hour record, once held by Coppi himself, and Baldini took the world title that day, with the support of the older man. It was Coppi who advised Baldini to infiltrate an early escape – although there were malicious whispers later that he had done so in an attempt to make the young man burn himself out – and he managed seventh, a considerable feat at almost thirty-nine years old.

In one sense Coppi's 'slow sporting suicide', as Jean-Paul Ollivier terms it, was not that remarkable. It was not uncommon in the post-war years for cyclists to continue racing up to and beyond the age of forty. Bartali was the most celebrated example; he rode his last race in November 1954, four months after his fortieth birthday. Other stars of the period such as Brik Schotte, Rik Van Steenbergen and Jean Robic also continued until they were over forty. What was surprising about Coppi's final years was how poorly he raced in major events, when he could bring himself to start them. In contrast, Bartali rode one poor Giro, 1954, when he was thirteenth, and retired the following winter.

Journalists of the time, who had followed Coppi in his glory days, clearly could not fathom why he now kept going. One commentator, Indro Montanelli, wrote after Coppi's death that there was a kind of glory in his stubborn refusal to accept reality. In his prime, Montanelli felt, it had taken only Bartali's shadow to sap Coppi's willpower; now, he refused to surrender in the face of impossible odds. 'At forty, he had found the grit he lacked at the age of twenty or thirty.'

Biagio Cavanna, for one, appears to have believed that physically Coppi was still capable of victories in major races: in 1953 he had told a magazine that his protégé would go on winning past the age of forty and he continued to supply advice and massage until Coppi's death. However, Cavanna had a vested interest in the *campionissimo* continuing to race: he was receiving a percentage of his winnings until shortly before Coppi died. Even for 1959, his share was 740,000 lire.

Those close to Coppi have various explanations for the slow, depressing coda to his career. Most say that he could not contemplate life without competing. 'He asked me, "What will I do if I stop racing?"' recalls Michele Gismondi. 'You imagine it: you are used to being constantly on the move, travelling to races, training, you are always in cars and trains, everything imaginable, and suddenly you are sitting looking at the walls. He loved the bike too much.' Perhaps he went on racing in the same way that his father worked the fields in Castellania. It is the oldest principle in farming: if the weather is good when the crops are coming in you keep going because it might rain overnight. There was no reason for Coppi to stop, as long as the race organisers still wanted him and he could still earn more in an afternoon than a manual worker earned in a month.

That did not make it any less painful. During the disastrous Vuelta a España of 1959, after one particularly poor performance a French journalist asked Coppi if he understood that he was risking his reputation. He replied that he understood what was at stake: 'I have signed contracts and I have to honour them. If I had understood how hard the Vuelta was, I would not have agreed to ride. Up to now, I have been privileged as a cyclist. Everything came easily to me. I did not know what suffering was.' He added that Giulia was calling him every day asking him to stop racing.

Nino Defilippis, for one, does not believe that Coppi tarnished his reputation by continuing in this way: 'Perhaps he didn't actually need the money. The bike was his life. He had come from obscurity; stopping racing would have meant going back to the past, being forgotten, leaving that world behind. He raced for the people, the public, and they respected that. He went to the races as Coppi [rather than as a competitor]. People knew he wasn't winning, and we [the other riders] knew that as well. It wasn't a question of his looking bad, even when he had to plead with other riders to slow down. The people didn't look at who won, didn't go to them for autographs. They only wanted Coppi.'

*   *   *

Inevitably, the White Lady was castigated for Coppi's decline. It was easy to blame her for emasculating the champion. His son Faustino dismisses this. 'His decline was in the normal order of things, because he was old and had other interests.

My mother would certainly have preferred him to stop earlier, but it was his life, his work.'

Speculation about the corrosive effect that Giulia Occhini had on Coppi goes further than this. Some claim that he had to keep racing to earn the cash to subsidise her extravagant lifestyle, while paying money both to Bruna and Dr Locatelli. Others suggest that he raced for small contracts in order not to spend time at home with her, which seems far less likely. Raphael Geminiani is adamant: 'He was ruined financially – he had to pay off the doctor and Bruna, assure the future of his children, and the White Lady was expensive, and what's more at the end of his career he earned less money.' He had settled 50 million lire on Bruna; the attempts to get his and Giulia's marriages annulled via the Holy See cannot have come cheap.

Life with his White Lady bore little resemblance to his old existences, either the peasant childhood in Castellania or the gentle routine of Sestri with Bruna and little Marina. Visits to two former team-mates on successive days fifty years on showed how that new life was viewed. On the first day, I was told that at the Villa Coppi there were silver plates on the table. The following morning's interviewee remembered the under-dishes being gold. Perhaps there were both in the cupboard, if Coppi adopted the same belt and braces policy as he did with his cars, of which he had four: two distinctively curved, powerful Lancia Aurelias (as driven by Formula One drivers Mike Hawthorn and Juan-Manuel Fangio), a Fiat Seicento and a Millecento, which he used as a support car in races.

'Fausto was a simple man, with uncomplicated tastes, but he was discovering another world,' says Raphael Geminiani. 'Giulia transformed him completely. Everything changed! Fausto used to dress elegantly, soberly, but now – check suits, cravats. I remember going to dinner there, there was a *maître d'hôtel* with white gloves. I said, "Fausto, this is not where you should be," and he shook his head like a man who has no power. But he liked it because he was discovering new things.' Another team-mate is more succinct: 'She polished him up and at home she acted the fine lady.'

A former team-mate and his wife clearly felt the Villa Coppi was scandalously lavish by the standards of the post-war years; there were five servants, the bed linen was changed every day. When the cyclist asked for water a servant boy brought a large silver jug, inadequately filled. Giulia shouted at the lad, and he explained that the jug was so heavy that he had thought it was full. Her response was, 'Fausto, you must sack him tomorrow.' And they claim Fausto did just that.

Just how far Coppi had come from his natural element – wandering the hills around Castellania with his dog and his gun – was shown by a curious television appearance, on the variety slot *Il Musichiere*, where he sang 'Nel blu, dipinto di blu', the song that had won the San Remo Music Festival Prize in 1958. Coppi is ill at ease, appears strangely diminished (those who knew him say that he usually seemed taller than might have been expected), and his slightly hoarse voice sounds infinitely unhappy as he sings the words, the tale of a man who paints his hands and face blue and is whisked away by the wind. He is truly a man alone.

*   *   *

Coppi was chasing more than his old form when he set off to race in 1958 in a new Bianchi jersey. He was in search of the happy little world that had cocooned him in the five years before Serse's death. Bianchi had taken him back in 1958, after an agreement was reached at the end of 1957 giving the bike manufacturer the right to make machines bearing the name Coppi. But this Bianchi team bore little resemblance to that of his heyday. When Coppi left to form Carpano-Coppi the team had split, some *gregari* remaining with their leader, others remaining with the team, others quitting altogether. He would return to his own team on his own bikes in 1959, when he raced for Tricofilina-Coppi.

His relationship with Giulia had done more than tear his family apart; it had wrecked his 'second family', the close-knit inner circle within his team. Briefly, he fell out with Biagio Cavanna, but they resumed working together in his final season, 1959. Sandrino Carrea and other team-mates wanted nothing to do with the White Lady ('There was a point when I just said, "enough is enough"') but it was more than that. 'The White Lady said we were just trying to take things from him, so we got angry and didn't see him any more,' says the wife of one former team-mate. 'What can you say? When you come to my house, I don't say you are going to steal something.' In the glory days of Bianchi, they had all lived in each other's houses, coming and going as they wished. 'She eliminated his old companions, although I was allowed to visit, because I was a foreigner,' says Raphael Geminiani. Masons and peasants were probably a little too sweaty for the world Giulia was building; and anyone who had been close to her Fausto amounted to competition.

Bruna had been unobtrusive but the presence of Giulia at Coppi's side at bike races led to friction. Alfredo Binda's and Fiorenzo Magni's disputes with her were not isolated instances. *La Dama* or *La Damazza*, the riders nicknamed her. The first has overtones of 'a fine lady', the second is simply offensive. Predictably, she did not get on with Cavanna, although equally predictably she persuaded him to massage her. She threatened to shoot him during one of their arguments; he responded that if he didn't have dark glasses on, he would rip her head off before she lifted the pistol. Michele Gismondi also had words with her on several occasions – the only incident he will speak of is on one occasion in Naples when she wanted him to take little Faustino home and he refused. Another Bianchi rider, Guido de Santi, recalled that he was training with Coppi for the Giro di Campania in Naples when Giulia came alongside in a team car and accused him of talking about Fausto behind his back. He replied with 'rude words', adding that 'Fausto, next to me, said nothing.'

Raphael Geminiani feels that Coppi continued racing because he was isolated. 'Champions' lives are built on personal success to such an extent that they lose touch with the outside world. They need to be kept in touch by having a band of close friends around them. They need an entourage.' There was no one to advise Coppi against racing, or at least no one he trusted. His closest confidant, Serse, was long dead; his *gregari* were banished. Ironically, the person he was closest to, Giulia, most probably did not want him to go on racing. Letters she published in 1980 in the magazine *Occhio* indicate that his absences made her insecure: she accused him of infidelity and of not bothering to write.

The letters, written while Coppi was on a lengthy racing trip to South America in early 1958, reveal more about Giulia than they do about him, although clearly he is 'racing and earning' as ever, even if he is winning less. She makes constant declarations of love, pleads for attention, details her ill health. He appears distant; she sounds desperate. The letters suggest that there was a cooling in the relationship, at least on Coppi's side, after the initial heat due to the pleasure of mutual discovery, the shared feeling that the world was against them. There are only hints of this elsewhere; Louison Bobet, for one, was shocked when he heard the way Giulia addressed Fausto at a race in 1959. There are persistent stories of arguments between the couple, often over money, according to Italian biographers. At times their squabbles could be overheard in the factory next door to Villa Coppi.

One reason for the lack of stability was the issue of the children. Giulia had given up access to Lolli and Maurizio, under conditions that stated she was permitted to see them every three months, at a religious school, with a nun in attendance so that she would not corrupt them. Faustino, on the other hand, had been registered as Dr Locatelli's son immediately he was brought back to Italy, because in Argentina his mother had had to acknowledge that she was still Locatelli's wife; according to Italian law, unless he formally gave up the child, Faustino was his. The doctor, not one to smooth his wife's exit from the marriage, refused and his claim to paternity was to remain ongoing until well into 1960, several months after Fausto had died. Faustino did not bear the name Coppi, legally, until 1978, when the doctor was dead. When we discussed the issue a quarter of a century on, he did not once utter the name 'Locatelli'.

*   *   *

Rumours that Coppi and the White Lady were going to part company first emerged in the Italian papers in October 1959. Those close to him are divided on the issue: some say he planned a quiet life on his own without her, others that he could never have left Faustino. That seems certain, given his love for his son, who was pictured in magazines surrounded with toys such as the massive pedal car he received on his first birthday, or waving at his father when the 1958 Giro d'Italia passed in front of the Villa. Coppi, it was said, persuaded a friend with an aeroplane to fly over the villa on Faustino's fourth birthday, dropping flowers from the sky.

Faustino, naturally, is adamant today that there is no chance his father would have ended the relationship with Giulia. However, this is not the view of two men who knew his father well. Raphael Geminiani recalls a conversation with Coppi

not long before his death, in which he told the Frenchman
of his desire for a quiet, simple life, with his family and his
old domestiques, some of whom, such as Carrea, he had not
seen for years.

'I was his confidant. He said, "Raphael, I'd like to go back
to my little bit of land, somewhere among the vines, make
wine, go hunting, have a small meal with friends and I'll be
happy. I'll end my life as I began it." He realised that he had
made a mistake. He had fallen in love with the White Lady,
discovered a whole new world, and had had a horrible time.'
Coppi told Geminiani: 'In the evening after *Carosello* [a popular
television programme] I want to lie down in my big old bed.'
He was longing for a simple life.

Nino Defilippis says similar things: 'He had a problem with
the White Lady. He wanted to go and live in Milan and he
wanted to go on his own. They were going to split up because
they didn't get on any more. In the beginning there was love,
Coppi only saw himself and the White Lady. That passed with
the years. He told me when we were away racing together in
France in his final season that he was moving out. He said
he didn't have the same feelings for the White Lady, that he
felt distanced from her.'

In her only interview after Coppi's departure from her
house, Bruna Coppi described clandestine meetings with
Fausto, carried out as if she, not the White Lady, was his
mistress: 'I never said anything because I hoped he would
come back to me, and it wasn't just the hope of a woman in
love who won't admit defeat. I met my husband, even when
he wasn't living with me. Sometimes, at night, furtively, like
at the time of our first meetings, with a feeling of embarrassment in our minds, our eyes lowered. But when we shook
hands, there was the same tenderness between us that there
always had been.'

Together the witnesses suggest that Coppi was now not

quite sure what he wanted, torn between his two families. Perhaps, having drifted into the relationship with Giulia, only to find her a tougher proposition than he expected, he was now wondering whether he had made the right decision after all. If that were indeed the situation, his persistent attempts to race at his old level slot neatly into place: amid the chaos – even the son he had so wanted could not bear his name – what could be more natural than his reliance on the one thing he knew he had been able to control in the past?

At the end of 1959, a year after Pope Pius's death, the Catholic Church was involved in an attempt to reconcile Fausto with Bruna. The intermediary was a young priest, Don Piero Carnelli, who was close to Bartali, and who had known Fausto since 1947. Bartali was also involved. The upshot was a two-hour meeting in Milan in October 1959, between Coppi and the priest, news of which was leaked to the press.

Carnelli did not suggest an immediate return to the estranged wife, but a period of reflection. When the priest read the parable of the Prodigal Son, Coppi broke down. He spoke of his love of his children, of his fear of what the world might do to Giulia if he abandoned her, of his mother's daily walk to the church to light candles on his behalf. The priest recalled later: 'He was worried above all about the way Marina was distancing herself from him. He seemed a man exhausted, completely disillusioned, a man who could not take any more.'

CHAPTER 15

GIVE ME AIR

'What else can I do? They look after me, they pay me.
This is my world. My life is the bike' – Coppi to Giancarlo
Astrua, before leaving for Africa

For elevenses, Raphael Geminiani opens a bottle of champagne.
Outside, the April morning sun shines on the green cones of
the Puys, the chain of extinct volcanoes that rears up into the
sky outside the French town of Clermont Ferrand. Inside
Geminiani's disorderly bachelor home, with its paintings of Coppi
and other cycling stars, we discuss disease, adultery and death.

Clermont is best known as the home of Michelin tyres,
but it has produced one famous cycling son: Geminiani, a
volatile, charismatic man of Italian extraction. Gem', also
known as 'le Grand Fusil', the 'Big Gun', raced at a level just
below the greats, coming close to winning the 1956 Tour.
He remains one of French cycling's larger than life figures,
having managed stars as diverse as Jacques Anquetil and
Stephen Roche in a lengthy career. But he has another role
in cycling history: unknowingly, he was the man who took
Fausto Coppi to his death.

Geminiani left Bianchi after Coppi's triumphant 1952 season,
but they remained close friends and he looked on as Coppi's
powers slowly ebbed. 'With Coppi it was le vélo, le vélo, le vélo
– he met la Dame Blanche in 1953, won the Giro, then had
his swansong at the world championship in Lugano – it was
the final mountain he climbed. The world championship, which
had always escaped him before and the change in his lifestyle . . .

you could say that he had realised his ambitions. He rode on, for money, but wasn't the unstoppable cyclist of 1949–52. He was not the same rider.'

When Geminiani telephoned Coppi in November 1959, Coppi was preparing for one more season of racing before retirement. He had already discussed with Cavanna how he would prepare for Milan–San Remo the following spring. His hotel on the Italian Riviera was booked for that February's training camp. He had interests in two teams for 1960: at San Pellegrino, sponsored by the mineral water company, he would be senior pro, guiding the younger riders. Bartali was to be team manager; much was made of the fact that the two great rivals were to be reunited in the same colours. Coppi was also involved in setting up a squad of younger riders. Coppi-Espressmatic would ride his own bikes, and had a French sponsor. Geminiani was advising him about talented young French cyclists for the team.

Now, Geminiani offered his old friend a place on a trip he and a group of fellow French professionals – Jacques Anquetil, the world pursuit champion Roger Rivière, the national champion Henri Anglade, the comedian of the cycling circuit Roger Hassenforder – were due to make in mid-December to the Republic of Upper Volta. It was a jaunt that would combine sightseeing and big-game hunting with a couple of easy criteriums to celebrate the first anniversary of the foundation of the republic (which became Burkina Faso in 1984). Coppi was not one of the first choices; Louison Bobet had dropped out owing to illness so Geminiani had to find a stand-in. It was, Gem' says now, *la fatalité* – pure fate. The Frenchman emphasises that Coppi did not make the trip for money, but because he loved travel. The bike racing was essentially an excuse to see a new place and indulge his passion for hunting. 'Coppi was not meant to come on that trip but Bobet pulled out.

I called Coppi and he said, "I'll come." The chain of events starts there.'

*   *   *

It was an exotic voyage in novel surroundings, with the feel of a school outing. Anquetil and Rivière had brought their wives. The cyclists ate cobra, buffalo, and a gazelle shot by Rivière. There is a celebrated photograph from the trip of Coppi using his hunting skills to stalk a crocodile. On another occasion, he and the other riders watched children luring the giant reptiles with a dead chicken on a string. He collected two elephant tusks to take home, took his big Rolleiflex cine camera everywhere, and told Anquetil, 'I've seen a lion; I can die happily now.' The riders posed with bare-breasted local women and with the antelope they had bagged lying in the back of a pick-up truck. Amid a lengthy series of receptions, they were presented to the president of the young republic, Maurice Yamegoo, and to the French High Commissioner.

For the races, held on a flat circuit around the presidential palace in the capital Ouagadougou, in 42-degree heat, Coppi was billed as 'the greatest cyclist of all time'. He took the events as seriously as any other, giving his assistant Adriano Laiolo elaborate instructions about where and how his bottles of water were to be handed up. He sprinted in second to Anquetil in the first race; in the second he allowed a local amateur, Sanu Moussa, to win the sprint, because Moussa had been promised a brand new Citroën by a sponsor if he won.

The day after the races, 14 December, the president made two planes available to the party, and they flew 250 kilometres south-west to Fada n'Gourma, capital of the central area of the republic and the jumping-off point for the best hunting grounds, further south towards Togo and Benin. As they flew, the planes swooped low to watch herds of zebra and elephant. Coppi and

Geminiani stayed with one Signore Bonanza, an expatriate Italian builder. At the evening's reception *L'Equipe* journalist Maurice Maurel spotted Coppi 'with what seemed an immense lassitude weighing him down. In the crude electric light, his face was no longer the same . . . it looked heavy, with bags under the eyes, pale cheeks and expressed a manifest desire to be somewhere else.'

That night, Coppi shared a room with Geminiani, Laiolo and the third Italian in the party, a vice president of FC Torino named Cillario. 'We were woken up by the mosquitoes,' recalls Geminiani. 'I remember Fausto swearing in Italian, "*Porca miseria, bim, bam, boum*". I'd had a bit to drink, some Scotch, and said, "Just leave it alone", but he kept going "bim bam boum". We had a disastrous night – there were no mosquito nets which was a mistake by the organisation . . . When we woke up we had mosquito bites all over, but it wasn't the first time we had woken up like that. You never imagine it can kill you.'

After one day's hunting, Geminiani and Coppi decided that they had had enough of Africa and re-arranged their flights so that they could return early. Giulia Occhini had been against the enterprise from the start, which may well have influenced Coppi's decision to cut the trip short. He returned home on 18 December, via Paris. His plane was diverted from Turin to Milan because of fog, so he got a lift with a young cyclist of his acquaintance, Romeo Venturelli. He was desperate to get home; Giulia was outraged that he had not been in touch while he was away. He did not receive a warm welcome: 'Oh, here you are. Couldn't you have stayed in Africa?'

What followed was routine: Coppi gave little Faustino his presents, a collection of miniature aeroplanes. He went to see Genoa play Alessandria in a local derby on 20 December. He met a journalist from *La Gazzetta dello Sport*, Cesare Facetti, for an interview, in which he spoke of his plans for the following year: in 1960 he was to ride the Tour of Flanders for the first time, as well as the usual major races such as Milan–San Remo, Paris–Roubaix and the Giro.

With those targets in mind, he set off on 23 December with a young local rider named Walter Almaviva for what would be his last training ride. Coppi was in high spirits, and the pair were sprinting behind lorries. Coppi still had the enthusiasm of a young rider even though he was three months past his fortieth birthday. They took on a Shell tanker – and the driver lowered his window and raised his cap.

On Christmas Eve, Fausto, Giulia and Faustino carried out the annual ritual of releasing helium-filled balloons into the air from the garden of the villa. Each bore a copy of Faustino's Christmas present list addressed to St Nicholas. On Christmas Day, Father Christmas duly appeared, in the person of Ettore Milano, wearing the red suit with the white beard. The little boy received new cars and a large toy monkey. Coppi's mother had come down from Castellania for the day, and Fausto presented her with a large purse, full of money. Aunt Albina and Uncle Giuseppe were there, too. After lunch, they went to the cinema.

The first of Coppi's companions from Africa to fall ill was Laiolo, who spent Christmas Day in hospital. Coppi, however, was well enough on Boxing Day to drive with Giulia to Nice, where he met a potential sponsor to finalise plans for his new team. He loaded up his Lancia Aurelia with champagne. Giulia remembered him driving home singing 'L'amore è una cosa meravigliosa' – love is a wonderful thing. However, at some point around this time, he was in touch with Raphael Geminiani, who recalls: 'I said to him "I'm tired, I don't feel well." He said, "I'm not good either. I've got a fever. I'm not well. I'm not well."' That night, at his home in Clermont, Geminiani woke up with a sore throat, violent shivering, vomiting and heavy sweating. The next morning he had a temperature of over 40 degrees.

On 27 December, Coppi went hunting on his estate at Incisa Scapaccino, twenty-five miles east of Novi, where his favourite spaniel, Dick, was ready and waiting for him. Coppi missed birds that he would usually have shot easily, and could not work out why. He came back to the villa and found Giulia having lunch with the lawyer who had defended them both in the court case at Alessandria. He excused himself, saying that he felt ill. He had had a dizzy turn in the car as he drove home. 'I couldn't get my boots on, so I came home,' he told Sandrino Carrea. Giulia called his physician, Dr Allegri, whose diagnosis was straightforward: it was flu, he told her, as might be expected at this time of year.

*   *   *

Three of the four men who had shared that mosquito-infected room on the trip to Upper Volta were now ill. They all had the same sickness: malaria. In Clermont Ferrand, Geminiani's temperature was still over 40 degrees, and the doctors were debating whether he had typhoid or jaundice. Laiolo was already being treated with a quinine-based medicine, Clorochine; it is not clear whether his doctors had a hunch that he might have malaria, or simply decided by lucky coincidence that this was the best way to reduce his fever.

On the following day, 28 December, Coppi was well enough to show a cine film that he had shot in Africa to a select audience including Ettore Milano and Walter Almaviva, who had just been told he would race for the *campionissimo* the following season in the Tricofilina team. But Coppi did not set foot out of doors. That evening, he complained of vomiting and pains in his legs. Doctor Allegri was perplexed, as Coppi's temperature would not respond to treatment. He recommended that Giulia call Professor Astaldi, another doctor who worked with the cyclist from time to time.

This was not Coppi's first attack of malaria. He had had the disease while he was a prisoner of war, most probably the less severe *Plasmodium vivax* type which can disappear before recurring some months later. It has immunosuppressant effects so the recurrent bouts Coppi had in 1944 may have undermined his health in the long term, and may have contributed to illnesses and spells of weakness throughout his career. But the form that had now struck Coppi and his companions was *Plasmodium falciparum*, the most virulent of the three forms. The illness usually has an incubation period of around seven days; it was, however, at least eleven days between the night Coppi was probably infected and the first signs of sickness on 27 December.

Malaria is caused by a minute parasite, transmitted by infected mosquitoes such as those which had bitten Coppi, Geminiani and Laiolo. The parasite invades the body's red blood cells and multiplies inside them, until the red cells burst and the parasites go back into the bloodstream to invade more red cells. As the immune system reacts the symptoms appear: fever, temperature spikes, chills, sweating, headaches, vomiting, diarrhoea, delirium, coma, respiratory distress. Death is rapid. The parasite's lifecycle of reproduction and reinfection causes intermittent symptoms, with the paroxysms coming when the corpuscles burst, releasing a new cohort of parasites, which happens simultaneously for each generation, on a twenty-four, forty-eight or seventy-two-hour cycle.

Coppi's decline was spectacularly rapid, the doctors' confusion total. According to Gino Bailo's impeccably researched account of Coppi's final days, *L'Ultimo Dicembre*, Walter Almaviva, who returned to visit a couple of days later, recalled Coppi as being barely recognisable; he was unshaven and unwilling to get out of bed, his voice was hoarse and he had a raging thirst. Almaviva was left to watch over him for an hour on the evening of 30 December while Giulia went to the hairdresser's. Coppi began to be sick, and Almaviva called the doctor, whose advice was to find some anti-vomiting medicine and inject it, fast. They had no solutions: as Giulia told it later, 'Astaldi visited on the evening of 30 December and was worried. He thought it was pneumonia: then he began talking about a virus, an infection that he might have caught hunting in Upper Volta.' There was talk of taking a urine sample, but nothing more.

Laiolo, meanwhile, was responding to quinine. So was Geminiani, although, as may have happened with Laiolo, the medicine had initially been administered by pure chance. Malaria does not seem to have occurred to his doctors, who thought he was suffering from a tropical fever of some kind. His temperature was coming down, but he was still vomiting. He had a blood test on 31 January, but there was no equipment in Clermont Ferrand that could detect the malaria parasite.

On New Year's Eve, Coppi's relations came to visit. First was Uncle Giuseppe, who advised the cyclist's brother Livio to go to see him. Their mother, Angiolina, said later that she could tell he was trying to force himself to seem normal to prevent her worrying. On her way home, she went to the church and prayed, offering to give up her seaside holiday in Alassio if her son were to get better. Coppi remained convinced that he had flu, as the doctors had said.

The final decline set in as 1960 dawned. Fausto's breathing became harsher, more laboured. Giulia stayed to watch over him as the servants went out to party and returned home in the small hours, trying not to wake him. She spent the night wiping his brow with a facecloth packed with ice, and dampening his lips with orange juice. At times, it seemed to her that he had stopped breathing. On New Year's Eve he had advised Almaviva, over the telephone, to 'enjoy himself'; on New Year's morning he was not capable of recognising his brother Livio. His pulse had risen to 130 beats per minute. In the villa, panic began to set in; one specialist after another was called, but there was thick fog, and it was not easy for them to get to his bedside. At Mass that morning in Castellania prayers were offered for the village's celebrated son.

By now the doctors numbered three – Allegri and Astaldi having been joined by Aminta Fieschi from Genoa – but collectively they still had no idea what illness they were treating. Fieschi later told a reporter: 'Coppi's sudden decline meant I was brought in eighteen or nineteen hours before he died. His deterioration could be seen from severe symptoms in almost all his vital organs, a kidney problem with a serious reduction in his urine volume and pathogens in the urine; obvious jaundice which indicated that his liver was involved; variations in his pulse rate.' The most serious symptom was his rapid, shallow breathing: Fieschi said it was akin to that of a patient being suffocated in the final phase of fatal influenza.

Coppi was dying in front of the mystified doctors. They could see that whatever illness he had was attacking his respiratory system. His breathing was rapid and shallow, so he was administered oxygen. The decline in his state had taken them by surprise: by the evening of New Year's Day he was too ill to be transported to Pavia, the preferred hospital. Instead he was taken to Tortona, twenty-two kilometres from Novi. As the *campionissimo* was transported out of the villa, four-year-old Faustino saw his father for the last time. 'He came down the stairs in a wheelchair because his muscles were so weak. He stopped and said to me, "Be good, don't do anything to make your mother cross".'

*   *   *

Between Serravalle, just south of the villa, and Tortona was a stretch of motorway that was on the point of being opened; Giulia asked for special dispensation to permit Coppi's ambulance to use it, to avoid bumping down the main road. It was a fine thought but ultimately to no purpose. The doctors were still in the dark. A hospital worker later admitted they tried everything they could think of, even if it was possibly detrimental, although by this stage it was debatable whether anything could have saved Coppi. 'We injected 150 milligrams of cortisone, something that can change everything in a normal man. We did it because there was nothing else to do, because when you are fighting a crazy, diabolical virus, you have to use all means available. There was nothing to lose; the only hope was to try things, even if that went beyond the limits of prudence.'

He was administered antivirals, antibiotics, antitoxins and medicines for the liver and heart, as well as cortisone. In a room down the corridor, a hysterical Giulia was being administered sedatives. In the background, there was the constant ringing of the telephone. The news that he had been taken to hospital was released that evening; Rino Negri was among the reporters who were summoned from whatever they were doing – La Gazzetta's man was at the theatre – to travel to Tortona. Initial despatches spoke of food poisoning.

At some point that evening, as Coppi lay in hospital descending slowly into his final coma, a celebrated telephone call – or calls – took place. It – or they – came from France, and the episode has been amplified and modified in a never-ending version of Chinese whispers that adds a final twist to the Coppi legend. It is the telephone call from Geminiani's family that, it is widely and probably wrongly claimed, could have saved the campionissimo. Geminiani told me: 'I had blood samples taken, they were sent to the Institut Pasteur in Paris where they diagnosed Plasmodium falciparum, they gave me quinine in big doses and saved me. My brother, who spoke Italian, phoned the clinic where Coppi was being treated and said: "They have found out what is wrong with Raphael – he has malaria, so Fausto must have the same thing." And the doctor said, "You deal with whatever your brother has, we will treat Coppi for what is wrong with him."'

It is inevitable given the way the White Lady has always been viewed that there is another variant which has Giulia Occhini taking the call. Her response is said to have been something along these lines: I used to be married to a doctor, so I know what is wrong with Fausto.

It is not, however, quite that simple. Geminiani's first interview after his illness, with *Oggi*, does not mention any diagnosis being communicated to Coppi's doctors. Instead, Gem' says that his father found out that Coppi was also ill, and his family decided to call the hospital in Tortona to see if the two cyclists had the same illness. According to Don Lorenzo Ferrarrazzo, the hospital chaplain, he took 'at least' two calls from Geminiani's family that evening, asking for information. According to Bailo's *L'Ultimo Dicembre*, the diagnosis of malaria did not reach Geminiani's doctors until 3 January.

As news emerged late that night that Coppi was dangerously ill, fans began to gather in little groups outside the hospital. It was the ever-faithful Ettore Milano who took his master's last order: 'He said, "Give me air." There was an oxygen mask and I changed the cylinder, it was two thirty in the morning.' One of the final acts of the *gregario* was to go to the villa and collect Coppi's most elegant suit. It was ultimately to be used to dress his corpse; as most accounts tell it, Milano left when Coppi was already dead. But in the version Milano told me, he went and found the suit 'for superstition, not for his death'; he did it before Coppi actually passed away in the hope that, if he prepared for his boss's death, he still might not die.

The controversy that had marred Coppi's final years spilled over into his final hours. As he slipped in and out of a coma in the small hours of 2 January, the issue of his last confession was hotly debated. It might seem bizarre to argue over such a thing as a man lies dying, but it mattered, immensely, to both the priests and Giulia. For Coppi to receive final absolution, he had to repent all earthly sins, which included his relationship with his lover. The matter had to be taken to the bishop, who took a while to respond via his secretary: after a long negoti-ation with Don Lorenzo, they decided that Coppi was to be asked one single question, and only a sign from him would be necessary for absolution to be given. Just before 2 a.m. Don Lorenzo asked him if he wished to confess and Coppi, he said, squeezed his hand. The priest made the sign of the cross over his forehead, hands and legs. It was sufficiently ambiguous for Giulia to remain convinced that her Fausto did not confess. She was adamant after his death: 'Fausto did not answer.'

There was also Bruna, still Coppi's legitimate wife. In a complex manoeuvre, to ensure she did not encounter Giulia, she was conducted to his bedside by Uncle Giuseppe and Milano at around 3.30 a.m. According to one version, her husband is said to have recognised her and covered his face in shame, but this seems fanciful; according to Negri he was unable to tell who she was. At 8.45, as day began to break, he stopped breathing; Giulia threw herself on to his body, screaming to the doctors to leave her alone with him.

*   *   *

As Rino Negri saw it, the entire crowd outside the hospital that morning had one thought: 'He could have been saved.' The questioning continues nearly fifty years on, and with good reason. Coppi's life has acquired huge symbolic importance over the years, and his killer had huge importance in twentieth-century Italy as well. It is no coincidence that its name is Italian: *mal aria*, bad air, from the fetid swamps and pools where the mosquitoes bred. The diagnostic failure seems understandable now, but was shocking at the time; Italy was home to the world's leading malaria experts. In the late nineteenth century the disease had affected the whole country, with almost 10 per cent of the population infected annually, and up to 100,000 deaths a year. The dire effect on Italy's economic performance prompted huge efforts to eradicate the disease; Italy became the centre of malaria science worldwide. By the end of the 1950s, malaria had been wiped out. Its elimination was symbolic of the country's advance into modernity; brief re-emergences coincided with the social breakdown of the world wars, hence the unwillingness to believe that, undiagnosed, it had killed the greatest Italian sportsman. Surely something else was to blame?

Ettore Milano, for one, is clearly still seeking explanations for the death of the man with whom he shared a room. He talks of blood transfusions that should have been done, incorrect diagnoses, a temperature which confused doctors because it wasn't high enough to indicate malaria, tests that were carried out for Geminiani, but not for Coppi. The searching underlines the fact that people are still trying to come to terms with this inexplicable, unlikely and avoidable tragedy.

Blood tests on Coppi's samples were completed only after his death and meant the cause of death was not established until several days later. Clearly, the great mistake was that the doctors assumed he was suffering from severe influenza and never thought of malaria. Perhaps they were convinced it was a thing of the past, although the last major outbreak in Italy had taken place just four years before Coppi's death. Tellingly, none of the experts consulted by *L'Equipe* in their reports of his death mentioned malaria, but they assumed Coppi and Geminiani had contracted something on a stopover on the way home.

Giulia Occhini twice told interviewers that she had suggested to the doctors it was malaria, but had been dismissed. This has to be taken with a pinch of salt, as the interviews were carried out a long time after the death (seven years and twenty years), and in her first interview, a week after the tragedy, she told Gianni Roghi of *L'Europeo* that she had suggested to Coppi it was malaria, only for him to reply that he had influenza.

As Roghi told it, malaria came as a shock to her. The most likely explanation is that once influenza was in the doctor's minds, and in Giulia's mind, it was not readily displaced.

Giulia also blamed the doctors for not responding to her worries. 'I was constantly concerned, asked them to tell me something. Fieschi answered that they weren't there for the fun of it.' She was specific about the doctors' alleged incompetence when interviewed by Jean-Paul Ollivier in 1978: her words, 'They killed Fausto', open his biography of the cyclist. She added: 'The doctors and professors were not up to the job. They did not treat him as they should have. But you don't need to be a great scientist to diagnose an unhealthy man who has just come back from Africa.' However, this is at odds with her initial reaction: 'When he was put to bed, Fausto insisted that he had influenza and he was treated for influenza until the Friday night when he was taken to hospital.'

The White Lady's accusation has its inevitable counterpart: she was responsible. Nino Defilippis is more forthcoming than most, with hints of foul play: 'Today they would open an inquest and do an autopsy. Write that in your book. Why didn't that happen? We believe there is something more serious there. Coppi's death is a mystery. How did he die? Was it malaria? Did someone want him to die? It was a mistake by the doctors, but did they understand or not? That is our doubt. Why? With the cash that Fausto had, with the acquaintances he had made, the connections, why couldn't they take him to a big hospital, a big clinic? That is my question.'

'Did someone want him to die?' The implication here is that Giulia Occhini kept Coppi at home an invalid too long. Another biographer makes a similar hint. 'The decision to take Coppi to hospital right at the last moment, with a coma imminent, after two weeks' decline at home, cannot solely be put down to ignorance,' he writes. However, far from taking two weeks, Coppi's final decline was so rapid that there was no time to take him anywhere but Tortona. Once he got there, it was too late to stabilise him, with the malaria parasites rampant in his system. According to Fieschi, who saw the analysis of Coppi's blood samples after his death, there were so many malarial parasites in his blood that by the time he was taken to hospital 'and even a few days before, no course of medicine, not even a specific one, could have had the slightest result'. Comparison with Geminiani's treatment indicates that his doctors were barely more successful than those who were treating Coppi.

Another theory has been put forward: suicide, or something akin to it, the notion that Coppi had lost the desire to live, that his was a 'willing' death. One biographer writes that, 'incredibly, in those two weeks [after his return from Africa] Fausto behaved like a person who definitely had the intention of dying'. Another believes Coppi must have known he might have malaria, and should have mentioned it to the doctor.

Whatever doubts Coppi may or may not have had about his life with the White Lady, his behaviour before he fell ill does not tally with this. Nipping off to France and returning with a carful of champagne is not the act of a man who is tired of life. Similarly, before his death he told Cavanna that he wanted to go and look at the route of Milan–San Remo, in which a new hill had been included. He told the masseur: 'I have ideas for San Remo.'

The detailed account of Coppi's final days published in *L'Ultimo Dicembre* does not suggest a man who simply sat down for two weeks and waited to die. The theories have one thing in common: they are different ways of rationalising an event that was just grotesquely unlucky. As the writer Gianni Brera put it: 'A tube of humble quinine would have been enough to prevent this man being killed.'

*   *   *

In his house outside Clermont Ferrand, Raphael Geminiani offers me another glass of champagne and reflects on the quirk of fate that ensured he survived where Coppi died. 'When I had regained some of my strength, about a week after he died, my wife said, "OK, Raphael, you are strong enough to know now", and they put the papers under my nose, explained everything to me. There I was in a coma, Fausto was dead, the papers were full of the funeral, all the front pages. I just couldn't deal with it.'

In a 1990 interview, Geminiani said he still could not believe that Coppi was dead. He felt that any day the *campionissimo* might turn up to drink a bottle of wine and eat a bowl of spaghetti with him. Even now, the normally ebullient 'Big Gun' cannot square the circle: Coppi died after a chain of events that he had instigated, yet he survived. 'It was a pleasure trip and it ended in tragedy. I couldn't imagine that you could die on a jaunt like that. My God . . . Fate is a strange thing. It was not an accident, but an illness that kills two million people a year.'

He throws his hands in the air. 'You cannot live off "ifs". Fate was responsible. There is such a thing. Something happens to one person, not the next.' He runs a finger across his palm. 'I'm sure your life is written on your hand. Your identity card is there. Why did he die, and not me? I wondered whether I was guilty . . . I felt guilty for a long time. We are all guilty of something or other. But it has no sense. The doctors should feel the guilt. They could have taken a decision and didn't. I was properly looked after . . . It was negligence that killed him. The thought destroyed me. It's fate and you can do nothing to stop it.'

CHAPTER 16

THE ICON AND THE MYTH

'Today ends the mortal life of Fausto Coppi; and a sporting cult of his name and his exploits begins' – Jacques Goddet

Coppi was laid to rest in Castellania on 4 January 1960. The tiny village was swamped. Estimates of the attendance at the funeral begin at 20,000; they rise as high as 50,000. The lines of parked cars on both sides of the road ran back four miles to the bottom of the hill and beyond. The constant stream of vans from overwhelmed local florists was the only traffic allowed through the police roadblocks into the village. There they deposited their load, turned round and went down again. The special buses laid on by the local cycling club stopped at the bottom of the hill, and the *tifosi* climbed up on foot, as they might have climbed mountain passes in the Alps and Pyrenees to watch the Giro and the Tour.

The mud was to remain Gino Bartali's abiding memory of this day. In the weak midwinter sunshine on the old snow-drifts in the ditches, fans began walking up the hill to Castellania at 6 a.m. As more and more of them did so, cutting across the verges and the fields to save a few seconds here and there, their feet sank deeper and deeper into the ooze. 'I remember it as the most solemn occasion: the people coming up on foot, straight up the hill to the cemetery, thousands of them,' says Jean Bobet, who was at the funeral on behalf of *L'Equipe*. 'The silence, the little bells of the church. It was fitting for the image of Fausto, a tragic person.'

The day before, gravel had been laid up the 500-metre

track to the church of San Biagio, which stands half a mile outside the village on a shoulder of the same hill. Among the cortege headed by Coppi's old team-mates, *gregari* and rivals was the *ammiraglia*, the Bianchi team car, with its fantastic curved lines and vast headlights, festooned with racks to hold spare cycles and wheels. The journalist Bruno Raschi imagined he could see Tragella standing in it with a microphone calling encouragement to Coppi on his final journey.

This was not merely a matter of saying farewell to Italy's greatest sports star. 'Even when dead he did not belong to himself. People appropriated him,' says Jean Bobet. To whom did the dear departed belong? The formal Italian ceremonial of bidding farewell to the dead could not accommodate the bitterly divided camps that Coppi had left behind him. As soon as the cyclist had drawn his final breath, the question arose of who was to publish the death notice. In Italy, this remains a far more public matter than in Anglo-Saxon countries: today, as in those days, death notices are posted in public places throughout the home town of the deceased. Was it the right of the family who bore the name Coppi, of Bruna and Marina, or of the White Lady and Faustino, who had actually lived with Coppi when he died?

Don Sparpaglione, Coppi's confessor, suggested that, to fudge the question, neither Bruna's name nor Giulia's should appear on the announcement. Giulia Occhini was apparently told that she had no right to issue the notice, as she was not legally Coppi's wife, but she put out the elaborately bordered sheets of paper all the same. '*La Signora* Giulia and *il piccolo* Fausto announce with profound pain the sudden loss of their much loved Fausto' read the inscription, alongside a picture of Christ in his death agonies on the cross. Significantly, no surnames were printed, which might have left the casual reader with the impression that *la Signora* Giulia was Coppi's wife. But in the Italy of 1960 any passer-by who glanced at the notice would have been aware of the background.

The emotions Coppi had unleashed accompanied him to the edge of the grave in the cemetery in Castellania. Writing in the magazine *Settimo Giorno*, the journalist Carla Ravaioli said she felt that many of the crowd were there to watch the public confrontation between Coppi's mistress and his misused wife. The press saw it in the same terms: while Coppi lay in state the day before in Tortona, one photographer was heard to say that a picture of the White Lady and Bruna alongside the body would be the shot of the year.

For Giulia Occhini, meanwhile, this was the final, and most public, opportunity to lay claim to her Fausto. 'Where is Bruna?' the crowd had murmured when Giulia defied convention and followed Coppi's body into his mother's home. The two women's paths crossed in the house; Bruna left by the back door. Clad in an elegant, diaphanous black lace veil, the White Lady followed the coffin, together with Coppi's team-mates, his old rivals and the team car. Bruna was already in the church, senior family members having agreed beforehand that the woman who had supplanted her in Coppi's heart and his bed would follow the cortege as far as the church, but would then not be present at the funeral service and burial.

The mistress and the wife did not meet face to face, but, as Ravaioli saw it, the White Lady would not give in. 'On the threshold of the church she collapsed into the arms of the people who tried to direct her away, went among the crowd and kneeled in a corner at the left, continually emitting an almost inhuman groaning.' Her keening could then be heard over the Elevation of the Host and Bruna eventually withdrew from the main part of the church. The White Lady would not be moved.

At the grave the first oration from Don Sparpaglione – in his round, rimless glasses and his Trotsky beard – included a clear reference to Coppi's confession. As the priest saw it:

'We know from the testimony of the hospital chaplain that [Coppi] found grace and eternal health in his soul when he declared that he was now removed from earthly temptations and was ready to renounce these.'

Not surprisingly, given the tension of the occasion so soon after the trauma of the death, Giulia Occhini fainted and was carried out of the cemetery over the heads of the crowd. As the champions dispersed and returned down the hill into the vast traffic jam on the roads around Castellania, the crowd applauded them as they might have done after a track meeting or a criterium.

*   *   *

It would have been foolish to expect the principal players in Coppi's turbulent life to fade quietly from the public gaze. Every Saturday Giulia Occhini made the trip to Castellania to put flowers on the grave, but she did not simply don widow's weeds and disappear with her grief. She gave her first press interview a week after Coppi died and continued to make headlines over the next thirty-three years, right up to her death in 1993. Immediately after Coppi's death, there were serious fears for her health.

The newspapers made much of the controversies that marked her next few years. Giulia was involved in several court cases, one for threatening a legal official who authorised bailiffs to remove property from Villa Coppi in respect of unpaid lawyer's fees. There was a dispute with a funeral parlour; she fell out with her lawyer. When she removed flowers put by fans on the tomb to make room for her own the result was an altercation with Uncle Giuseppe Fausto and the matter ended in the hands of the police. The press covered every last detail of her love life and progress in the custody cases involving the Locatelli children.

It was not merely a case of the papers dogging her every step. As Bobet said, even in death Coppi had to be 'appropriated', her claim to him confirmed in the face of public hostility. It was even claimed that she and Fausto had been secretly married by a friendly monk in a scene reminiscent of *Romeo and Juliet*. Giulia made persistent attempts to get her side of the story across: magazine interviews, the publication of what appears to be the later part of her correspondence with Fausto. She also adopted the role of protectress to her late lover's memory, castigating any depiction of his life which might be remotely construed as disrespectful, be it the play *Un uomo solo al comando* (1980) or the television series *Quando Coppi correva in Bicicletta* (1981).

Giulia's death, on 6 January 1993, made headlines across Europe. It came after she had spent almost two years in a coma following a car accident. Not long before the incident, she told a journalist, 'My life today is represented solely by the past because the present counts for absolutely nothing.' Some ten years earlier, she had lost her daughter Lolli to cancer; her photographs joined those of the beloved Fausto on the walls of the villa by the Serravalle road.

Coppi's son also spent his early years in the media spotlight. The papers reported rumours of an attempt to kidnap him in April 1960, and even mundane events such as his marks on leaving middle school were considered newsworthy. Faustino was never really told about his father's death, he said to me; with a child's insight, he worked it out. 'One day neither my mother nor my father was there any more. My father had died and my mother was not there. There was a period of solitude. Then my mother took me to the cemetery, said a few words, we saw the picture . . .'

Due to the vexed issue of Faustino's paternity, it took a while to settle his father's estate. Coppi had made his property over to his son soon after his birth in 1955, including the estate at Incisa Scappaccino and the villa plus its contents. But the problem was that in strictly legal terms, when Coppi died, Dr Locatelli was still his father. The legal question of his paternity was not resolved until well into 1960, when a court ruled that Dr Locatelli was not carrying out his responsibilities as a parent.

Bruna Coppi avoided media attention until her death, of a heart attack, in September 1979, but she too was unable to leave the past behind. Fiorenzo Magni described the one occasion they met, almost twenty years after Fausto had left her: 'Bruna just talked about Fausto, Fausto, Fausto as if they were still together. She was still in love with him.' She said next to nothing in public, and explained why only once: 'I was his shadow, so I tried to remain discreet. I remained quiet when the papers announced that Fausto had left me. I never spoke out in spite of everything that happened, because I wanted to share in his love, not his fame.'

*   *   *

'Il Mito Coppi', Coppi the myth, reads the graffiti on the wall below the cemetery in Castellania. But il campionissimo is a ubiquitous presence far beyond his birthplace. In 1987, on my first visit to an Italian bike shop, a single room full of dusty chainrings and fading tubular tyres in the Venice suburb of Mestre, run by a little old man in his seventies – presumably a contemporary – there Coppi was in a torn black and white photo pinned on the wall. Look hard enough in any Italian bike shop, and a similar image will be there somewhere. The same goes for the faded writing on the roadsides.

Coppi has become an inspiration, to novelists, artists, fashion designers. The British designer Paul Smith has a picture of Coppi on his desk, and is a fan of the campionissimo. Speaking of his first experiences of cycling in the 1950s, he told me: 'The aesthetics of the whole sport were very appealing . . . there were the clothes. Who could resist the modernity of white kid gloves with knitted backs, special shorts or black shoes that laced to the toe with big holes drilled in the leather to keep your feet cool?' The image is that of Coppi, whose kit has inspired a retro revival in recent years with the British clothing company Rapha to the fore.

As with all style icons, it is only partly because of what Coppi wears in the photographs – the perfectly cut suits, the Bianchi winter training tops with huge lettering on the chest, the turned-up wool collars, the simple designs of the jerseys with only one or two sponsors' names, only on the chest and back, the elegant tropical shorts. It is also the fact that he is rarely seen without sunglasses (in fact due to his fears of conjunctivitis) which in turn adds to his detachment from the world. As a model should be, he is tall and has no jarring features that distract from the clothes (Bartali has that broken nose, Magni is bald with a leathery face). There is his distant, ambiguous Mona Lisa smile, the perfect white parting in the black Brylcreemed hair.

Coppi's iconic status is a product of his time: before a multiplicity of sponsors made cycling jerseys a mish-mash of logos; when a cyclist's value was dictated not by how often his jersey appeared on the television screen, but how he looked and performed for the crowds at a track meeting or a circuit race. The mythology is not merely visual; before blanket television coverage of races, the mystery of what actually happened on the road enabled writers such as Orio Vergani and Dino Buzzati to give full vent to their imaginations. Vergani defined Coppi as a heron, awkward on the ground, graceful in flight. He coined a phrase now synonymous with his death, 'the great heron closing his wings'.

No cyclist has inspired so many writers. Gianni Brera's *Coppi and the Devil* is a fictionalised version of Coppi's life, intermingled with Brera's accounts of how he met Coppi later in life. It is never made clear what the devil is: fate? Cavanna? The act of bike racing? Or a malignant force that presents temptation in the form of Giulia? Brera also makes the parallel between Dr Enrico Locatelli and Gustave Flaubert's cuck-olded country doctor, Charles Bovary, in the classic French love triangle.

Coppi's Angel, recently translated into English by Michael McDermott, is a short story by Ugo Riccarelli, in essence a description of Coppi's realisation that he is past his best, with forewarnings of his death, prompted by his meetings on a hill (symbolically named *il Padre*, the Priest) with a mysterious blond youth who could be guardian angel or nemesis. Mauro Gorrino's *Serse and the Beast* is similar – it traces a fictional breakaway made by Coppi's brother in Milan–Turin. The 'beast' may be the peloton unleashed in pursuit, or the Grim Reaper, waiting for Serse at the end of the race. For some, Coppi simply riding his bike was an artistic act in itself. 'From this fastidious act, which consists of turning the pedals at a regular rhythm, he manages to create an artistic spectacle,' wrote the Frenchman Louis Nucera in *Mes Rayons de Soleil*.

As Nucera says, Coppi has been 'deified'. There are places of pilgrimage, including memorials on some of the greatest Alpine climbs used by the Giro and the Tour: the Stelvio, the Col de l'Izoard, and the Sella Pass, between Val Gardena and Canazei. More obscurely, there are stones commemorating Coppi on the Bocchetta Pass between Genoa and the town of Gavi, a key point in the Giro dell'Appennino, and on the Agerola climb (between Castellamare and Amalfi), as well as outside the chapel of the Madonna del Ghisallo. In Turin, not far from the Autovelodromo, an elaborate memorial incorporates stones from cycling's most celebrated roads: the cobbles of Paris–Roubaix and the Crespera climb from the 1953 world championship circuit at Lugano as well as the great climbs of the Alps and Pyrenees.

There are also religious overtones in the fans' and writers' devotion. At his greatest triumphs, the Lugano world championship and the Cuneo–Pinerolo stage win in the 1949 Giro, there are reports of *tifosi* crossing themselves as he passed, while at Lugano they were kissing the tarmac, kissing pictures of the *campionissimo* torn from newspapers. The writers depicted him as they might an Italian saint. For Gian-Paolo Ormezzano, he was a champion 'with a cross on his back'. For Pierre Chany his eyes were 'fixed, staring out of their sockets as Piero della Francesca liked to paint them'. To Roger Bastide, Coppi was 'like a church window, all length and thin-ness; the lines on his face, drawn by suffering and effort, were like those of an ecstatic monk. When he was suffering one thought of the road of the cross.' And to his *gregari*, of course, he was God. As the obscure Valerio Bonini said: '[Being near Coppi] was like being next to Jesus Christ. I don't want to speak ill of Jesus Christ but Fausto was a bit like him: a being outside the norm, a saint in flesh and blood.'

*   *   *

The White Lady and Bruna are long dead, but the *polemica* about Coppi's relationships never seems to stop. In 1995, nine million viewers watched the two-part television biopic *Il Grande Fausto* starring Ornella Muti as a pouting, sensual Giulia. It was as controversial as could have been expected – Faustino Coppi attacked the film as poorly researched and inaccurate. Bartali was 'furious'.

The Coppi myth has a momentum of its own. The man still makes headlines, with new twists to his story uncovered every year, usually on the anniversary of his death. There have been and still are lesser murmurings over the champion's spiritual inheritance: the mausoleum, the establishment of the

Casa Coppi museum and documentation centre, the cycle path built in his memory from Tortona to the village, which is better engineered than the road used by the residents.

Most bizarre was the 'revelation', in January 2002, that Coppi had not died of malaria but had been poisoned by a witchdoctor during his racing trip in Upper Volta. The tale, which made the front page of *Corriere dello Sport*, hung on the evidence of an Italian Olympic Committee member, Mino Caudullo. He claimed to have been told by a Benedictine monk that, in the confessional, the latter had been informed that Coppi had been poisoned. 'The monk explained to me that the potion was well known in Burkina Faso because it is derived from a local herb. It acts slowly and the fevers it induces can lead to death.' This being Italy, a judicial inquiry was organised, amid speculation that the body of the *campionissimo* might be exhumed. Almost a year later, inevitably, the magistrates' office in Tortona decided that Coppi had died of malaria after all.

The best example of the mythologising is the never-ending debate about the 'bottle picture' from the 1952 Tour de France, in which a bottle of mineral water is being passed between Coppi and Bartali on the Col du Galibier. The moment itself is not important. This is a relatively common act. Cyclists continually pass bottles to and from each other as they ride up mountains. The bottle picture does not show a moment that defines an event, for example when a race is lost and won. In the context of the relationship between Bartali and Coppi, or of the victory in the 1952 Tour, the moment when the old man gave his young rival his wheel on the stage to Monaco the following day was more important. On that day Coppi could have lost the Tour, but Bartali was there and helped him out. But it is the bottle picture that has inspired the debate, the articles, the television programmes.

It is not even as if this is the only 'bottle picture': there is another from 1952, an earlier one from 1949. What matters is not the incident, but what the photograph of it has come to represent, the way its continual exploration and exposition has turned a banal moment into something legendary. As Daniele Marchesini wrote in his chapter about the photograph in *Coppi e Bartali*: 'It has become the defining moment of an unrepeatable season, the greatest cycling has ever known.' As Marchesini tells it, the debate began a few days after the photograph was taken when the magazine *Sport Illustrato* published it, and the readers began writing in to ask who was passing the bottle to whom. The key element in the picture, says Marchesini, is that it shows Coppi and Bartali, the great rivals, joined together by the bottle.

That has a deeper message: the photograph shows Italy united, in the cooperative act of sharing the bottle. That idea was important for a nation which had just been ripped apart by the war, and which was still uncertain about its physical boundaries. The picture shows Italians cooperating in spite of their apparent difference; in this Tour de France one of the deepest and longest rivalries cycling has ever seen was put aside in favour of shared national interest. It also shows Italy successful on the international stage, because the alliance ensured that Coppi and his Italians dominated that 1952 Tour de France.

The image also encapsulates an era. The Coppi and Bartali years have a particular significance in the collective Italian psyche, one that goes beyond the merely sporting and is similar to the 1966 World Cup, Stanley Matthews or the Bannister mile for the English. The nostalgia is heartfelt, but there is a paradox: the late 1940s and early 1950s were not easy years in Italy. The nostalgia is for the aspiration and inspiration the men represented, not for their time. Cycling in the post-war years, at its popular zenith, boils down to two men: Gino and

Fausto, the rivalry by which all others are judged. Whenever the Italian sports media whips up disagreement between two sports stars, their every pronouncement studied and hyped, it is done in the shadow of Bartali and Coppi.

On the hilltop, the old men gather in the clear winter air. They have come in their dozens, muffled up against the January cold in green Loden coats, dark puffa jackets and hats of every shape, size and colour, from trilbies to flat caps via black berets. Echoing the scenes at Coppi's funeral nearly forty-seven years before, their Fiats are lined up for half a mile, with two wheels in the verges among the sapless vineyards and the stunted oak trees. They gather, as they have done every 2 January for forty-seven years, since Coppi's death. Most are regulars at this annual Mass in memory of the great cyclist and his brother Serse. They must have aged together, getting a little older and stiffer at the joints at each annual meeting in the little square.

In fact, to call the space where the old men are gathering a square is an exaggeration: it is a car park. On one side is a small and apparently disused weighbridge; on the other stands the ugly brick chapel, a large wooden cross and the marble memorial where Fausto and Serse now repose. Their bodies were moved here ten years after Fausto's funeral, when the number of *tifosi* making the pilgrimage became too much for the little cemetery.

The gathering is solemn but not morbid, a reunion rather than a wake. The souvenir stand selling Coppi calendars, books, photographs and desk diaries is hidden tastefully behind the weighbridge hut. Coppi's former *gregari*, the men who built his victories by serving him body and soul on their bikes, line up for what resembles a team photograph, joshing and jostling a little as they do so. They pose for photographs and sign autographs; once in Coppi's shadow, now they can bask in reflected glory – ironically given that their *raison d'être* was to deny themselves any chance of glory and that they felt guilty if they so much as thought of victory.

'We are like the *Garibaldini*,' one told me, referring to the small army that began Italian unification in the nineteenth century. 'Whatever else we have done, we are known because we raced with Coppi. It doesn't matter that I won forty races including an Italian championship. I am known as Coppi's team-mate.' Like the *Garibaldini*, Coppi and his *gregari* stand for Italy at a certain stage in her history. They are the men of the reconstruction that finally united this diverse country after the Second World War.

Inside the little brick chapel next to the memorial and the souvenir stand it is standing room only, shoulder to shoulder, on this January day as 10.30 approaches. It is not the most formal of ceremonies. The doors remain open throughout; close family members turn up late; mobile phones keep trilling. This is Italy in the twenty-first century after all. The buzz outside is a constant background to the chanted responses and prayers.

It is hard to separate Roman Catholicism from cycling. The priest draws his own parallels: Christ as team leader, John the Baptist as the *gregario*. The denial of worldly temptation on the road to a Tour de France win compared with Christ's refusal to turn the stones into bread; Coppi's generosity to fellow competitors as a metaphor for his preparation for eternal life. *La Gazzetta dello Sport* is quoted as readily as the Bible. Behind the chapel, to the right of the monument to Fausto and Serse, stands the trophy room, its walls hung with glass cases containing jerseys donated by the men who have ridden in Coppi's shadow in the last half-century. Not one of the Italian champions of the past half-century is missing.

The inscriptions on the glass cases tell their own story about how Coppi is venerated. The ritual of dedicating a jersey to *il campionissimo* is described in terms that also refer to religious fervour: *'reverente pellegrinaggio'* – a reverent pilgrimage. Almost every cycling champion has made the same journey up to the shrine that the old men and I have made this January morning, leaving something of themselves behind in the same spirit the fans show when they leave drinks bottles, caps, inscribed stones, at the various memorials. The fallen of *il Grande Torino*, who perished when their aeroplane crashed into a hillside near the Superga basilica in 1949, have inspired a similar kind of 'civic religion'. Again there is a museum, again there is an annual Mass, again the fans gather on the anniversary. But *il Grande Torino* was an entire team, who died together in a single instant of appalling tragedy while at the height of their powers; Coppi was just one cyclist, the best in the world in his heyday, but a shadow of his former self by the time of his death. No other cyclist's passing is marked in this way; in the wider world of sport, few stars receive such honour.

Coppi's early death has preserved him in a state of grace that has remained undefiled by everyday reality. Other cycling champions have grown old or senile or fat. Some have been tarnished by drugs scandals or blatant commercialism. Coppi remains pristine. Were Coppi among us now he would be just another old cyclist with a highly distinguished past. Instead, his premature death, and the strenuous efforts of the Coppi industry – the Italian media, cycle makers and his former team-mates – have preserved *il campionissimo* as if in aspic, his aura intact, his story endlessly told and retold, in books, paintings, operas, films, music, statues, interviews.

There are reminders everywhere. The Anglo-Italian professional cyclist Max Sciandri tells the story that, while out training one day, he stopped to answer nature's call next to a near derelict building high on a lonely Tuscan hill. Scratched into the stone at eye level were the letters W Coppi – w for *evviva*, 'long live'. The graffito had been there at least forty years.

The Italian writer, Dino Buzzati, considered that in life the sporting champion, *il campione*, is a human being on a higher plane. 'After the race he does not go back to being just any man. He remains *un campione*, alien to our everyday world . . . we consider everything they do in a special way . . . [we are in] the presence of something mysterious, sacred, a kind of grace, [a] supernatural authority.'

In life, Coppi had the champion's mystique, the champion's aura, and his death has left that aura unadulterated. At the same time, however, the public display of his frailties meant that he was anything but 'alien to our everyday world'. His achievements on the bike were superhuman; he himself was all too human.

Only his remaining contemporaries can now truly understand what he achieved in sporting terms, because his greatest wins belong to a long gone era. We may feel we can imagine how hard it is to race up and down the mountains of the Great Tours, but the roads to the passes are now asphalted, not surfaced with clinging mud or choking dust, the descents are not littered with rocks and slithery gravel. Bikes have twenty-one gears instead of ten and are made of carbon fibre, not steel.

The context of the times in which Coppi raced is just as alien. Cycling will never again enjoy the popular monopoly it so briefly did in the post-war years. The focus is diluted. But the side of Coppi with which we can all empathise is the human side: his uneasy choice of a love that lay outside social norms, the abrupt change in his family life that could only cause pain to those around him and left him confused and not entirely happy, his love of his children, the protectiveness of his friends even now, his moments of crisis even as he rode to his greatest triumphs. These, and the lengthy rivalry with Bartali, are universal in any age.

The man who unknowingly took Coppi to that early death, Raphael Geminiani, has one final comment on his old friend. 'His life is a novel. If you wanted to create a real romance, you need only write his life story from A to Z.' The old men will gradually pass away, taking their stiff limbs and their memories with them. With the grace of a heron in flight and the scrawny physique of a skinned cat, Coppi *il mito* will ride on.

BIBLIOGRAPHY

The following list is by no means exhaustive. Of particular value as sources throughout were the following:

Le Drame de Ma Vie, Fausto Coppi, Editions France-Soir, 1950; *Fausto Coppi, l'Echappee Belle: Italie 1945–1960*, Dominique Jameux, Denoel, 2003; *Fausto Coppi: La Gloire et les Larmes*, Jean-Paul Ollivier, Glenat, 2006; *Fausto Coppi: La Tragedie de la Gloire*, Jean-Paul Ollivier, PAC Editions, 1979; *L'Italia del Giro d'Italia*, Daniele Marchesini, Il Mulino, 1996; *The Sweat of the Gods*, Benjo Maso, trs. Michiel Horn, Mousehold Press, 2005; *Gli Angeli di Coppi*, Marco Pastonesi, Ediciclo Editore, 1999; *Bartali e Coppi*, Rino Negri, Reverdito Edizioni, 2001; *Parla Coppi*, Rino Negri, Anannia Editrice, 1971; *Vélo Gotha*, Harry van den Bremt and Rene Jacobs, 1984; *Caro Coppi*, Orio Vergani and Guido Vergani, Mondadori, 1995.

Newspapers consulted: principally *La Gazzetta dello Sport*, *Corriere della Sera*, and *La Stampa*.

The following were of specific reference in particular chapters; again the list is not exhaustive.

1 The Letter and the Photograph

Author interview with Armando Baselica, 2005, and Piero Coppi, 2005 and 2007; *Quando Coppi Correva in Bicicletta*, DVD, *La Gazzetta dello Sport*, 2003; *Love and War in the Apennines*, Eric Newby, Hodder & Stoughton, 1971; Marco Pastonesi interview with Armando Baselica, in *La Gazzetta dello Sport*, January 2005.

2 To Race a Bike, You Need to Be a Poor Man
Cavanna, l'Uomo che Inventa Coppi, ed. Marco Pastonesi, Ediciclo Editore, 2006; author interviews with Michele Gismondi, 2006, Ettore Milano and Sandrino Carrea, 2005, and Alfredo Martini, November 2004.

3 The Blind Man and the Butcher's Boy
L'Armata nel Deserto, Arrigo Petacco, Mondadori, 2002; Les Woodland's interview with Len Levesley in *procycling*, 2004; *Le Vèlo a l'Heure Allemande*, Jean Bobet, La Table Ronde, 2007; *Les Rendez-voux du Cyclisme ou Arriva Coppi*, Pierre Chany, La Table Ronde, 1960; author interviews with Alfredo Martini and Ubaldo Pugnaloni, 2006.

4 'A very regrettable phenomenon'
Les Rendez-voux du Cyclisme ou Arriva Coppi, Pierre Chany, La Table Ronde, 1960; 'La Triste Felicita di Giulia Locatelli', *Oggi*, 9 September 1954; the image mentioned on page 65 can be found on pages 160–161 of *Guerra Civile: Una storia fotographica*, Pasquale Chessa, Mondadori, 2005; *L'Italia della Disfatta*, Indro Montanelli and Mario Cervi, Rizzioli, 2000; information on the state of Italian cycling in 1946 is quoted from *La Biblioteca del Ciclismo: Rinasce la Sfida, 1946*, Geo Edizioni; *Quando Spararono sull'Giro*, Paolo Facchinetti, Limina, 2006; *Il Sangue dei Vinti: Quello che accade in Italia dopo il 25 Aprile*, Giampaolo Pansa, Sperling, 2005.

5 Jousting in the Rubble
Author interview with Marina Bellocchi, January 2007; *Un uomo, un mondo, la bicicletta*, Giorgio Maioli with Gianetto Cimurri, GES Bologna, 1982.

6 The Imposter
Bartali: L'uomo che salvò l'Italia pedalando, Leo Turrini, Mondadori,

2004; *Bartali: Il mito oscuarato*, Giancarlo Brocci, Protagon, 2000; *Don Camillo and the Prodigal Son*, Giovanni Guareschi, Penguin, 1962; *Gino Bartali: 'Mille Diavoli in corpo'*, Paolo Alberati, Giunti, 2006; *Coppi et Bartali: Les Deux Visages de l'Italie*, Curzio Malaparte, Pascuito, 2007; Philippe Brunel's essay 'Il etait une foi, Gino Bartali' in *l'Equipe*, July 1998; Paolo Alberati's interview with Giovanni Corrieri, 'L'Amaro mondiale di Coppi e Bartali', Luciano Boccaccini, *Bicisport*, 2006; author interviews with Ubaldo Pugnaloni, Fiorenzo Magni, 2007, and Alfredo Martini.

7 The Mystic and the Mechanic

Author interview with Faustino Coppi, 2007; *Ero la Peccatrice de'Italia*, ghosted article by Giulia Occhini, *Oggi*, 25 March 1978; *The Giro d'Italia*, Dino Buzzati, trs. Velopress, 1999; *La Testa e I Garun, Alfredo Binda si confessa a Duilio Chiarada*, Ediciclo Editore, 1998; author interviews with Ettore Milano, Alfredo Martini, 2004, Raphael Geminiani, 2005

8 Summer Lightning

Author interviews with Jean Bobet, 2006, Ubaldo Pugaloni, Raphael Geminiani, Alfredo Martini and Fiorenzo Magni; Luciano Boccaccini's interview with Vito Ortelli, *Bicisport*, October 1989; the section on Paris–Roubaix quotes *Les Rendez-voux du Cyclisme ou Arriva Coppi*, Pierre Chany, La Table Ronde, 1960.

9 Extinction of the Worthy Brute

Coppi, ma Serse, Giuseppe Castelnovi and Marco Pastonesi, Litho Commerciale, 2001; author interviews with Nino Defilippis, 2006, Fiorenzo Magni.

10 Loss of the Lucky Charm

But et Club's special issue devoted to the 1952 Tour, particularly 'Le Roman du Tour' written by Felix Levitan; author interviews with Ettore Milano, Nino Defilippis, Ubaldo Pugnaloni, Michele Gismondi.

11 A Man Alone
Debating Divorce in Italy: Marriage and the Making of Modern Italians 1860–1974, Mark Seymour, Palgrave Macmillan, 2006; author interviews with Faustino Coppi, Jean Bobet, Raphael Geminiani; 'Ero la Peccatrice de'Italia', ghosted article by Giulia Occhini, *Oggi*, 25 March 1978; *Coppi e Bartali*, Daniele Marchesini, Il Mulino, 1998.

12 The Outlaws
La Triste Felicita di Giulia Locatelli, *Oggi*, 9 September 1954; 'Parla il Marito della "Dama Bianca"', *Oggi*, 9 September 1954; 'Non ho tradito nessuno', Coppi in *Epoca*, November 1954.

13 In the Dock
Author interviews with Fiorenzo Magni, Nino Defilippis, Keith Robins, Michele Gismondi, Raphael Geminiani, Sandrino Carrea, Faustino Coppi; Beppe Conti in *Bicisport* on Coppi's last Tour of Lombardy.

14 Decline and Falls
Author interviews with Raphael Geminiani, Ettore Milano; *L'Ultimo Dicembre,* Gino Bailo, Associazione Fausto e Serse Coppi di Castellania, 2004; *The Conquest of Malaria: Italy 1900–1962*, F.M. Snowden, Yale University Press, 2005; *La corsa piu pazza del mondo: Storie di ciclismo in Burkina Faso e Mali,* Marco Pastonesi, Cicloeditore, 2007.

15 Give Me Air
Author interviews with Jean Bobet, Faustino Coppi, Fiorenzo Magni and Paul Smith.

ACKNOWLEDGEMENTS

This book could not have been written without the assistance of the riders who gave up their time for interviews over the last few years, in some cases on several occasions. My most sincere thanks are therefore due to Alfredo Martini, Ubaldo Pugnaloni, Fiorenzo Magni, Sandrino Carrea, Raphael Geminiani, Jean Bobet, Ettore Milano, Nino Defilippis and Michele Gismondi.

Of the immediate Coppi family, Piero Coppi, Faustino Coppi and Marina Bellocchi *née* Coppi were unstintingly helpful. To Marina go particular thanks for showing me the letter quoted at length in the first chapter.

To my colleague Marco Pastonesi at *La Gazzetta dello Sport* I must add particular thanks for facilitating interviews with various former cyclists and members of the Coppi family, and opening the way to the archive at his newspaper.

At Yellow Jersey, I am indebted to Tristan Jones and Juliet Brooke for their patience and help. Thanks are also due to the sports editor at the *Guardian*, Ben Clissitt, and my agent John Pawsey, for their support.

As ever, though, it is to Caroline, Patrick and Miranda that I owe the most, for putting up with yet more absences and yet more hours chained to the desk.

INDEX